Charles River

Bartons Point

Copper Works

Rope Walk

Lee's Ship Yard

Eb. N. Mill Damm

N. Water Mill

Gees Ship Y'd

Ferry to Charles Town

Hudsons Point

Hunt & Whites Ship Y'd

Mill Pond

Water Mill

Bowling Green

Ferry Way

Burying Place

Bakers

Salem Street

Hanover

Back Street

Middle Street

North Street

Lyn

Thorntons Yard

Union

N Battery

Tramount St

Fifth Street

Ship Street

Clarks Ship Yd

Borough w.

Greenwood Ship Yd wharfe

Cornhill

Kings

Leakes W.

Burells W.

Clarks W.

Woodmansys Wharfe

Scarletts Wharfe

Old Wharfe

Clarks Wharfe

Marshalls w. Wharf

Olivers Dock

Farmers

Greenleass yd

Longware H

Wings sh Yd

Olivers Wharfe

Old Wharfe

Fort Hill

S Battery.

Hubbards w.

Long Wharfe

HARBOUR

Samuel Sewall: A Puritan Portrait

Samuel Sewall:
A Puritan Portrait

by

T. B. STRANDNESS

Michigan State University Press

1967

FOR

CLAUDE M. NEWLIN

In Grateful Memory

Preface

Anyone who writes on a diarist like Sewall must wonder whether he may not be doing what the man himself has already done better. Sewall's diary, however, though generally praised as the one work of its time still quick with life, is also a work most readers are willing to respect and neglect. One reason is that, to change the figure, Sewall's diary is a tangled skein. As with all good diaries, this is part of its appeal, but it means that innumerable entries need explaining for all but special students of the period. Also, though extensive, the diary leaves much unsaid. Sewall's letters in particular contain much which the reader of the diary needs and does not ordinarily have.

In writing about Sewall I have resisted the impulse to generalize about such things as "the typical Puritan" and "the Puritan spirit." Like clouds, they seem distinct only at a distance. The closer one gets, the better one sees that what appeared fixed is in process of change. "The typical Puritan" doesn't exist any more than does "the average American." This is important for anyone engaged in studying early New England to remember; should he forget, he stands a good chance of entering the realm of myth occupied by so much writing devoted to this period. To say this is not to rob the present work of point. Sewall in large degree epitomized the world in which he lived, and studying him one learns a great deal about that world.

The treatment long accorded Sewall by New England's fond sons offers an instructive example of filio-piety's way with fact. Here is Whittier's Sewall:

> Stately and slow, with thoughtful air,
> His black cap hiding his whitened hair,
> Walks the Judge of the Great Assize,
> Samuel Sewall, the good and wise.
> His face with lines of firmness wrought,
> He wears the look of a man unbought,
> Who swears to his hurt and changes not;
> Yet touched and softened nevertheless
> With the grace of Christian gentleness;
> The face that a child would climb to kiss;
> True and tender and brave and just,
> That man might honor and woman trust.[1]

So firmly established was this Sewall of flattering legend that a century and a half after the natural man was laid to rest, Moses Coit Tyler, distinguished historian of early American letters, wrote: "A strong, gentle, and great man was Samuel Sewall, great by almost every measure of greatness,—moral courage, honor, benevolence, learning, eloquence, intellectual force and breadth and brightness. . . . He was a man built, every way, after a large pattern. By his great wealth, his great offices, his learning, his strong sense, his wit, his warm human sympathy, his fearlessness, his magnanimity, he was a visible potentate among men"—an estimate which appeared, significantly, in 1897, shortly before publication of the diary.[2]

The reason for the Sewall legend is easy to understand. Though hardly "a visible potentate," he was, in the twilight years of the theocracy, a visible embodiment of what he called "the first ways of N.E.," *antiquis moribus, prisca fide.* The Rev. Mr. Prince's sermon on the occasion of his death contains the usual exaggeration, but he doubtless described what Sewall had come to represent when he called him "this venerable Judge of our Country whom the God of our Fathers was pleased to raise up and continue to the present Generation, as a memorable Instance of our primitive Glory."[3] Last of the old Charter magistrates, last of those first appointed to the Council of the Province, respected member of its highest court for as long as anyone could remember, he was from a more heroic time.

A final example of sentimental piety at work is Robert C. Winthrop's *A Difference of Opinion Concerning the Reasons why Katherine Winthrop Refused to Marry Chief Justice Sewall* (Boston, 1885). Winthrop tells how, having recently read an address on Sewall by George Ellis, venerable historian of early New England (Ellis spoke of Sewall's "pure and unstained soul"),[4] he rose in a meeting of the Massachusetts Historical Society to address its guilty author: "This is the pamphlet which, at the close of our last meeting, you handed to me to give to my father; and the reason why I preferred to await a more advanced state of his convalescence before doing so, is that I accidentally observed that, on the eighteenth page, you style his great-great grandmother a 'worldly-minded woman.'" Ellis had arrived at this horrid judgment because of Madam Winthrop's insistence that Sewall purchase a coach and wear a wig.

How refreshing to turn from this sort of thing to Sewall's own pages, for there we move in the honest realm of fact. I intend in this book to remain there. Sewall stands in no need of wings. If there be that about him which amuses and sometimes dismays us, there is more which wins affection and respect. If we lose the paragon, we gain a credible and interesting man. The loss in reverence for the gain in truth seems a fair exchange.

In the matter of sources, I have read everything Sewall wrote of which I was able to learn and such other primary sources as seemed relevant. I have not hesitated, however, to use the findings of others in dealing with Sewall's many connections with his age. It would be strange for a worker in this field not to incur a heavy debt to Samuel E. Morison, Edmund S.

Morgan, Kenneth B. Murdock, and Perry Miller, to name but four examples. In this connection I should also say that Ola Winslow's *Samuel Sewall of Boston* (New York, 1964) is a work I have read with pleasure and profit, but that I did so after my own work was done. Similarities between the two in both form and content are inevitable; dissimilarities in emphasis and appraisal are, I trust, sufficient to show their independent origin and, more important, their separate interest. Among the many other persons I might name, two are most important, Professors Norman S. Grabo of the University of California at Berkeley and M. Halsey Thomas of Princeton. The generosity of these two experts in the study of colonial New England has given me fresh appreciation for the meaning of the pleasant phrase gentleman and scholar.

In transcribing material from original sources I have retained peculiarities of spelling, punctuation, and capitalization. Since my purpose is historical more than antiquarian, however, there seemed little point in retaining abbreviations that would only bedevil the printer and so multiply the chance of trivial error. I have therefore expanded them as a printer in Sewall's own day would have done. Y^e thus becomes *the,* y^s becomes *this,* õ becomes *on,* etc. Also, *I*'s, *j*'s, *u*'s, *v*'s, and the long form of the letter *s* have been changed to suit with modern usage. Typographical peculiarities involving numbers have been kept (for example, 21st for *twenty-first,* 9^r for *November*). On the other hand, italics have not been kept for words that would not now have them. Dates are given according to the Julian calendar, and for the annual period between January 1 and March 25 the contemporary device of double-dating (e.g., 1719/20) is employed.

T. B. S.

Michigan State University
East Lansing, Michigan

Acknowledgments

I have used the resources of the Michigan State University Library, the Widener Library of Harvard University, the public libraries of Boston and New York City, the Boston Athenaeum, the New England Historical and Genealogical Society, the Essex Institute, the Massachusetts Historical Society, and the New York Historical Society, not to mention offices of public record at Boston and Salem. To the staffs at all these places I owe much thanks. My debt is especially great to the Massachusetts Historical Society, whose library holds nearly all the Sewall manuscripts. I recall with some amazement the interested and unfailing assistance afforded me by persons at that admirable institution.

Contents

Contents

xiv

*And Samuel
judged Israel all the
days of his life.*

I SAMUEL 7:15

CHAPTER ONE

Background and Early Years

The Family Pattern

Riding the Bristol Circuit in September 1698, Samuel Sewall, then forty-six years old and a member of the Superior Court of Massachusetts, was held up at Bristol by rain. "So," he wrote in his diary, "after dinner at Mr. Saffin's, Not knowing better how to bestow my time, Look'd on Mr. Saffin's Books, and lit on Dr. Fullers History of the Worthies of England, and in p. 116. 117. found mention made of the Inundation at Coventry, on Friday April, 17. [1607] in the Maioralty of Henry Sewall my Father's Grandfather."[1]

Born in 1544, this Henry Sewall of Coventry was the first of three generations of eldest sons to bear the name. A man whose lines fell in pleasant places, his life was long, prosperous, and filled with honor. Being, in the words of his great grandson Samuel, "a prudent man," he married "a well-dowered maiden of very respectable degree, to wit Margaret, daughter and co-heiress of Alvery Gresbrook . . . of Stoke Hall, Middleton, in his own country of Warwickshire," the first of many such prosperous alliances in the generations of Sewalls that followed. By means of his marriage and his business, that of linen-draper, he "acquired a great estate," a fact shown in his will's list of "messuages," "closes," "lands," "annuities," "parcels of ground," and "tenements." That he enjoyed the trust and regard of the people of Coventry may be inferred from his not only serving them as mayor (in 1589 and again in 1606) but as their representative in Parliament

(1620-1622). The Puritan disposition of him and his constituents shows in a disputatious correspondence with King James over the manner of receiving holy communion, Sewall defending one's right to remain standing, a practice irritating to the pedantic king.[2]

So stands the first Henry Sewall, rich in lands, successful in his calling, prudent in marriage, long of life, busy for his town, all under the great Taskmaster's eye. A member of the "country party" whose leadership the Puritan gentry did so much to supply, we see him heavy with years (seventy-six when he first entered Parliament) sitting among those at Westminster who looked with loathing on the corruption of James's court and heard with alarm his ever-renewed demands for extension of royal prerogative.

He died in 1628 and was buried in the Drapers' Chapel of St. Michael's Church at Coventry. His wife Margaret died the next year and left to their eldest son "twelve pence in money," adding that she forgave "his offences." The father's will also mentions these "offences" and instructs the son "to continue obedient,"[3] the first evidence we have of a trouble-begetting disposition in the second Henry Sewall.

Though cut off by his mother with the conventional shilling and unsuccessful in a long suit at law to recover his share of her property from his brother Richard and sisters Margaret and Anne, he was in no financial difficulty. Besides having property from his father, he had made a prosperous marriage to Mary Cawarden, "daughter and heiress of Thomas Cawarden, of Manesgyn, Ridware." This wife dying childless, he married an Anne Hunt, to whom the third Henry was born in 1614, their only son and father of Samuel.[4]

In 1634 the tide of Puritan emigration had reached its height. Few weeks went by without news of men, touched in their pockets by the exactions of Charles and in their consciences by the regulations of Laud, leaving "the pleasant land of England," as Cotton Mather said, "to transport themselves, and families, over the ocean sea, into a desert land in America."

One such emigrant was the second Henry Sewall, who, as his grandson later wrote, "out of dislike to the English Hierarchy sent over his onely Son . . . to New England in the Year 1634, with Net Cattel and Provisions for a new Plantation. Mr. [John] Cotton would have had my father settle at Boston; but in regard to his Cattel he chose to goe to Newbury, whether my Grandfather soon followed him."[5]

The character of this "Pitch at Newbury" is worth noting. Guided by the rule that "to him who hath it shall be given," the founders allowed each of the ninety-one grantees two hundred acres for each fifty pounds contributed. Henry Sewall thus got six hundred thirty acres, more than anyone except Richard Dummer, who received one thousand eighty. The smallest holder got ten. In the first company's list of names only Sewall's carries the words "and servants."[6]

The economic base was stock-raising, in recognition of which the General Court ordered on July 8, 1635 (the actual settlement not being made until June of that year), that land be laid out at Newbury "for the keeping of the sheepe and cattell that came over in the Dutch shipps this yeare, and to belong to owners of said cattle." While the people of Newbury may have differed from those at Marblehead—who told John Cotton that whatever *his* purpose had been in coming to New England *theirs* was "to catch fish"—one doubts that they all joined the enterprise, in Cotton Mather's words, "meerly on the account of pure and undefiled Religion."[7]

While the "offences" which kept the second Henry out of his mother's will are not specified, we are hardly prepared to learn that on October 6, 1635, the General Court ordered his wife to be "att her owne disposeall, for the place of her habitacion, and that her saide husband shall allow her wearing apparell, and twenty pounds annually, to be paide quarterly, as also a bedd with furniture to it." Apparently the two did not stay apart, for on April 5, 1638, he was "presented by the grandjury for beating his wife." (The Puritans did not hold with the common law idea of permitting a man to beat his wife so long as the stick was no thicker than his thumb.) In 1638 he had a "business and difference with the town of Neweberry" referred to the General Court, and two years later, "for his contemptuous speech and carriage to Mr. Saltonstall," he was "enjoyned to acknowledge his fault publicly at Ipswich Court, and to be of good behavior."[8]

In 1650, according to evidence presented to yet another grand jury, the old man (now seventy-four) "was walking in the meeting-house neare the pulpit and Mr. Rogers being present and ready to step into the place to begin prayer, said, Mr. Showell [sic], cease your walking. Mr. S. answered, you should have come sooner." Pastor: "Remember where you are, this is the house of God." Sewall ("with a lowd voyce"): "I know how to behave in the house of God as well as you." Pastor: "Putt him out." Sewall: "Lett us see who dare."[9] This was in Rowley, for when the Newbury meeting house was moved in 1646, he sold his house and land (again outraged, no doubt) and moved to this nearby town, where he died in March of 1657, eighty-one years of age.[10]

While the old man's antic behavior suggests that he was a bit deranged, his proud and truculent spirit appears in grateful relief against the sober half-tones of the generation around him.

On March 25 of the year the elder Henry moved to Rowley, his son, now thirty-two, married nineteen-year old Jane Dummer. Like most Sewall marriages, the alliance was "prudent," for, as already noted, the Dummers were Newbury's largest original proprietors and a family of long and worthy record in England.[11]

Shortly after the marriage, father and mother Dummer decided that the climate of New England was "not agreeable" and returned to England, taking the younger couple with them. There, at Tunworth, Bishop Stoke, and Baddesley in Hampshire, five children were born, to which three more were added when the family later returned to New England. Of these, Samuel, the eldest son, "came abroad," as he said, on March 28, 1652, at Horton in the parish of Bishop Stoke, "so that the light of the Lord's Day was the first light that my Eyes saw, being born a little before day-break. I was baptised by Mr. Rashly, (sometime member of the Old Church in Boston) in Stoke Church May 5, 1652. Mr. Rashly first preached a Sermon, and then baptised me. After which an entertainment was made for him and many more."[12]

At Baddesley, to which the family moved shortly after Samuel's birth, the father apparently served as minister; for when, in 1659, he returned to New England—his father having lately died and "his rents at Newbury coming to very little when remitted to England"—he carried a letter from Richard Cromwell, Protector, addressed to the Governor and magistrates of Massachusetts Bay which read:

Loveing Friends,
We being given to understand, that Henry Sewall of Rowley in Messeytusick bay in New-England, dyed about four years since [actually one], possessed of an estate . . . in the colony aforesaid, and that the said estate did and ought to descend and come to his only sonne Henry Sewall, minister of North Baddesly, in our country of Southampton in England, who now purposeing to make a voyage into New-England, there personally to make his clayme to the said estate, hath desired our lycence for his absence, as also our letters recommendatory unto you, that when (by the helpe of God) he shall be arrived in New-England, he may have speedy justice and right done him . . . soe he may the sooner returne to his ministeriall charge at North-Baddesly . . . he being personally knowne to us to be laborious and industrious in the work of the ministry, and very exemplary for his holy life and good conversation. . . .
Your very loving friend,
Richard P.
Whitehall, the 23d of March 1658[13]

Why he did not return to England we do not know, but Richard's abdication must have been a determining factor. A friend of the Protector would have little to look forward to in Restoration England whereas in Massachusetts the elect still ruled.

There can be no doubt where his sympathies lay. He told his son Samuel "many times," for example, how in 1637, when Governor Winthrop's authority was being challenged by the party of Sir Henry Vane during the Anne Hutchinson controversy, "he and others went on foot from Newbury to Cambridge [where the election was held 'upon the Plain in the open Aer'], fourty miles, on purpose to be made free [made freemen, that is, and so allowed to vote], and help to strengthen Governor Winthrop's Party."[14] The esteem in which he was held by the people of Newbury is shown in their six times choosing him to be their deputy in the General Court at Boston. His estate, like those of his forbears, was large—numerous "houses," "barnes," "lands," "tenements," etc., both in old and New England.[15]

In the winter and spring of 1700 he "grew very decrepit and sickly" and died on May 16 of that year, eighty-six years of age. Shortly before, when there was talk of going to meeting, "he shewd his inability, and said he hopd he should shortly go to a greater Assembly." A few months later his wife Jane died, and on a tombstone in the burying ground of the First Church at Newbury one reads these words:

HENRY SEWALL SENT BY HENRY SEWALL HIS FATHER
IN THE SHIP ELIZABETH AND DORCAS, CAPT. WATT
COMMANDER
ARRIVED AT BOSTON 1634
WINTERED AT IPSWICH, HELPED BEGIN THIS PLANTATION
1635
FURNISHING ENGLISH SERVANTS, CATTLE AND PROVISIONS
MARRIED MISTRESS JANE DUMMER, MARCH 26, 1646
DIED MAY 16. 1700. AETATIS 86.
HIS FRUITFUL VINE BEING THUS DISJOINED
FELL TO THE GROUND JANUARY 13 FOLLOWING, AETATIS 74.[16]

The son Samuel's feeling for his parents was one of affection and warm regard, and after he moved to Boston there was much visiting back and forth. When he stopped to see his father two days before the old man died they kissed each other's hands, and he was pleased to note that at the funeral, Mr. Tappan, the minister, termed his father "a true Nathanael," which is to say a man without guile. A characteristic reference to his mother appears in a letter to his aunt Alice Dummer in England. He asks if his mother's home community continues to be "fruitfull in such Christians as my dear mother was. If it doe, it must needs be a happy place." And the following diary excerpt from a long description of her funeral says much of both mother and son:

> Nathaniel Bricket taking in hand to fill the Grave, I said, Forbear a little, and suffer me to say That amidst our bereaving sorrows We have the Comfort of beholding this Saint put into the rightfull possession of that Happiness of Living desired and dying Lamented. She lived commendably Four and Fifty years with her dear Husband, and my dear Father: And she could not well brook the being divided from him at her death; which is the cause of our taking leave of her in this place. She was a true and constant Lover of Gods Word, Worship, and Saints: And she always, with a patient cheerfullness, submitted to the divine Decree of providing Bread for her self and others in the sweat of her Brows. And now her infinitely Gracious and Bountiful Master has promoted her to the Honor of higher Employments, fully and absolutely discharged from all manner of Toil, and Sweat. My honoured and beloved Friends and Neighbours! My dear Mother never thought much of doing the most frequent and homely offices of love for me; and lavished away many Thousands of Words upon me, before I could return one word in Answer: And therefore I ask and hope that none will be offended that I have so ventured to speak one word in her behalf; when shee her self is become speechless. [Speaking at the grave

was not customary at Puritan funerals.] Made a Motion with my hand for the filling of the Grave. Note, I could hardly speak for passion and Tears.[17]

Of Samuel's brothers and sisters, only his brother Stephen ("Frater Charissimus") figures with any importance in Sewall's diary and letters. He was prominent in the affairs of Salem, and a visiting English bookseller, John Dunton, wrote of him: "His care is to live so as to be an example to the people; he is the mirror of hospitality, and neither Abraham nor Lot, were ever more kind to strangers." A second brother, John, enters the record as little more than Samuel's notation at the time of his death that the family's three brothers and five sisters were at last "broken in upon." The sisters, all of whom married and lived at Newbury or Rowley, figure chiefly as begetters of "many desireable Children."[18]

The figure of the "fruitful vine" applies to all eight; for all married, none had fewer than four children, and together they replenished New England with no fewer than seventy-three. "Many children and Grand-children are Sprung of my Father's Eight," Sewall wrote toward the end of his life, "insomuch that I cannot reckon them up."[19]

Newbury

When, in 1661, Sewall's father decided to remain in Massachusetts and so sent to England for his family, the mother "quickly . . . went to Winchester with 5 small Children . . . and John Nash and Mary Hobs her Servants there to be in a readiness for the Pool Waggons." Relatives "took leave with Tears," and (Sewall writing this as an old man remembering what impressed the nine-year-old boy) "Capt. Drummer of Swathling treated [the company] with Raisins and Almonds." They boarded the *Prudent Mary* at Graves End, took on sheep at Dover, and stood out to sea.[1]

Little is known of shipboard conditions in the seventeenth

century, but it is agreed that they were "well nigh intolerable." The vague illness termed "ship fever" was familiar to
every port physician. Ordinary passengers slept in canvas
hammocks below decks and helped themselves in the galley
while first-class passengers like the Sewalls shared the accom-
modations of the Captain's Cabin. "We were," says Sewall,
"about eight weeks at Sea, where we had nothing to see but
Water and the Sky; so that I began to fear that I should never
get to Shoar again; only I thought the Captain and Mariners
would not have ventured themselves if they had not hopes of
getting to Land again." When finally he did see land he was
"overjoyed" and, going ashore in a boat, was "carried out in
arms July 6, 1661," at a place near the later Scarlett's wharf.
Thus, as "a poor little Schoolboy of Nine years and 1/4 old,"
he entered Boston, the town of which he later liked to say he
had "grown a little fond," and for more than half a century
the day was the occasion for anniversary notes in his diary.[2]

Sewall's father "hastened to Boston and carried his Family
to Newbury by Water," where young Sam was taken ashore
in a canoe. For the next six years, until he entered Harvard
College in 1667, he lived in Newbury, developing for it a
characteristic affection. Since the town was less than thirty
years old when he arrived, he doubtless heard stories of its
founding: how the first small company came up from Ipswich
by water, through Plum Island Sound, up the Quascacunquen
(a river later named Parker), then across country to the place
where the town now stood; how religious services were first
held "in the open air under a tree"; how a rude meeting
house was built, to the services at which all able-bodied men
brought firearms for watch against Indians; of the hard winter two years before his arrival, when snow stood four feet
deep on the level; and why a law was passed imposing a fine
of five shillings on any man who should "discharge a gunn
in the meeting house . . . or ride a . . . horse into [it]."[3]

Matters which must have engaged the boy's attention were
work on the new meeting house in the year of his arrival, a

prison break at Ipswich the next year, and, in 1663, Lydia Wardwell's being "severely whipt" for coming naked into the meeting house, "being given up to the leading of the Lord." On January 26 of this year also, just "at the shutting in of evening," occured an earthquake which he long after remembered as shaking him while he sat "in a Jam of the Chimney." This was the year, too, when Elizabeth Webster sat before the meeting house on lecture day with a paper on her head bearing the words, "For TAKING A FALSE OATH IN COURT." On July 6, 1664, Giles Cromwell was ordered "to keep the boys in order in the meeting house, and to give notice to the selectmen of such as are out of order, and to have six shillings for his paynes." (Sam was then twelve.) In 1665 the town voted to pay forty shillings for "every wolf . . . killed within the Towne," and seven were turned in that year. In 1666 the wheat crop failed for the third season running.[4]

Prison breaks, religious fanatics, shooting of guns in meeting, rough justice, harsh winters, bounties on wolves, unruly youths, crop failures—all add up to what became a standard feature of the American frontier, namely the raw, isolated community. The picture is of course somewhat distorted, for the violent and unruly aspect of things rather than the sober and conforming part is what finds its way into a town's records. But it is a picture, nevertheless, which differs considerably from the conventional one of the staid and orderly Puritan community.

What young Sam was like we can only guess, our single contemporary source being highly dubious, namely the Rev. Mr. Prince's sermon preached on the occasion of Sewall's death. In it we find distortions playing their usual part in the cause of conventional piety—pious legend in the making:

Let the very Children first come along with me, and look thro' the Glass of his Life, and see his Early Piety. Look O Children, and see, How quiet and modest our

Young Samuel sits at the feet of his pious Parents; how full of Reverence and Affection to them, how ready and dutiful in all his Carriage: and how full of the Fear of GOD, how afraid of sinning against Him, how careful to read the Scriptures, and to Pray in Secret in his early Days!

Look into the School, and see, How submissively He behaves Himself; how full of Veneration and Love to his Master, how mindful of every Instruction, how diligent in Learning his Books and improving in Knowledge: behold how pleas'd his Master is to observe it, and how greatly loves Him. There you may see the hopefull Bloom of his future Usefulness: And do you O Children, Learn to follow Him.[5]

Schoolboy

Sewall says that at Baddesley he was "by the merciful goodness of God . . . taught to read English," after which he attended grammar school at the neighboring market town of Rumsey, where a Mr. Figes was master. Assuming the course of his studies followed that described by Charles Hoole, famous schoolmaster of the time, he entered Baddesly "petty school" at the age of five or six and possibly earlier (Sewall's own son, Joseph, was sent to school when not yet three). Arriving "fairly washed, neatly combed, and handsomly clad," he learned his letters and "a smattering of some syllables and words in the horn-book" by spelling them aloud in unison with the other members of the class, the master starting them off together with a blow of his strap on the desk. From horn-book he passed to his primer and learned by rote such things as the Lord's Prayer and Ten Commandments, after which he entered on the Book of Genesis and such other "remarkable Histories" as would be "most likely to delight him." Finally came catechizing in such a work as *The Foundation of Christian Religion gathered into sixe Principles* by William Perkins, noted Puritan divine.[1]

The petty school calendar provided no free Saturdays and no months of vacation. School began "before eight in the morning" with a prayer and, with a two-hour break from eleven to one, ended the same way "about five a clock in the summer, and four in the winter season," at which time the young scholars would "rise out of their places one by one with their . . . book in their hand, and make their honours to their Master as they passe[d] before his face, one following another at a distance out of School."[2]

When, after a year or two of petty school, he could read "in any place of a book that [was] offered him," he entered Rumsey grammar school and began the study of Latin. School hours were now longer, beginning at six or seven in the morning "both in Winter and Summer," and continuing, with a break from eleven to one, till five in the afternoon. Scholars who arrived before school began were permitted to "play about the Schoole, till the clock strike, on condition they [could] say their parts." Occasionally they might be excused to attend a writing school, which, unlike grammar school, was for "them that have a prejudice against Latine" and therefore taught things proper to "ordinary callings," like arithmetic and writing.[3]

Grammar school texts were Holle's *Nomenclature,* a small Latin-English vocabulary; one of the same author's *Colloquies* of Corderius containing texts in Latin and English whereby "children, by the help of their Mother-Tongue, may the better learn to speak Latin in ordinary Discourse"; Hoole's or Brinsley's *Sententiae Pueriles, or Sentences for Children;* and Brinsley's *Accidence.* In addition, there were the Grammars of Lily and Camden, and, if a venture were made into Hebrew, those of William Shickard or John Buxtorf. Rules were mastered by "patter[ing] them over by heart." In addition to Corderius, authors most read were Aesop, Cicero, Ovid, Homer, and Virgil, not to mention the Bible, of which there was "a Chapter every morning, and every noon in the *New Testament,*" for, says Hoole, "variety in the Mastery of . . . Accidents."[4]

Moving to Newbury probably meant an improvement in Sewall's education. We know nothing of "Mr. Figes," master of the grammar school he attended at Rumsey, but he would have had to be truly heroic to compare with the Reverend Thomas Parker of Newbury, to whom, the town not having a regular grammar school, Sewall was sent.[5]

Son of a renowned father, Parker was graduated from Magdalen College with a master's degree. His studies had cost him his eyesight, but he would remark "after a Christian and pleasant manner," said Cotton Mather, "Well, they'll be restored shortly, at the resurrection." His nephew, Nicholas Noyes, wrote: "He kept a school, as well as preached. He ordinarily had about 12 or 14 scholars. He took no pay for his pains, unless any present were freely sent him. Though he was blind, yet such was his memory, that he could in his old age teach Latin, Greek, and Hebrew, very artificially. He seldom corrected a scholar, unless for lying and fighting, which were unpardonable crimes." Since Noyes was four years Sewall's senior and Sewall was six years with Parker, one event described by Noyes might have found young Sewall present: "Once hearing some of us laughing very freely, while, I suppose, he was better busied in his chamber above us, he came down, and gravely said to us, 'Cousins, I wonder you can be so merry, unless you be sure of your salvation.' "[6]

Parker was to Sewall "my ever honoured Master," and when he died in April 1677, eighty-two years of age, the twenty-five-year-old diarist wrote: "The Lord give me grace to follow my dear Master as he followed Christ, that I may at last get to heaven whither he has already gone." The fact that Parker remained a bachelor gave Sewall his theme for some characteristic verse titled "A specimen of New England Celibacy":

> Though Rome blaspheme the marriage bed
> And vows of single life has bred [,]
> Chaste Parker, Stoughton, Brinsmade, Noyes,
> Show us the odds 'twixt force and choice.
> These undefiled contracted here,
> Are gone to heaven and married there.[7]

The details of Sewall's education, though interesting in themselves, merit consideration for the better reason that Sewall's nature was a conforming one. He had no inclination to decry with John Locke the practice whereby a youth was "chain'd to the Oar, Seven, Eight, or Ten of the best Years of his Life, to get a Language or two." The making of Latin verses, which Locke called "a foolish custom," was encouraged by Parker, and Sewall took life-long satisfaction in it. Grammar school did not give him, again in Locke's words, the "qualifications requisite to Trade and Commerce and the Business of the World," with the result that as a merchant, keeper of public monies, and possessor of one of the largest estates in New England, he suffered embarassment in keeping accounts; but he never thought to resent this limitation. Instead, he found pleasure in using an appropriate tag of Latin or Greek or in spending a "very entertaining" evening with a friend reading Latin verse.[8]

Parker took "extraordinary delight in singing of psalms" and "bent himself unto the study of the Scripture prophecies." So did Sewall. A matter of more immediate importance, however, was that at the age of fifteen he had so far advanced in mastery of Latin and Greek, "meet Testimony of his towardlinesse," that his father took him down to Cambridge to be examined by President Chauncy for admission to Harvard.[9]

CHAPTER TWO

Harvard College and Intellectual Life

Undergraduate Years

Before Sewall arrived in Cambridge the town and college was described as being "very pleasant, at the end of a spacious plain, more like a bowling green, then a Wilderness, neer a fair navigable river, environed with many Neighbouring Towns . . . so near, that their houses joyn with her suburbs." The timber building which the college occupied was judged "very faire and comely," having "a spacious Hall (where they daily meet at Commons, Lectures, Exercises) . . . a large Library with some Bookes . . . [and] Chambers and studies . . . fitted for, and possessed by the students." But it must have been poorly constructed, for soon after Sewall's graduation it had "fallen doune, a part of it, and thereby rendered not habitable." Work on the so-called New College was begun in 1672. "A fair pile of brick building covered with tiles," it was not yet completed when Sewall took his second degree in 1674. A third structure, the small, brick Indian College, from which one red man had been graduated, held the colony's printing press.[1]

During Sewall's years at Harvard (1667-74) the college had entered on sorry days. The average graduating class in the 1660's was seven, and though he entered with what his school-mate Edward Taylor described as "a great and yet civill class" (eleven being graduated in 1671), the resurgence was temporary. When he took his second degree, there were only twenty-five other students. The college was "languishing and decaying," the buildings "ruinous and almost irreparable." The year after he took his Master's degree three students remained.[2]

The causes for this are not clear. Sewall, who might have thrown light on them, fails almost entirely to do so. When he returned home to Newbury after his graduation in 1674, the General Court asked that he return and give his views on the "lowness of the College." This he did, saying the causes were "external as well as internal." What he meant is suggested by his observation two years earlier that the people of Newbury gave no more attention than "the pines on the beach" to the college's pleas for support. Frontier conditions were apparently having their effect, so that children of the founders did not feel their fathers' concern over who might occupy the pulpits when their present ministers should "lie in the dust."[3]

The "internal causes" seem to have led to a student rebellion. Charles Chauncy, who died in 1671, was succeeded by Leonard Hoar, Harvard's first home-grown president. Generally thought a worthy man, he "fell under the displeasure of some that made a figure in the neighbourhood," wrote Cotton Mather, and "the young men in the Colledge took advantage therefrom, to ruine his reputation, as far as they were able. . . . The young plants turned cud-weeds, and, with great violations of the fifth Commandment, set themselves to travestie whatever he did and said, and aggravate every thing in his behaviour disagreeable to them, with a design to make him odious; . . . several very good men did unhappily countenance the ungoverned youths in their ungovernableness." Things came to such a pass that students began to leave the college; finally the unhappy Doctor resigned in the spring of 1675.[4]

Since 1672 to 1674 were the years when Sewall served as a teaching fellow, we expect some word from him on all this, but again we get only a suggestion, the kind of oblique reference to something troublesome which the discerning reader must learn to recognize. On June 5, 1674, Urian Oakes, pastor of the Cambridge church and college president after Hoar's retirement, told Sewall "that though he respected and loved me as formerly, yet he desired that I would refrain coming to his house, and that he did it *se defendendo,* least he should be mistrusted to discourage and dissettle me." That is all.

But when Sewall was an undergraduate, the redoubtable Chauncy was still President. Like Parker of Newbury, he was a man of large learning, particularly in Oriental languages, a fact which may account for Sewall's fondness for study of Old Testament Scriptures "in their inspir'd Originals." And also like Parker, Chauncy was dauntless in pursuit of his calling, pushing through the snows of a Cambridge winter when past eighty and telling concerned students how happy he would be to die in the pulpit. As college president, says Cotton Mather, "How learnedly he . . . conveyed all the liberal arts unto those who 'sat at his feet'; how wittily he moderated their disputations and other exercises; how constantly he expounded the Scriptures to the College-Hall; how fluently he expressed himself unto them, with Latin of a Terrentian phrase, in all his discourses; and how carefully he inspected their manners . . . will never be forgotten by many of our most worthy men, who were made such by their education under him."[5]

Entering Harvard, the fifteen-year-old Sewall had to satisfy Chauncy in oral examination. Having done this, he then transcribed a copy of the college laws, which the President and one of the fellows signed to evidence his admission. These stipulated, among other things, that he board at commons, be diligent, speak in public eight times during his freshman year, be present twice a week at the public debates, keep good company, leave town only with permission of the president or a tutor, stay out of taverns, avoid "rich and showy clothing," not go out of the yard "unless in his gown, coat, or cloak," and "abstain from dice, cards and every species of gaming for money." His hair was cut to conform with a rule against "wearing of long haire after the manner of Russians and barbarous Indians," a practice "uncivil and unmanly whereby men do deforme themselves . . . and corrupt good manners."[6]

Assigned a tutor and a place in the Long Chamber where he would sleep and keep his chest of belongings, Sewall began his life as a college freshman. Since he was not a fellow-commoner, he acted as "a kind of Servitor . . . to the whole College . . . to go of Errands &c." except during study hours. On a typical day he appeared in College Hall at six o'clock for morning prayers, led by the tireless Chauncy, who had been up since four and had already spent an hour in private devotions. Here, besides a short prayer to begin with and a long one to close, was exposition by Chauncy of a chapter from the Old Testament and sight translations of the text, each scholar in turn, from Hebrew into Greek—unless he were a freshman, in which case he translated from English into Greek. Not surprisingly, cribs were much used, a practice called "hogueing."[7]

After prayers came "morning bever," the first of four meals. Unlike dinner and supper, which were eaten as "commons," it and "afternoon bever" were "sized out" at the buttery hatch and eaten in chambers or, given pleasant weather, in the yard. Staple items were bread and beer bought for a ha'penny, though for another farthing or two cheese and butter might be had. Once Sewall notes having spent three pennies for milk.[8]

Classes met from eight to eleven, followed by dinner in the Hall, when beef was generally added to the bread and beer. Hours from two to four were devoted to public disputations moderated by Chauncy or one of the teaching fellows and, on Friday, declamations. Evening prayers at five were like those in the morning except that the scripture expounded was from the New rather than the Old Testament. Supper came at seven-thirty, and at nine the day ended for all except seniors and fellows, who might stay up till eleven.[9]

The pattern that one associates with this life, that of early-to-bed-and-early-to-rise, of much work and no play, was doubt-less more fiction than fact. We know, for example, that Sewall allowed himself the pleasure of a pipe and that on one occasion his friend Daniel Gookin missed hearing Sir Thacher preach because he was "gone a fishing with his brothers."[10] How-ever, a few days earlier he noted an episode with grimmer suggestion. Thomas Sargeant, "being convicted of speaking blasphemous words concerning the H.G.," was ordered to be "publickly whipped before all the Scholars . . . suspended as to taking his degree . . . sit alone by himself in the Hall uncovered at meals, during the pleasure of the President and Fellows [one of whom was Sewall], and be in all things obedient . . . or else be finally expelled." The whipping took place in the library before the assembled students. The culprit knelt down and "Goodman Hely attended the President's word as to the performance of his part in the work. Prayer was had before and after by the President."[11]

Harvard's curriculum, except for emphasizing Oriental lan-guages and slighting natural philosophy, was essentially that of Oxford or Cambridge. The Chaunceian Code, drawn up in 1655 and in effect until 1686, read in part as follows: "In the first yeare after admission for foure dayes of the weeke all Students shall bee exercised in the Study of the Greeke and Hebrew Tongues, onely beginning Logicke in the Morning towardes the latter end of the yeare unless the Tutor shall see Cause by reason of their ripenesse in the Languages to read Logicke sooner. Also they shall spend the second yeare in Logicke with the exercise of the former Languages, and the third year in principles of Ethickes and the fourth in meta-phisiks and Mathematicks still carrying on their former studyes of the weeke for Rhetoricke, Oratory and Divinity." In addi-tion there were periodic disputations (twice a week for under-graduates), declamations every two months, and twice-daily exposition of Scripture.[12]

At the end of four years Sewall stood for his degree by appearing at appointed hours during a period of three weeks for "visitation" by all who would "examine into his Skill in those Languages and Sciences, that he pretends to be master of," a procedure known as "the Sitting of Solstices." If he could "logically . . . explain the Holy Scriptures, both of the Old and New Testament," was "thoroughly acquainted with the principles of natural and moral philosophy," and was "blameless in life and character," he proceeded to commencement, where he displayed his ability in formal disputation by upholding a thesis.[13]

Master of Arts

Staying on for the M.A. meant Sewall was headed for the ministry. He paid no tuition and received no regular instruction, but read divinity with President Hoar. In graduate student fashion, he gained appointment as a teaching fellow and borrowed against pay day. Unlike his present-day counterpart, however, he held a position of considerable dignity and privilege. He could live, as Sewall did, outside the college, was addressed as "Sir," and enjoyed the respect of town and colony authorities. He and his friend Gookin, for example, were consulted by the "Townsmen of Cambridge" about the seating of students at meeting and were treated "very civilly." They also "were invited and went to dinner with the Magistrates in the Court Chamber." After his graduation, as already noted, the General Court asked for his views on the state of the college.[1]

While the President and Board of Overseers had governance of the institution, the teaching fellows had day-to-day responsibility for instruction and discipline. They were, in fact, the only regular instructors. Leading undergraduates "through all the liberal arts," their instructions were "to advance in all learning, divine and humane, each and every student . . . according to their several abilities; and especially to take care that their conduct and manners be honorable and without blame." The instructional methods might well have left something to be desired. Sewall, for example, teaching a lesson in Heereboord, the physics text, "went to the end, and then red it over from the beginning," in doing which he was following standard practice.[2]

Besides teaching, Sewall was ordered by the Corporation on March 1, 1674, to "be from hence forth the keeper of the Colledg-Library." Whether this put him in charge of "nothing in particular" (a visiting Dutchman's phrase) or of something "handsome" (the word of a visiting Englishman), we can only guess. Certainly facilities were better for divine than for secular studies. Also, since there had been no keeper for seven years before Sewall's appointment, it is not surprising that one of his first tasks was to search out missing books.[3]

Requirements for the M.A. read as follows:

What Bachelours soever shall present unto the President a written Synopsis, or Compendium of Logicke, Natural Philosophy, Arithmeticke, Geometry or Astronomy within a weeke of the Summer Solstice in the third year after taking his first degree (which Synopsis shall be kept in the Colledge Library) and shall bee ready to defend his positions, and be Skilfull in the Originall Tongues as aforesayd, having Staid three yeares after his first degree, and herein thrice problemed, twice declaymed, and once made a Common place or else some answerable exercise in the Studyes that he is most Conversant in and remayning of a blameless Conversation, at any publique Act having the approbation of the Overseers and the President of the Colledge, shall bee Capable of his Second degree, viz to be Master of Arts.[4]

In the days before his graduation in the summer of 1674 Sewall performed his sermon, or "commonplace," to a disappointing audience of six and worked up a thesis on the subject of "Whether original sin be both sin and its punishment?", handled in Latin and stated as "An Peccatum Originale sit & Peccatum & Poena?"[5]

Commencement was an important social occasion, and for it persons of high and low degree made the trip to Cambridge, as Sewall himself often did in later years. Its nature may be seen in his description of one he attended in 1685: "Besides Disputes," he says, there were "four orations, one Latin . . . two Greek, one Hebrew . . . and Mr. President after giving the Degrees made an Oration, in Praise of Academical Studies and Degrees, Hebrew Tongue. . . . Governour there. . . . After Diner the third part of the 103 Psalm was sung in the Hall." At his own commencement he doubtless felt as he did at his son Joseph's ("could not hear one word while the degrees were giving") some thirty years later, when he was "concern'd" lest in his presentation Joseph might fail; "but God helped him and he managed . . . very well."[6]

At least one person in Sewall's commencement audience was impressed, namely sixteen-year-old Hannah Hull, daughter of John Hull, wealthy Boston merchant and master of the colonial mint. "She saw me when I took my Degree," says Sewall, "and set her affection on me, though I knew nothing of it till after our marriage."[7]

Studies Sacred and Profane

So, after spending "seven long years . . . in studious toil," Sewall received from President Hoar the ceremonial book and heard him pronounce the words: "Admitto te ad Secundum Gradum in Artibus, pro more Academiarum in Anglia . . ." —"I admit you to the second degree in Arts, according to the custom of the English Universities; and I deliver to you this book, with the privileges of practising a profession, whenever you shall be called on to do so."[1]

Since the profession of the twenty-two-year-old graduate was to be, he thought, the ministry, the effect of Harvard on his later intellectual interests was chiefly theological. Anywhere but in a community like seventeenth-century Boston the extent of those theological interests would have been singular for a man whose occupations were to be those of merchant, magistrate, and judge. Even in Boston they were notable. The arcana of scriptural prophecy, so dead to present-day concern, were his special delight and the source of his most ambitious intellectual effort, *Phaenomena quaedam Apocalyptica Ad Aspectum Novi Orbis configurata,* the thesis of which is that "America's Name is to be seen fairly Recorded in the Scriptures . . . that it stands fair for being made the Seat of the Divine Metropolis [and] . . . that the New-English Planters were the Forerunners of the Kings of the East."

If some of his interests now seem the trivial concerns of a provincial Puritan mind, it is partly because we fail to place them in context. Sewall's concern with the "Hebdomadal Revolution," for example (arrangement of the week into seven days), seems unimportant, but implications made it otherwise. The Puritan had long been interested in demonstrating the rationality of that "Hebdomadal Revolution." Then in 1704 Jeremiah Dummer, recently returned from his studies abroad, preached a sermon in which he made rationality the test of its divine institution. Sewall was understandably shocked, for the sermon betokens the "Age of Reason" emerging from the "Age of Faith." This was not trivial.[2]

The effect of Sewall's education is equally clear in what he read. "Dr. Calamy's Abridgment of Mr. Baxter's Life," "Dr. Owen upon the Hebrews, all the 4 Books," "*Cosmologia Sacra* by Nehemiah Grew," "Po[o]les Synopsis criticorum in five volumes," "Mr. Henry's Annotations so far as he has gon," "All Calvin's Commentaries," "Dr. Calamy of the ejected Ministers two Vol. and his Answer to him that insulted him," "Mr. Thomas Ridgley's body of Divinity"—such are the books, to name a random few, which appear in overwhelming preponderance in the long order lists he sent to agents in England. The lists are not a completely reliable index to his reading, however, because the student was also a merchant, a fact which results in items like "12. Colsons Seamans Kalendar," "6. Wakely's Compas rectifier," "6. Norwoods Epitome of Navigation," and a "gross of Horn-books."[3]

The books he gave his friends better indicate the kind of reading he enjoyed. Here again the number is great and the nature mainly theological. Receiving seven "Folios of Dr. Owen's Life," for example, he gave one to Mr. Appleton, at whose house he was when he opened the bill of lading, one to Increase Mather, one to his "dear Son, Mr. Joseph Sewall," one to his "loving Son-in-law Mr. William Cooper," one to his "dear and only Brother Stephen Sewall esqr of Salem," and one, he says, "I keep for my self." At a meeting of Superior Court at Cambridge he gave his fellow judges copies of "Maroll's Martyrdom, Marbled." The speaker of the House of Representatives received "Mr. Colman's Book of the Virgins"; his pastor, Mr. Willard, "two volums of Rivets works"; Edward Taylor, his college roommate, "*Centuriae Magdeburgenses,*" a church history in thirteen volumes; his cousin Coffin at Dunstable, "Ainsworth on the Pentateuch"; and so on, indefinitely. Occasionally, by way of relief, he might give almanacs or old copies of the London *Gazette* and Boston *News-Letter*. This was the great day in New England of published sermons, and these he distributed with a generous hand. At home, at court, in council, on circuit—always there were sermons, drawn from their company of "Chockalett," figs, almonds, and other pleasant edibles in the roomy pockets of his outer garments and given to a needy world.[4]

Still better evidence of his reading is in the commonplace book he kept between 1677 and 1686. Here, gathered under such headings (common places) as "De Honore," "De Obedientia," "De Sabato," and "De Conselatione," are extracts from such Puritan favorites as Augustine, Foxe, Calvin, Owen, Pareus, Perkins, Barrow, and Melancthon. Only one secular extract appears, some verses from Dryden's *Indian Emperour,* which he "accidentally met with" at Samuel Green's and read on his way to Hogg Island out in Boston harbor. But while the verses are secular, Sewall's interest was not. What concerned him was the spread of the Catholic faith in Mexico, for which reason he records some dialogue between Montezuma and the conquering Cortez and set about getting "a Smattering of the Spanish tongue." His interest in Turkish and Italian was the same.[5]

Sewall's fondness for writers like Horace, Ovid, and Virgil may surprise one not acquainted with the Puritan's attitude toward his intellectual heritage. Like the schoolmen of thirteenth-century Paris, the Puritans believed in the unity of knowledge. If theology was queen, all other subjects were her servants. Classical authors provided much teleological and moral instruction and were studied with this in mind. As was said of the Boston's famous schoolmaster, Ezekiel Cheever, his students he "from Virgil did to David train." The study of Greek and Roman authors might be seen as ultimately secular, but the purpose of the Puritans was religious.

Once on the way to examine boundaries of his Narragansett lands Sewall stopped for dinner and, waiting, "read in Ben johnson, a Folio":

> Wake, our Mirth begins to dye:
> Quicken it with Tunes and Wine.
> Raise your Notes; you'r out; fie, fie,
> This drowsiness is an ill sign.

These are followed in the diary entry by a dozen more similarly secular lines, and no "improvement" is made. But such instances are rare. Another occurs when he encloses to Governor Saltonstall of Connecticut the lines of Prior's epitaph:

> Monarchs, and Heraulds, by your leave
> Here ly the bones of Matthew Prior;
> The Son of Adam and of Eve:
> Let Bourbon, or Nassau, goe higher![6]

More extensive evidence of secular poetic interest appears in an unpublished memorandum book, where, in addition to the usual pious and memorial "tributes of tears" of the kind he turned out on funereal occasions, he set down some for which the reader is hardly prepared. One, for example, is a "Letter written from a young man in the Country to a Boon Companion in the City concerning a Mourning Cloak; and his conceited Answer thereunto," four lines of which read:

> You say that I shall Smart for the Cloak
> Tho I care not a fart for the Cloak
> I'le study the black Art in the Cloak
> Rather than yeald [?] to part with the Cloak.

One stanza of another runs:

> There is but one and only one
> and I am only he
> That Loves but one and only one
> and thou art only She.

Still another, titled "Wit and Folly in a Map," consists of scrambled lines of verse followed by the invitation to

> Come try your wits for a merry Pot
> In half an hour you read it not,
> In its true sence as it ought to be,
> Then lay a wager stake and see.[7]

Whatever such items say of Sewall's critical taste, they certainly add a fresh touch to the man of stereotyped legend.

Alumnus

Sewall said of Cambridge that "Rome, in all her Pomp and Glory . . . could not be so much . . . to her Julius and Augustus . . . as that Town must needs be to me," and the concept of "our class" was dear to him. During a visit home, while yet a student, he wrote asking his friend Daniel Gookin to

"Remember me kindly to all our Class; jointly and severally." Fifty-five years later he sadly noted having been "at the Interment of four of my Classmates[.] First, the Rev'd Mr. William Adams of Dedham, Midweek, Augt. 19, 1685. Second, Mr. John Bowles, at Roxbury, March, 31, 1691. Was one of his Bearers. Third, Capt. Samuel Phips at Charlestown. . . . Inter'd Augt. 9. 1725. Fourth, the Rev'd Mr. Thatcher at Milton. Now I can go to no more Funerals of my Class-mates; nor none be at mine; for the survivers, the Rev'd Mr. Samuel Mather at Windsor, and the Reverend Mr. Taylor at Westfield, [are] one Hundred Miles off, and are entirely enfeebled."[1]

The next year Mather died, leaving only Sewall and his "dear Colleague, and Chamberfellow," Edward Taylor, who was bedridden and "waiting for his Dismission." In these circumstances Sewall prayed "that as my dear Classmates have run their Race, I also may be made ready." Finally, with the passing of Taylor in the summer of 1728, Sewall found himself, with his "Disorder[ed] . . . Back," "weak Hands," and "feeble Knees," the last surviving member of his class.[2]

Harvard's languishing state in the year after Sewall's graduation did not mean that those in authority failed to recognize its importance in their Wilderness Zion; quite the contrary. In the struggle at the turn of the century between the conservative Mather forces (which included Sewall) and the more liberal forces of the Brattles and John Leverett, the great object was control of the college. With it slipping from his grasp, Increase Mather cried: "O New-ENGLAND! NEW-ENGLAND! Look to it, that the Glory be not removed from thee. For it begins to go. . . . And if the Fountain should fail: I mean the COLLEDGE . . . the Glory is like to be gone . . . in less than one Generation." Leverett's inauguration in 1708 was a victory celebration. The walls of the old conservatism had been breached at their most strategic point.[3]

As an Assistant of the Colony and later as a member of the Council of the Province, Sewall automatically became one of the Overseers of the College. This was not the comparatively meaningless body it later became; it was the governing board. As such it was actively engaged in the Mather-Leverett struggle for control, a struggle which saw Sewall in the role which he repeatedly played as the Puritan state changed, that of the sad, rear guard resister. As he wrote when the colony lost its Charter, "When the foundations are destroyed, what can the Righteous do?"

His most effective action against the Leverett-Brattle forces was in advising those at New Haven who planned to establish a new and untainted stronghold of the faith. In 1701 they appealed to Sewall and his friend Isaac Addington (then Secretary of State for the Province and, like Sewall, a man of the old cast) for help in framing a charter. The two wrote expressing great concern that "the president be enjoined to read and Expound the Scripture in the Hall morning and Evening," a practice at Harvard which had been declining. Also, they were dissatisfied with the vague injunction in Harvard's charter for "the instituting, guiding, and further-ing . . . of piety, morality, and learning." They wanted some-thing more definite and asked that students be required to recite "memoriter" from the Westminster Catechism and from Dr. William Ames's *Medulla* and *Cases of Conscience,* in all of which, as in the expounding of Scripture, Yale's charter reflects their wishes. The letter they wrote to accompany these "Hints for an Act" expresses the conservative attitude. "We should be very glad," it says, "to hear of flourishing Schools and College at Connecticut; and it would be some relief to us against the Sorrow we have conceived for the decay of them in this Province."[4]

Expounding of Scripture by the college head was a sore point with Sewall and one which brought him into conflict not only with the Leverett forces but with the Mathers as well. Increase Mather, though eager to assume control of the col-lege, was unwilling to give full time to the job. He wished instead to commute from Boston. "Should I," he asked, "Leave off preaching to 1500 souls . . . only to expound to 40 or 50 children?" Sewall not only felt that he should, but that even were he to reside in Cambridge and yet "not Expound the Scriptures, and Pray in the Hall . . . the Example of it would doe more hurt, than his going thither would doe good." When he spoke in Council to this effect, Cotton Mather came to Mr. Wilkin's shop, where Sewall's son Sam was working, and said that Sewall "had used his father worse than a Neger; spake so loud that people in the street might hear him." Sewall recalled "Mr. Dod's saying; Sanctified Afflictions are good Promotions," which he found a "cordial." He also recalled that a few days earlier he had sent Increase Mather "a Hanch of very good Venison" and hoped that in that he "did not treat him as a Negro."[5]

Next day he wrote Cotton Mather suggesting that they meet at Wilkins' with some mutual friends and "try to give an Instance of the Truth of that old Proverb; *Amantium Irae Amoris Redintegratio est.*" They met the following morning and Sewall "expostulated with him from 1 Tim. 5.1. Rebuke not an elder." Mather replied that "he had consider'd that" and, says Sewall, went on to charge the Council with "Lying, Hypocrisy, Tricks, and I know not what all. I ask'd him if it were done with that Meekness as it should; answer'd yes. Charg'd the Council in general, and then shew'd my share, which was my speech. . . . I ask'd him If I should suppose he had done somthing amiss in his Church as an Officer; whether it would be well for me to exclaim against him in the street for it (Mr. Wilkin would fain have had him goe into the inner room, but he would not.) I told him I conceiv'd he had done much unbecoming a Minister of the Gospel." At this point Sewall was called away to Council, where he "Hammer'd out an Order for a Day of Thanksgiving," something for which the events of the morning had not offered much encouragement.

Next day, again at Wilkins', Increase Mather announced that "if I am a Servant of Jesus Christ, some great Judgment

will fall on Capt. Sewall or his family."* Two days later, after
Sewall had circulated a copy of his speech in Council "that
all might see what was the ground of Mr. Mather's Anger,"
the storm began to subside, so that Sewall could note: "They
seem to grow calm." This was toward the end of October.
On December 31, in "consideration of this being the last day
of the year" and inasmuch as Cotton Mather had honored
Sewall's pew by sitting there in meeting "last Tuesday was
fortnight," Sewall wrote to say that he did "now Remise,
Release and forever quit claim, as to any personal Controversy
we were lately managing at Mr. Wilkins's" and signed himself "your truly loving friend and humble Servant." Besides
showing Sewall at work in Harvard politics, the episode shows
in part why the Mathers were finally pushed from their
dynastic place.

Seventeen years later Sewall was still waging his fight for
more regular expounding of Scripture. On November 12, 1718,
the business before the meeting of Overseers concerned the
proposed dimensions of Massachusetts Hall. The motion being
called for, Sewall rose and said that though the matter in hand
was of "great moment," he "apprehended there was an affair
of greater moment." "I had heard," he says,

> Exposition of the Scriptures in the Hall had not been
> carried on [and] . . . enquired of the President [Lev-
> erett] whether 'twere so or no. Was silence a little while;
> then the President seem'd to be surprised at my Treating
> of him in that Manner; I did not use to do so. . . . Many
> spake earnestly that what I did was out of Season. . . .
> When I was fallen so hard upon, I said I apprehended
> the not Expounding the Scriptures was a faulty Omis-
> sion, and I was glad I had that Opportunity of shewing

---

* The title of Captain refers to Sewall's role in the South Company,
one of Boston's train bands, and in the volunteer organization called
the Ancient and Honourable Artillery Company. Though he had at
this time been a judge for many years, he was commonly known as
Captain Sewall.

my dislike of it. President said, he had begun to take it up agen; I said I was glad of it. . . . Mr. Belcher stood up, and mov'd earnestly that Exposition might be attended. At last Mr. Wadsworth stood up and spake in favour of it, and drew up a vote that the president should *as* frequently *as he could* entertain the students with Exposition of the holy Scriptures. . . . I mov'd that *as he could* might be left out; and it was so voted. Mr. President seem'd to say softly, it was not till now the Business of the President to Expound in the Hall. I said I was glad the Overseers had now the Honour of declaring it to be the President's Duty.

A week later Leverett spoke to him again "and intimated that twas not the President's Duty to Expound before this Order." Sewall replied that "twas a Shame that a Law should be needed; meaning *ex malis moribus bonae Leges.*"

Three years later he was less successful in opposing the course of change, the issue this time being a stipulation in the Hollis endowment for a divinity professorship that the occupier of it should be "in Communion with a Church of Congregational[ists], Presbyterian[s], or Baptists." Sewall objected to such a condition, "chusing rather to lose the Donation than to Accept it." But when it came to the vote, "very few appear'd in the Negative." Edward Wigglesworth was shortly appointed to the post, and it was Sewall, characteristically enough, who administered the oath at his installation. As was so often the case, he registered resistance and, failing, resigned himself.[6]

Despite his opposition to developments at the college, Sewall's allegiance remained unshaken. Even when giving advice to Yale, he worked to get Harvard's charter of 1700 passed in the right form, and though he continued to be "a Well-wisher" to the new college in Connecticut, he also sent up prayers for his *alma mater*. It was to Harvard that he gave five hundred acres of his Narragansett lands, and to it he sent in precious trust his son Joseph to be trained for the ministry.[7]

On the subject of Sewall and Harvard there remains only

to be considered his marriage, which, in a practical sense, was the most important result of his college years. Abruptly it changed the course of his life, as the minister-to-be found himself born, willy-nilly, into the world of property and merchandise.

CHAPTER THREE

Merchant and Man of Property

Father Hull

In 1680 Governor Bradstreet noted that "two or three" men in Massachusetts might be worth "sixteen or eighteen thousand pounds a piece, some few others worth eight or ten thousand pounds a piece, a third sort worth four or five thousand pounds a piece. . . . He is accounted a rich man in the Country that is worth one thousand or Fifteen hundred pounds." Shortly before this John Hull set down an inventory of his estate in which he valued his "lands," "shares in ships," "dwelling houses," "money and goods," and "Debts owing" at twelve thousand and sixty pounds. He was, in short, one of those Boston merchants who struck an English visitor as "damnable rich."[1]

We shall not here treat in detail Hull's rise from silversmith to colonial worthy, but some knowledge of the man's career helps one understand the society in which he prospered and the man who became his son-in-law. It is worth noting, for example, that Hull's youthful care of his aged mother, "then weak in body, and poor in estate," caused the Reverend John Wilson to prophesy: "I charge you to take notice of what I say; God will certainly bless that young man; John Hull . . . shall grow rich, and live to do God good service in his generation!" Cotton Mather tells the story and ends by saying: "It came to pass accordingly that this exemplary person became a very rich, as well as emphatically a good man, and afterwards died a magistrate of the colony." Hull thus stands as an impressive example of that happy combination of riches and righteousness so admired in Puritan New England, a man of whom John Danforth could write:

> Choice HULL the fifth Command observ'd so well,
> His Carriage to His Parent did Excell;
> Wilson Pronounc'd the Promis'd Blessing then;
> The LORD of Providence too said AMEN.
> The Hull, soon Built upon, became an Argo;
> Deep fraighted with Terrene & Heav'nly Cargo;
> Immortal Vertue gave Immortal Name;
> Long Life, Power, Honour Added to his Fame.
> Stretching his Course, Refresh'd with Prosperous Gales,
> Quitting New-England's Coasts, to Heav'n he sails.[2]

In Puritan Massachusetts piety and wealth meant public office. Thus Hull, between 1668 and 1680, was deputy for Wenham, Westfield, Concord, and Salisbury at meetings of the General Court. For three years (1676–79) after King Philip's War he served the hard-pressed colony as its Treasurer, digging into his own coffers to support its shaky finances, and from 1680 to his death in 1683 he was annually elected to the oligarchic Court of Assistants. Also, as a good citizen of Boston, he served at various times as one of its selectmen and as a member of both the South Military Company and the Ancient and Honorable Artillery Company. In the latter organization he was Captain from 1671 to 1678, a post of much honor.[3]

As regards Sewall, these details show how largely he inherited not only Hull's wealth but his responsibilities. When, in 1683, Sewall became a member of the General Court, it was as representative of the town of Westfield, which Hull had represented ten years before. When Hull's death left vacant his seat on the Court of Assistance, Sewall was elected to that lofty post the following year. Hull being a founder and chief pillar of South Church, Sewall became one of its principal supporters. In his service with the South Company and the Ancient and Honorable Artillery Company, he followed in the steps of "father Hull." He was, in short, Hull's political, religious, and social, as well as his financial, heir. Except for his career on the bench, Sewall did not create his public life, he entered on its duties.

The legendary part of Hull's career had chiefly to do with his work as Mintmaster of the Colony, in which capacity he and his partner, John Sanderson, turned out some five million dollars worth of pine-tree shillings. The colony first undertook to supply itself with specie in 1652 and contracted with Hull to supervise the job, allowing him "to take one shilling out of every twenty." The authorities soon recognized the extravagance of this arrangement and sought to reduce Hull's seigniorage, but Hull declared himself eminently satisfied, and not till 1675 was it lowered to twelve pence per twenty shillings. Since his gross return on the project was about two hundred thousand dollars hard money, an enormous sum in the specie-short colony, it is no wonder that gossip put his daughter's dowry at thirty thousand pounds or that Hawthorne, suiting fiction to legend, gave him a strong box "large enough to play at hide-and-seek in" and "full to the brim of bright pine-tree shillings fresh from the mint."[4]

The Meaning of Prosperity

John Hull's swift rise to affluence epitomizes that of the colony. Cotton Mather's "howling wilderness" had become, after fifty years, a place of which a visiting Englishman could write:

The merchants seem to be rich men, and their houses [are] as handsomely furnished as most in London. In exchange of fish, pipe-staves, wool and tobacco, they have from Spain, Portugal and the islands, the commodities of those islands; their wool they carry to France and bring thence linen; to England they bring beaver, moose, and deer skins, sugar and logwood, and carry

home cloth and ironwares; to Barbadoes, in exchange
for horses, beef, pork, butter, cheeses, flour, peas, biscuit,
they have sugar and indigo; when they trade with
Jamaica, as they do sometimes, they bring home pieces
of eight, plate and pigs of silver.[1]

As early as 1654 Edward Johnson, first historian of the Bay,
exclaimed over "this City-like Towne . . . whose continuall
enlargement presages some sumptuous City"—and this where
but a few years back "Wolfes and Beares nurst up their
young."[2]

The earth is the Lord's, and the saints of New England set
to work possessing it in his name. *Laborare et orare.* That
wealth should follow was a cause for thanks but not surprise.
As Cromwell wrote when trying to persuade New Eng-
landers to remove to Jamaica, where they would "better . . .
their outward condition," God intended that "his people
should be the head and not the tail."[3]

John Josselyn, in his *Account of Two Voyages to New-
England* (London, 1675), describes the Boston in which
Sewall began his life as John Hull's protégé:

The houses are for the most part raised on the Seabanks
and wharfed out with great industry and cost, many of
them standing upon piles, close together on each side
the streets as in London, and furnished with many fair
shops [;] their materials are Brick, Stone, Lime, handsomely contrived, with three meeting-Houses or
Churches, and a Townhouse built upon pillars where
the Merchants may confer [;] in the Chambers above
they keep their monethly Courts, Their streets are many
and large, paved with pebble stone and the South-side
[where the Hulls lived] adorned with Gardens and
Orchards. The Town is rich and very populous, much
frequented by strangers. . . . There is a small but pleasant
Common where the Gallants a little before Sunset walk
with their Marmalet-Madams as we do in Morefields,

&c. till the nine a clock Bell rings them home to their respective habitations, when presently the Constables walk their rounds to see good orders kept, and to take up loose people. Two miles from the town at a place called Muddy-River the Inhabitants have Farms [one of them Hull's, later Sewall's] to which belong rich noble grounds and meadows where they keep their Cattle in the Summer, and bring them to Boston in the Winter; the Harbour before the town is filled with Ships and other Vessels for the most part of the year.

With its twenty-five hundred houses, busy shipyards, wharves, shops, and counting houses, its military installations, churches, and governmental pomp, Boston was something to excite satisfaction in its founders, such as were yet alive. Certainly Sewall, returning to it from drowsing Newbury, must have looked about him, considered his sudden prosperity, and remarked God's kindly providence in his life.[4]

But good Puritan that he was, Sewall could not simply enjoy prosperity. The doctrine of stewardship by which Puritans came to terms with the world, setting out to subdue it for God's glory instead of rejecting it for the same reason, was logically right and theoretically righteous. Its practical effects, however, were disturbing: diligent stewardship brought wealth, which in turn brought temptation. It was easy for John Cotton to speak of "diligence in worldly businesses, and yet deadnesse to the world" as a "combination of vertues" desirable in "every lively holy Christian," but the second of these virtues had a way of getting lost in the first, so that prosperity brought with it a sense of "falling away" from "the primitive glory."[5]

When, for example, Edward Johnson was waxing eloquent over the colony's wealth, the Reverend John Norton was expressing his fear that in forgetting it was "a Plantation Religious, not a plantation of Trade," it would earn the name of Ichabod. By the turn of the century, Increase Mather thought it had earned that name. In fact, he called up the

37

memory of John Norton to mark the sad change in Boston. When would the town see his like again? "And almost every where 'tis so, whether in our Ecclesiastical, Military, or Civil State. So that what our Great Hooker long since predicted, that the People of New England would be punished with the want of Eminent Men to manage Publick affairs, both in Church and State is in part sadly verified already." The first generation lived for the church, their sons for "Trade and Land." As the unclerical Ned Ward put it, "Interest is their Faith, Mony their God, and Large Possessions the only Heaven they covet."[6]

In the 1670's, when Sewall was troubled by having to choose between the ministry and merchandise, Eleazar Mather reminded his congregation that while prosperity might be a sign of God's blessing, "when men have prosperity, outward riches, and know not what to do with them, besides making gods of them, this is a sign that the Lord's gracious presence" is not among them. He called for "less Trading, Buying, Selling . . . more Praying . . . more close walking," and asked: "You had once another Spirit, had you not? A right New-England Spirit. . . . Are you the same men you were? Are you not strangely changed?" Ezekiel was commanded to prophecy over dead bones, but, said Mather, "I have dead hearts to deal withal." And Sewall's college friend, Urian Oakes, declared: "All sides are agreed that things are in a declining posture, that there is a great degeneracy . . . that there is a defection and declension." He reminded his audience, as he may well have reminded Sewall, that ministers were now reckoned "Bills of Charges" and hoped he might never see the time when "houses and lands, lots and farms and outward accomodations are of more value . . . than the Gospel and Gospel ordinances. . . . Surely there were other and better things the people of God came hither for than the best spot of ground, the richest soil." In 1679 Increase Mather observed that "God sifted three Nations . . . so he might bring over choice grain into this wilderness." Never was there a group of men who "did so perfectly shake off the dust of Babylon." But "this Generation is not like the first," and the change "from a Religious to a worldly Interest" was "the great Radical Apostasy of New-England."[7]

In 1679 also, *The Necessity of Reformation* appeared. The work of a group of Boston elders and ministers, it ranks with loss of the charter as a mark of change in the Bible Commonwealth—the one chiefly political, the other moral and religious. It spoke of the "Great and visible decay of Godliness," of "Oathes . . . in ordinary discourse," of selling at "excessive rates," of neglect of schools, of Sabbath breaking and irreverence at worship, of the debauching of Indians by "those who call themselves Christians," of increase in adultery, of "farms and merchandising . . . [being] preferred before the things of God." All of which may be thought no more than the sort of thing expected from clerics in any age. Many facts, however, give it the look of truth. The most revealing have to do with loss of the charter, which, to use Sewall's word, embodied the very "foundations" of the Puritan state.[8]

Attacks on the charter by enemies of the colony were nothing new. What was new was the spirit with which men of Sewall's generation faced these attacks. In 1634 the threatened appointment of a Royal Governor elicited from the magistrates a grim decision "not to accept him, but defend our lawful possessions," and a wrathful Endecott tore the hated cross from the English flag. Fortifications were begun out on Castle Island and a military committee was appointed as the colony prepared for the worst. Fortunately for it, events in England kept the threat from materializing, and the colony entered on a century of almost complete self-rule.[9]

When the threat was renewed, men of Endecott's generation were mostly gone, and resistance of the kind they planned seems never to have occurred to their sons—certainly not to Sewall. He merely records, sadly, fatalistically, developments pointing to the old order's passing. His feelings are of sadness and resignation, and his voice is the voice of submission. His affections are touched, moving him to tears, but of passion there is nothing. On January 7, 1684/5, the town "had the newes of . . . [the] Charter's being condemned, just as going to Meeting." On July 24 following, there were "very sharp debates about submission &c. upon a Governour's Arrival, occasioned by a vote from the Deputies to the purpose that the Court be Adjourned till third Wednesday in August except some demand of the Government from His Majestie be made before." The decision, finally, was to adjourn, Sewall not voting.

In December, Samuel Shrimpton refused to appear at court because it "proceeded upon a Law made since the vacating the Charter . . . so that," remarks Sewall, "we begin palpably to dye." Controversy in the Shrimpton case dragged through several months, with much "Heat between the Members of the Court"—and no decision. "Such discourses and arguing before the People," says Sewall, made the government "grow weaker and weaker." "The symptoms of Death are on us."

On May 21, 1686, magistrates and deputies went to the home of Governor Bradstreet. There "Adjournment . . . was declared by the Weeping Marshal-Generall. Many Tears Shed in Prayer and at Parting." Sewall felt "moved to sing, so sang the 17. and 18. verses of Habakkuk." Two days later Joseph Dudley took office as provisional President under orders from England, and on December 19 following: "As I was reading the Exposition of Habakkuk third, which this morning sung and read in the family, I heard a great Gun or two . . . which made me think Sir Edmond [Andros] might be come." He was right, and five days later: "About 60 Red-Coats are brought to Town, landed at Mr. Pool's Wharf, where drew up and so marched to Mr. Gibbs's house at Fort-Hill."

The charter government was dead, so that on the day for meeting of the Court of Assistants, the deposed Sewall could only record that it had been "a great day of feasting on Board Capt. Head." Similarly, when the General Court should have met, there was instead a celebration of the King's birthday, with firing of guns and people marching through the streets "with Viols and Drums, playing and beating by turns."

Such is Sewall's record of the great change that came to Massachusetts under James II. Of anger or outrage, there is not a word, but the feeling rather than "we . . . deserv'd to be turn'd out long ago." There was the feeling, too, that God had somehow failed his people, the Wednesday night meeting of the South Church Society asking: "How shall we attend known Duty with cheerfullness and Constancy: though God impart not so much of his Counsel as we could desire?" When papers condemning the charter were formally shown the General Court, Sewall spoke against any protest—"The foundations being destroyed what can the Righteous do?"[10]

It would be oversimplifying matters to say that adherence to radical principle in the fathers had been supplanted by concern for property in the sons. The situation was complex. For example, foreign trade and the rapidly growing number of "strangers" had ended the colony's sense of sanctuary and isolation. Concentration of authority in ministers and magistrates had lessened as villages became towns and towns became cities. Most important, the great Puritan movement had largely spent its force. The creation of the fathers was the inheritance of the sons, and the confidence of the builders had become the caution of the conservators. No one can doubt Sewall's love of "the first ways of N. E.," but it was a cautious love. He and his friends were no less devoted than their fathers, just lesser men in different times. Endecott's rending an idolatrous cross from the English flag, Hooker's readiness to "put a king in his pocket"—such things were memories. What was wanted now was safety, and safety said *Submit*.

But however we account for what took place, we finally return to the change "from a Religious to a worldly Interest." Sewall's inability to act when the charter government fell was suddenly overcome when he learned that Andros meant a threat to property.* On July 16, 1688, Sewall was told of "a Writt out against [him] . . . for Hog-Island [a property out in the bay], and against several other persons for Land, as being violent intruders into Kings Possessions." Next day he tried to go to the island to see if a writ had been served on its tenant but had to give up because of bad weather and a broken oar. This was Friday. On Saturday he wrote to friends in England through his London agent, Edward Hull, enclosing fifty pounds "to pay them . . . if they call'd for it." The following Monday he wrote to Ephraim Savage, from whom he had purchased the Hogg Island property, asking him to "consider seriously what may be most proper for defence." Then, after a few days' thought, he tried to make peace with Andros through a petition "humbly praying" for "Grant and Confirmation of the said Hogg-Island . . . upon such moderate Quit-Rent as your Excellency shall please to order."

This was not easy to do, for, as he wrote Increase Mather, now Massachusetts' agent in England, "I was urg'd by my friends two contrary wayes; but at last have . . . petition'd. . . . Mr. Dudley, Stoughton and several principal men having taken Patents . . .; some of which were formerly most averse." Then he makes this comment: "The generality of People are very averse from complying . . . and look upon me very sorrowfully that I have given way." That is, he had identified with Dudley and Stoughton, leaders of the party of submission, men who, for property's sake, stood ready to do Andros' bidding. Later the same year he again wrote Increase Mather, repeating the facts and adding: "Am so sensible of the miseries this people [are] like to undergoe, if that course be follow'd [the course he had already taken], that I shall be very willing to give more than comes to my share, if some general way of Relief might be obtain'd." His concern was such that he wished to "cast [himself] on the sea to come for England before petitioning, but knew not how to get away," his wife being "very near her time." He ends by "Praying God you

---

* The new government held that when the charter was cancelled, so were property rights granted under it.

may hapily finish what you have so well begun, especially about Property. . . ."[11]

Finally, in November, 1688, he took passage and arrived in an England that had undergone its Bloodless Revolution. Increase Mather was at court working to obtain a new and more favorable charter, and Sewall did his best to help, consulting about "a virulent Libel" which had appeared against New England, visiting influential persons "to promote our Interest," going to Westminster "to give Evidence for N.E.," and appealing for a new policy in the name of "Religion, Liberty and Property." Plainly it was the third of this trinity that brought him to a course of action more effectual than prayer.

The Marriage of Wealth

On leaving Harvard, Sewall went home to Newbury with his two brothers, Stephen and John. There he passed the next year and a half doing nothing in particular—watching his brothers and friends marry and get settled, visiting his old master, Thomas Parker, and tending to such odd jobs as writing family letters, getting in the beans, and felling an oak near the house while his mother and sister stood by weeping ("*Matre et Sorore valde plangentibus*"). He received a call to a church at Woodbridge, New Jersey, a town settled by people from Newbury, which he did not accept. Once he took over Parker's pulpit and had a discouraging time ("Being afraid to look on the [hour] glass, ignorantly and unwillingly . . . stood two hours and a half"). When and why he gave up plans for the ministry he does not say. Certainly his approaching marriage was a factor. He would have been less than human did he not tell himself that he was, in the words of the Reverend Thomas Prince, "by the call of Providence directed from it," and that his being "put into the early possession of Secular Wealth" offered "a larger Sphere and Power of Employing his Talents for the Glory of God."[1]

His decision, or indecision, caused him some distress. Shortly before his marriage, for example, he wrote: "Morning proper fair, the wether exceedingly benign, but (to me) metaphoric, dismal, dark and portentous, some prodigie appearing in every corner of the skies." Not until four months after his marriage did he go with Hull "to Mr. Smith's, there to see the manner of the Merchants," and eight months later his "calling" was still not fixed: "Feb. 23, 1676/7. Mr. [Samuel] Torrey spake with my Father [Hull] at Mrs. Norton's, told him that he would fain have me preach, and not leave off my studies to follow Merchandize." Two months before this the Reverend John Reyner of Dover, a relative by marriage, had expressed the opposite view. Walking with Sewall in the orchard, he urged him "not to keep over much within, but goe among men." He would thereby "advantage" himself.

A year had passed since his marriage and more than two since his graduation from Harvard; still he hesitated. Gradually, however, uncertainty ended, less through decision than through accepting what seemed inevitable. By the spring of 1677 he was in active apprenticeship with Hull, drawing up a "Joynt Account between my Father in Law, and me" involving "three Bayles and two Hoggsheds of English Goods received from on Board the Blessing." Items like "Calico," "Blankets," "Ruggs," "Blew Linnen," "green Serge Cortains" with "French Fringe," "Mens Felts," "Mens Castors" (a kind of beaver hat), "Black Taffata," "Lawn," and "Cambrick" were reminders of how far he now was from the ministry.[2]

Though Sewall's intellectual interests remained chiefly theological, his commercial involvement exemplifies the triumph of wealth in the Puritan community and the movement away from the pulpit as a seat of power. Jaspar Danckaerts, a Dutchman who visited New England at about this time, noted the growing secular spirit and wrote: "When we were there, four ministers' sons were learning the silversmith's trade." Sewall's course was more direct: he married the daughter of the richest silversmith in the colony. This is not to say that he followed a course of shrewd ambition (according to Sewall it was she who first "set her affection" on him, not the other way around), only that some men act upon life while others are acted upon by it. Sewall was among the latter.[3]

If the diary says little of Sewall's decision to abandon the ministry, it says even less of his courtship and marriage. If he ever went down from Newbury and "had a discourse" with Hannah Hull, as he notes his brother doing with Hannah Fessenden at Cambridge, he never noted the fact. During the month before his marriage, even on the day itself, he is silent. His only word on the subject is in a letter to his son Sam, many years later: "Gov. Bradstreet married us . . . in the Old Hall [of the Hull residence on High Street]; 't was then all in one, a very large Room."[4]

John Hull's biographer describes the wedding—busy preparation of cakes, puddings, and ale, wedding apparel arriving from England, the aristocracy of the colony gathering, flames leaping in the fireplace and silver tankards reflecting the glow. All of which is pleasant speculation of a more believable sort than the legendary weighing-in of the bride, but still only speculation. (If, incidentally, the dowry was indeed thirty thousand pounds paid in pine-tree shillings, she could hardly have been weighed against it. Such an amount, rating a silver pound as four ounces, comes to something over three tons. As a matter of fact, the settlement was probably five hundred pounds. Such, at any rate, was the amount Sewall entered in his account book as from "My Father-in-law, Mr. John Hull, to his Free Promise."[5] This amount makes the weighing-in possible, for its weight would have been one hundred twenty-five pounds.)

In estimating Sewall's position in the colony after his marriage, it means little whether or not popular belief about the dowry was true. What is significant is that Hull's wealth was the stuff of legend.

Apprentice Years

Because, through the loss of a manuscript volume, a gap occurs in Sewall's diary from March, 1677, to February, 1685, and because, too, regular entries in his letter-book do not begin until 1686, the record is scanty for the years when he was beginning his business career. It is clear, however, that toward the end of his life Hull turned more and more of his earthly affairs over to his son-in-law. When, for example, a business correspondent wrote suggesting a cargo of hoops, fish and pipe-staves for the Canaries, Hull replied that he wished more "to embrace oppertunyty of getting out rather than running into the business of this world Speacially forraigne traffique as desirous to be more thoughtfull of Launching into the vast ocian of Eternity whether we must all shortly bee carried." That Sewall was taking over Hull's accounts is shown in Hull's writing to an agent in London on December 27, 1680, that he had received his shipment of "glasses and hats" and had turned the matter over to "my Son-in-law, Samuel Sewall. . . . He hath sold your hats and some glasses; and as he can sell the rest, and receive in, so he will render you an account, and make you a return; and I hope with prudence and faithfulness, for he is both prudent and faithful."[1]

Because of Sewall's inexperience one must doubt that he was always prudent. There is something plaintive in a set of entries which show him, fresh from his theological studies, having trouble with "Some petty Debtours . . . to whom I delivered goods of my Father's, trustingly"—such things as "a Barrel of Rum," "13 Bus. ½ of Malt," "2 Length. of Rope & a Bus. ½ of wheat." On one occasion Hull's impatience was such that Sewall retreated into Latin when writing of it. Someone had angered Hull by bringing him, as Treasurer of the Colony, oats in place of money for a tax payment. Then when Sewall threw a larger log on the fire than the old men thought proper, he was told that Hull could have no confidence in him if "his mind would be as unstable as if it were akin to the wind." Sewall patiently told himself that "no godly man hath any more afflictions than what he hath need of." Still, when Hull "watched his last" in 1683, Sewall's sorrow could hardly have been unmixed with relief. Thirty-one years old and the father of four, he was still "son Sewall."[2]

Two years earlier he had made a move toward independence by undertaking the management of Boston's printing press. Located in a shop "over against the Sign of the Dove" (an inn on Snow Lane), it had begun operation in 1674 under John Foster. After Foster's death, Sewall, "at the instance of some friends with respect to the accommodation of the publicke," took over. Though government documents and the score or so of books which appeared during the two years of his management were largely the work of his assistant, Samuel Green, Sewall sometimes worked at the case himself. Thus, on February 2, 1684/5, he wrote to his English uncle Nathaniel Dummer:

> It so fell out that not long since I was the owner of a printing press and Letters, and practised something myself in that science. Not to mention other things, I composed the Assemblies Cathechism with the proofs, Mr. Oakes's Artillerly Election Sermon at Cambridge. ... [I] have sent six hundred of them [the catechisms] in a small box, which intreat the young persons of Bishop Stoke [Sewall's birthplace] will kindly accept from him who cannot but affectionately remember his native soil. ... If you have to spare, let Baddesley [the town to which Sewall's family had moved from Bishop Stoke] next partake.[3]

The lost diary volume would tell us much about these years, concerning which we can only speculate. Apparently Sewall's interest in the press was somewhat casual. The last work published under his mangement was Samuel Willard's sermon preached at Hull's funeral. The General Court then released him from the post, which passed to Samuel Green.[4]

The World of Business

At John Hull's death, Sewall came into what he describes as "an Estate that might afford a competent Subsistence according to our manner of living in N. E." By agreement among the heirs (Hull having died intestate), something more than a third remained in the hands of mother Hull, but she and her son-in-law were on the best of terms, so this was nominal. When she died in 1695 all she had went to Samuel, Hannah, and their children.[1]

Rentals, both in money and kind, flowed in. Few men owned more Boston property than Sewall (four in 1687, one of the few years for which tax lists survive), and income from it was considerable. In the large, close-packed pages of his ledger appear such items as sixteen pounds a year from "Walker's House," fourteen from the "House at Cotton Hill," six from "the new Warehouse," four from "rent of the stables," sixty from Hogg Island, six from the shop occupied by cabinet maker William Howell, three from "a shop at the warehouse," ten shillings from a "Lot in Hull Street," four from shoemaker Joshua Lane for the "Shop next Mr. Poles," twenty from "Hoar's House," four pounds ten shillings from "Part of the house by the Dock," and so on, innumerably. Around twenty pounds a year came from property at Rumsey in Hampshire, England, given him by his father in 1680. Narragansett holdings brought anywhere from fifteen pounds in 1694 to forty-six in 1711. Hogg Island revenue stayed at sixty pounds for several years after 1715, but by 1729 was up to eighty. Typical rentals from other outlying properties were twelve shillings from his "Share of Meadow in the Land of Nod" (at Woburn), one pound for "Rent of the Saw-Mill Stream at Braintry," ten pounds from the lands at Muddy River, one pound for a "Meadow in Shrewsbury," two pounds ten shillings for "Ram Island in Merrimak River," six pounds from Moses Adams of Sherborn for his farm there, one pound ten shillings for "5 acres of Salt-Marsh at Newbury."[2]

Some of these amounts seem small, but even the smallest had a purchasing power for local products which is hard to believe. This is shown when payment was in kind. In 1694, for example, Sewall rented four acres of "Marsh" to Thomas and Joshua Gardener at one pound ten shillings a year. In the next five years they supplied him some twenty loads of oak and walnut firewood, three pigs, and numerous "fowl," for which they received a credit of four pounds, leaving them three and a half pounds in debt![3] Sturgeon, corn meal, sides of pork, tubs of butter, hay, cider, malt, turkeys, cattle—everything New England produced and the Sewall household could use came from tenants at such places as Muddy River, Sherborn, Hogg Island, Shrewsbury, and Newbury.

If Sewall's income made possible a life of leisure, he ignored the fact, knowing that the Christian must have a calling and "walk diligently" in it. One who did not, though he have "two thousands to spend," was "an uncleane beast." Man was sent into this world, not "as into a Play-house, but a Work-house," and those who did not sweat on earth would surely sweat in hell.[4] Sewall bent to his work.

Information on New England trade for the period is meager, but its pattern, size, and importance to the colony are all clear enough. Since the balance of trade between old and New England was heavily in favor of the mother country, Boston merchants had to find a means of gaining credit abroad. This they did by maintaining with the West Indies a balance of trade heavily in their favor. Thus emerged the triangular pattern of Boston to West Indies, West Indies to England, England to Boston. It appears in the dealings of John Hull and later in those of Sewall.

Everything about Sewall's commercial activities, in fact, is a copy of Hull's—routes, commodities, ships, and agents. He simply took over where Hull left off. In small square-rigged ketches like the *Seaflower, Hopewell, Pomgranet,* and *Fidelity,* New England staples "for the proper account and risque of Mr. Samuel Sewall" went to Port Royal, Jamaica, St. Christopher, Barbados, Antigua in the West Indies, and occasionally to Bilbao, Spain. Most important was fish—barrels, hogsheads, and "quintals" of "good sound Mackarell," "good merchantable codfish," "dry Bass," "pickled Bass," "Alewifes," and "scale fish." For West Indian rum and sugar there were staves—white oak for rum casks, red oak for sugar —fashioned into barrels and hogsheads by a ship's cooper on the outward voyage. In smaller amounts went barrels of pork and beef, hogsheads of "bread and pease," "firkins" of butter, "sidar," "unyons," apples, and occasionally candles, "train oyll," and tar. Proceeds from their sale were sometimes converted to goods for return to Boston, but generally either money or bills of exchange went to Sewall's agents in London, chief of whom was his "Loving Cousin," Edward Hull "at the Hat in Hand within Algate." Since the need was English credit, such things as "oyle," beaver, "Cramberries," molasses, sugar, and "logwood" were sometimes sent, but more often "fine silver," pieces of eight, "dust gold," "money of England," "Spanish pistolls," "Arabian Gold," and "Mexico pieces melted down." For the same reason, income from Sewall's property in England went to his London agents.[5]

From England, in return, came "hard mettald" sithes, "rub stones," "good strong serviceable knives," "worsted Damask stuffs, several colors," "Castors," "Good black Broad-Cloth," casks of the "best sweet-Meats," "Nailes," various kinds of "sive Bottoms," "cod hooks," "blew duffals," "mixt sad coloured searg," "coloured callico," "Wickar Fans to fan Corn with"—everything, in short, which the mother country had and the colony lacked. Some was used in the Sewall household, some was resold on commission, some he ordered because "importuned to" by Boston citizens.[6]

Besides being a merchant and property owner, Sewall sometimes acted as banker, money-lender, and pawnbroker. One page of his accounts, for example, carries the note that "at the latter end of the Summer [of 1679] Mary Howen pawned a Warming Pan for ten shillings of Mother Hull." Needing the pan during the following winter, she brought "in the room of it . . . two Platters." Later she brought "two small Platters for Six Shillings," "a whole Apron laced at the gathers, and an old Scarf" for four shillings, and "three small Pewter platters" for five shillings. In 1680 scarf and apron were redeemed for four shillings, and ten years later "the Seven Platters" for one pound, Sewall thus standing a money loss of one shilling on the transaction! In accord with the principle that nothing needed for livelihood should be taken from the poor, the pawn was generally an object of silver. Widow Bridgham, for example, received twenty-five pounds and four pence for "one Silver Salt Maker . . . one Silver plate . . . one Silver Cup . . . three Porrengers, one Dram Cup, [and] . . . a Duz. gold Rings," all of which were kept "in a Linnen Bagg in the closet." Seth Perry received two pounds two shillings for "a Silver Goblet," Bethia Collucott fifteen pounds nine shillings for "a Silver Bowl and small scollopt cup," Abigail Johnson five pounds for "a wrought Silver Serving Plate."[7]

Persons wanting a place of safekeeping for large sums of money found it in Sewall's "Iron chest," the same chest which John Hull had filled with pine-tree shillings, silver bullion and colony funds. Out of it now came shillings and pounds for those wanting loans.

Much controversy has centered on the idea advanced by Max Weber, German economist of the last century, that Calvinism freed the businessman from rule of the priest, justified usury, and both sanctioned and sanctified economic success. We need not here speculate on the general applicability of this thesis to the Puritan businessman. It would seem to need, at the very least, some qualifying. Certainly it does as applied to Sewall.

The marked effect of economics on Sewall's life has already been shown. He came to terms with the world, abandoned the ministry to live "among the merchants," married great wealth, loaned money at interest. His actions when the colony faced the loss of its Charter were chiefly determined by concern for property. His "Lines for a Sun dial"—

Keep in God's way; keep pace with evry hour
Hurt none; do all the Good that's in your Power.

Hours can't look back at all; they'll stay for none
Tread sure, keep up with them, and All's your own.

—anticipate Poor Richard. His prayer that he "might have
an Interest in God, Signed, Sealed, and Delivered" nicely
expresses the mercantile mind. But while all this is true, it is
far from the whole picture. Just as true is the fact that any
sanction given to business by Puritan doctrine did not, in
Sewall's case, result in eager devotion to economic gain. On
the contrary. Within a decade after Hull's death his mercantile activity had come almost to a standstill. Apparent reasons
were his growing preoccupation with public affairs (in 1692,
for example, he began his long career on the judicial circuit,
the duties of which frequently took him away from Boston
for weeks at a time), increased risks of ocean commerce as
a result of renewed war with the French, and lack of ability.[8]

For Sewall's managerial talents were of a rather low order.
In 1704 he noted in his diary that henceforth his wife should
"keep the Cash," adding: "If I want I will borrow of her. She
has a better faculty than I at managing Affairs: I will assist
her; and will endeavour to live upon my Salary: will see what
it will doe. The Lord give his Blessing." When he became
treasurer of the Society for the Propagation of the Gospel, a
job which called for annual accounting to the society's London commissioners of funds spent in New England, he ex-
perienced all the difficulties of the amateur, and this despite
the fact that he had then been keeping his own accounts for
many years. On January 14, 1703/4, for example, he got the
society's New England overseers together to pass on his work,
but they "could not get through with it; met with so[me]
gross mistakes or such as fear'd were so; and had not time.
Col. Foster offers me to carry all I have done, into Leger
parcells." Four years later Foster again lent a hand.[9]

Sewall's limitations as a man of business appear again in his
record as property owner, for he continually had to sell this
or that holding to keep in funds. In a letter to Cotton Mather

dated December 10, 1706, he wrote, for example: "When I
returned from England, I had some thought of carrying out
the Wharf, so as to fit it for a Building yard; that fell
through. . . . About the year 1701, I found myself under a
necessity to sell it for the payment of my debts; and to that
purpose a Note was publickly affixed: yet no Chapman appeared, which put me upon selling other Lands to my great
Loss." Another time he "importunes" his agent at Rumsey
to send to his agent in London "all that it due to me" because "next Summer we must make some new Cloaths . . .
and this little Spring [the Rumsey income] is our Supply."
In 1719 he sold "the Malt-house and land" for three hundred
pounds, and forty acres at Newbury went for a hundred more.
In 1727 he disposed of his holdings at Woburn for something
over two hundred pounds.[10]

The point of this recital is that it invalidates much of the
very cogent essay on Sewall in Vernon Louis Parrington's
The Colonial Mind, where he serves as a "worthy representative" of the "rising world of mercantilism," one who plied
"the gospel of thrift with notable success" and "made full use
of his opportunities to worship God, to thrive and rise," who
reveals "the newer practice of incipient capitalism" as John
Winthrop had revealed "the older ideal of theocratic stewardship," who spent his years "busily adding new acres to his
holdings," who "with excellent thrift . . . fixed his young
affections upon the only child of a wealthy merchant" and
"proved himself a shrewd husbandman," "a capable executive
and administrator," "a Puritan embodiment of Defoe's merchant ideal," "progenitor of a practical race that was to spread
the gospel of economic individualism across the continent"[11]
—views either wholly wrong or in need of so much qualification as to be worthless.

The notion that Sewall represented the "newer practice of
. . . capitalism" as John Winthrop did the older ideal of
"theocratic stewardship" deserves a word of comment. In
1682 Ned Ward said it was a proverb among "those that

know them" that "whosoever believes a New-England Saint, shall be sure to be cheated: And he that knows how to deal with their Traders, may deal with the Devil and fear no Craft." If, as seems reasonable, this is the sort of "newer practice" Parrington had in mind, the reader of Sewall will be hard put to find it demonstrated in his pages. When Sewall quotes the hard dealing old Thomas Dudley (father of Governor Joseph Dudley), saying, "A bargain's a Bargain and must be made good," he is not speaking to a delinquent creditor but to George Lason, mariner, who had left his wife and "lay with another woman." The hardest bargains Sewall drove were the oft-cited marriage settlements of his last years, the niggling character of which hardly merit the name of "capitalism." If he let money at interest, he never did so in amounts large enough to suggest the true-born money-lender, and it was far exceeded by what he either "forgave" or listed as "gratuities."[12]

The number of such "gratuities" is, indeed, so large that it seems fair to credit him with a real sense of being God's steward, even if his careful noting of shillings and pence suggest at the same time that, as the saying went, he was "a little near." His largest benefactions involved his Narragansett lands in southern Rhode Island: five hundred acres to Harvard for youths "whose parents may not be of sufficient ability to maintain them there, especially such as shall be sent from Pettaquamscutt . . . English or Indians"; five hundred more "towards the Support of a School there"; one acre for "a meeting house in Kings Town," Rhode Island, where the word of God "may be Received Offered and kept pure and Entire." Eleven acres at Sherborn went for the maintenance of that town's minister. Part of his "Elm Pasture" he deeded to Boston for an annuity during his life "for the Use of the School at the South End." Five pounds went toward a meeting house at Shrewsbury and a pound ten shillings for its minister. In 1692 and 93 he sent a total of more than one hundred pounds to Nicholas Morey of Taunton "for his encouragement." For help toward "Rumney Meetinghouse" he gave eight pounds, six shillings, and six pence; toward a new meetinghouse in Cambridge seven pounds; for the inside finishing of one at Sandwich two pounds more; etc. Seth Shove, son of George Shove of Taunton, was taken into the Sewall household, educated at Harvard with Sewall's help, and finally established as a minister of the church at Danbury.[13]

One could go on almost indefinitely listing Sewall's cautious efforts to do good, and while the amounts are generally small, their number is large. On a single page of his ledger, for example, appear more than sixty separate "gratuities," none of which has here been mentioned.[14] As to his motives, they were doubtless influenced by the thought that in the right use of one's possessions lay promise of divine reward. On the other hand, he was a kindly man, sufficiently guileless to do good simply because he thought God wished it.

In his career both as business man and property owner what Sewall most enjoyed was the chance to play countryman and farmer. "Grafted the Button-pear tree stock, which lies at the lower end of the Garden, and several Apple Trees." "Friday April 3rd, Mr. Joseph Eliot and I graft some Walnut Trees." "Set sweet-briar seeds at the Pasture by Mr. Saunderson's." "Plant Six Chestnut trees at Hog Island." "April 13, 1688. Grafted a Stock next John Wait's, pretty high out of the Cows reach, with cions from Mr. Moodey's Orange Pear, and grafted Two Appletree Stocks with Mr. Gardener's Russetings." Such entries appear throughout the diary. At the age of sixty-seven he helped his farmer son, Sam, to "cut his Stalks" and gather in apples, and at sixty-eight he "Cock'd Hay at Saunderson's pasture."[15]

On a page of the account book kept during the years of his Hull apprenticeship, after entries having to do with such things as an "interest in the John & An," "Cash Recd," etc., appears one which reads, "Gather the Pears." On another page is a note about "Cherry the red cow-calf" and the cost "to ty her Legs, & carry . . . to Braintrey." Another concerns five cherry trees "well wrapt up in wet straw (the roots)." Had Sewall felt the same interest in trade that he did in gathering pears and planting cherry trees he might have been "a worthy representative" of the "rising world of mercantilism." But since he didn't, the figure he presents as he rides off to Watertown on his "Sorrel Horse" to see about some hay, or to his lands at Newbury to view "the sheep shearing," is much more the conventional country squire than "Defoe's merchant ideal."[16]

CHAPTER FOUR

Servant of Colony and Province

The Biblical Authority

John Eliot, remembered as Massachusetts' "Apostle to the Indians," wrote in his *Christian Commonwealth* (1660) that a people should "submit themselves to be ruled by the Lord in all things, receiving from him, both the platform of their Government, and all their Laws." These they should "fetch out of the Word of God, making that their only Magna Charta." John Cotton had already thus fetched out "Moses his Judicials" (1636), the aim of which was "to show the complete sufficiency of the word of God alone to direct his people in judgment of all causes." This body of laws, supplied when freemen of the colony were demanding a codification for protection against the magistrates, the General Court did not accept, one reason being the charter provision against any laws "repugnant to the laws of England" and another the wish to supplement God's word with their own "right reason." Nevertheless, Cotton did in a general way reflect the colony mind. This is shown by the fact that while the Court refused his work, it also passed a resolution favoring a draft of laws "agreeable to the word of God" and stipulated that until such could be agreed on, magistrates were to go by laws already passed or "as near the law of God as they can." Though the code finally adopted (Nathaniel Ward's Body of Liberties in 1648) departed from Mosaic law, it departed still more from English common law—so much so that Thomas Lechford, an English lawyer visiting the colony, spoke angrily of the "slight[ing of] all former lawes of the Church or State, cases of experience and precedents, to go hammer out new . . . upon pretence that the Word of God is sufficient."[1]

Reliance on Biblical authority had several results. For one thing, it gave the clergy enormous power. In the colony's early years "the preachers made . . . all the magistrates," wrote John Winthrop, "and kept them so entirely under obedience that they durst not act without them." Magistrates were like-wise of awful stature, for the civil power they embodied expressed the will of God. They were His "vice regents." The Boston Synod of 1680 declared that any who resisted them "resist the ordinance of God" and instructed that people pray for them, "honour their persons . . . pay them tribute . . . obey their lawful commands, and . . . be subjects to their authority for conscience sake." On January 2, 1717/18, speaking of the death of one of his judicial colleagues, Sewall reminded his audience that "Councillors and Judges [are] . . . by the Supream Authority called gods" and that when the court speaks "the Judgment is the LORD'S."[2]

Another result was a neglect of ordinary legal training. Indeed, since it was thought more important that a judge be instructed in the word of God than that he be skilled in common law, feeling toward lawyers ranged from suspicion to downright hostility. Item twenty-six of the Body of Liberties said a defendant might employ an advocate, but only without fee, which explains why those who appeared in the role were of every profession except the law. The General Court was English-minded enough to see a need for "better light for making and proceeding about laws" and hence sent to England for some necessary legal texts. In fact, several were men of some legal training, but not till 1712 did the first trained lawyer sit on the Massachusetts bench, and almost a century later Jefferson wrote apropos the appointment of a Massachusetts judge, "He is not thought to be an able common lawyer, but there is not and never was an able one in the New England States. Their system is *sui generis* in which the Common law is little attended to."[3]

Scarcity of trained lawyers often resulted in the kind of courtroom found on the frontier. Travelling in New England in 1704, for example, Sarah Kemble Knight wrote in her journal:

> A negro Slave belonging to a man in the Town, stole a hogs head from his master, and gave or sold it to an Indian, native of the place. The Indian sold it in the neighbourhood, and so the theft was found out. Thereupon the Heathen was Seized, and carried to the Justices House to be Examined. But his worship (it seems) was gone into the field, with a Brother in office, to gather in his Pompions. Whither the malefactor is hurried, and complaint made, and satisfaction in the name of justice demanded. Their Worships cann't proceed in form without a Bench: whereupon they order one to be Immediately erected, which, for want of fitter materials, they made with pompions—which being finished, down setts their Worships . . . and the inquiry proceeds.

Sewall was himself at this time just such a "tryer of Small Causes" (not to be confused with his more august duties as a member of the Superior Court), and his complaint that "persons often come upon me unawares" quite possibly meant they found him out hoeing beans or inspecting his "pippins." The Knight episode also suggests a number of occasions when impromptu action was called for, such as the time Mrs. Obinson presented herself at Sewall's door "complain[ing] of her Husband's ill usage of her; kick'd her out of bed last night"; or the time he fined "Widow Gutteridge's Negro Ned" five shillings for "breach of the Sabbath yesterday Robbing my Orchard"; or the time he fined James Barry the same amount "for his misdemeanour in Sounding and Halooing several times, at twenty minutes past six a clock—to my great disturbance as I was reading in my family the Lord's Day-Eve."[4]
The power of thus fining a man for "Halooing" on Saturday evening grew from an action by the General Court in 1648,

the year Sewall first took his place among the magistrates: "In the case of misdemeanor, or vehement suspicion thereof, where no Court is at hand, any magistrate . . . being present . . . may impower any person to make search and apprehend any disorderly person, whereby their misdemeanors may be brought forth & punished."[5] Magistrates, in short, were to be their own police. In the street as in the courtroom, what they lacked in knowledge was to be made up by "right reason."

Proceeding by rule of moral thumb brought surprising departures from traditional practice, such as the giving of private advice by magistrates before a case came to court, making juries the judge of both law and fact, and finding of guilt on "strong suspicion." Despite such practices, however, a rough kind of justice seems to have obtained. But the notion that it would be as well served by righteousness as by regular procedures held danger for all concerned, magistrates as well as the James Barrys and Negro Neds. "Take heede my brethren," wrote Thomas Lechford, "despise not learning, nor the worthy Lawyers of either gown, lest you repent too late." His warning went unheeded, and it took the loss of the charter and the subsequent threat to land titles to make clear the meaning of an untrained Bench and Bar.[6]

The picture Sewall gives of the magistrates' and deputies' last meeting under the old government is humorous and pathetic. Not knowing that they might challenge measures being taken by the Crown as illegal, Sewall could think of nothing better than to sing "the 17. and 18. verses of Habakkuk." When, later, land titles were threatened by Writs of Intrusion, they got John Higginson, a minister, to state their case. Not surprisingly, the best he could do was argue derivation of rights "from the grand charter from Genesis where God gave the earth to the sons of Adam and Jonah." Of whatever remote validity, such an argument was hardly as effective as would have been the citing of pertinent acts by Crown and Privy Council. But of this the Puritan leaders seemed unaware. As earlier noted, Sewall shared the helplessness of ignorance and submitted to Andros' demands.[7]

Magistrate

Sewall took his place among the magistrates as one trained for the ministry. This training, far from unfitting him for high public office, was thought desirable. "The Employment of the Magistrat and Minister" being, as he said, "so much akin," his qualifications appeared excellent for avoiding "the disagreement of Moses and Aaron." Furthermore, his Hull connection gave promise of concern with New England as well as with the approaches to heaven.[1]

The known facts of Sewall's public life in the last years of the Charter government, except for those having to do with its fall, are few and of no particular consequence. On March 30, 1676/7, he joined the Third or Old South Church, "making a Solemn covenant to take the L. Jehovah" for his God, and to "walk in Brotherly Love and watchfulness to Edification." Though "tormented" as to want of grace and not at all sure that South Church had been "in God's way in breaking off from the old" on the half-way covenant issue,* such concerns gave way before the fact that his father-in-law was a founder of Old South and also that his wife would soon bear him a child who would need baptizing.[2]

In May of the following year, having proved himself industrious and law-abiding and possessing the necessary two hundred pounds (or income equal to that from such an amount), Sewall was made a freeman. In taking the oath, he swore "by the Great and Dreadfull Name of the Ever-Living God" to bear faith and true allegiance, plot no evil against the state but "discover and reveal the same to Lawfull Authority," and use his vote as in his "own Conscience [he] judge[d] best to Conduce and tend to the Publick Weale." Being a freeman meant participation in the work of the Puritan state; it also meant membership in an elite of about a thousand in a population twenty-five times that num-

---

* Under the half-way covenant, children of church members could share the privileges of church membership even though unable to testify to conversion.

ber; above all, it meant public service. Office was more often given than sought, and one who chose not to perform "such public service as [he might] . . . be chosen to by the freemen of the severall townes, as cunstable, jurers, selectmen, and surveyors of high wayes" was fined for "every such refusall . . . not exceeding twenty shillings."[3]

In his first year as a freeman, Sewall was made constable, a post so unpopular that men often paid the fine rather than serve. Sewall, however, was willing. His chief duty was directing Boston's night watch, which meant seeing that the "Watch men . . . duely examine all Night walkers after ten of the clock at night (unless they be known peacable Inhabitants) to inquire whether they are going, and what their business is . . . to see all noises in the streets stilled, and lights put out." Any "night walker" who gave an unsatisfactory answer was held till morning and then taken before a magistrate.[4]

Sewall liked this work, and in one capacity or another—"perambulator of bounds for Muddy River" (Brookline), officer of the South Company (a Boston train band), "Overseer of the Poor" (an office he held for several years), or simply as magistrate—he made nighttime inspection tours for thirty years. His satisfaction often shows in the diary: March 12, 1684/5: "Watched with Isaac Goose and Sam. Clark, had a pleasant Night. Gave each Watch 12 *d.* to drink." November 23, 1685: "I go the Rounds with Cous. Quinsey and Isaac Goose, a very severe night for Cold, yet 'twas fair and comfortable: came home at 5. *mane.*" It might be "a very pleasant Moonshiny night" or one when snow was "extream deep," but in either case he would have a "very comfortable" time.

In 1683 Sewall served the town as assessor (one of seven) and as member of a committee to frame instructions for its deputies to the General Court. In this year also he became deputy from Westfield (residence requirements not being established till ten years later), and on May 7, 1684, he was chosen to the Court of Assistants, the oligarchic group of

eighteen which functioned as supreme court, executive council, and upper legislative house all rolled into one. Just what
brought thirty-two-year-old Sewall to such high office is not
clear, though one assumes it was less his performance in such
assignments as Constable and Deputy than it was the fact of
his being John Hull's heir. As so often in his life, he had
shown himself to be "not unworthy." Hull quit New England
to "sail for heaven" on August 14, 1683, and before another
year was out Sewall sat in his magisterial seat.[5]

The Charter government had not long to live, for on the
same day Sewall became deputy for Westfield (November
7, 1683), Edward Randolph, hated agent of the Crown, arrived with a *quo warranto* charging the colony with abuse of
its franchise. But the charter was not vacated until the next
year, and still another passed before the General Court made
its final adjournment, orders having arrived for Joseph Dudley
to head a provisional government pending arrival of a Royal
Governor. Meanwhile the old government, with ancient
Simon Bradstreet at its head, continued to function, drawing
up a "Humble petition & addresse" to the King in which they
"prostrated" themselves at his "majesties royal feete"; framing instructions for the colony's agent in England; and seeing
to such every day matters as licensing public houses "for . . .
enterteinement, and retayling wine & licquors," regulating
the size of bricks, and ordering a day of fasting and humiliation because of smallpox.[6]

In these years Sewall was twice elected magistrate and
faithfully attended meetings of the General Court and the
Court of Assistants. Since the latter had original jurisdiction
in "all Capital and Criminal Causes, extending to Life, Member or Banishment," its records show life in the Puritan community at its most violent. Rape, murder, piracy, stealing,
manslaughter, infanticide—all are there in amounts which
must have moved the young magistrate to ponder Satan's
awful power. James Morgan, for example, "not having the
feare of God before his eyes being Instigated by the divill . . .

63

in the house of constante worcester widdow in Boston did . . . wound kill & murder Joseph Johnson Butcher . . . by running a spitt into his belly a little above the navell." He was found guilty and ordered to "Goe hence to the place whence you Came & from thence to the Gallowes & there be hanged by the neck till you be dead & the Lord have mercy on your soule." John Balston "Commit[ted] a Burglary on the dwelling house of Sarah Noyse widow in Boston." For this he was to be "branded with the letter B on the forehead and have his Right eare Cutt of[f]," pay the costs of the trial, and "make treble Restitution to the party Injuried & in defect thereof . . . be sold to any of the English plantations." Joseph Indian "murder[ed] his squaw . . . and . . . drew her . . . on the ground to the lime house . . . and left her there with severall mortall wounds on her head." Found guilty of cruelty, he was sentenced to be "severely whipped with thirty stripes" and pay costs of the trial or be sold out of the country.[7]

If the pious Sewall felt distressed by these proceedings, it was for what they showed of natural man's unregenerate state more than for any severity of punishment suffered by the guilty. After James Morgan's execution, for example—he that killed Joseph Butcher "by running a spitt into his belly"—Sewall wrote: "Thorsday, March 11 [1685/6]. Persons crowd much into the Old Meeting-House by reason of James Morgan [who would be on exhibit and provide the afternoon's subject]. . . . Mr. Mather's Text was from Num. 35. 16. And if he smite him with an Instrument of Iron &c. . . . Morgan was turn'd off about ½ an hour past five. The day very comfortable." Puritan justice demanded eye for eye, tooth for tooth, and stripes laid on in the name of the Lord. The man at the whipping post who prayed that the "scourgineer" might remember the Scriptural saying "Blessed is the Merciful Man," got the Scriptural answer "Cursed is he that doeth the work of the Lord negligently."[8]

Under Dudley's provisional government, Sewall, passed over in the new Council appointments, was asked to continue as Justice of the Peace. He replied that there were many good men, and "besides, my Mother [Mother Hull, this is] and wife are incessantly importunat with me to accept at least a part of that Retirement which God hath dismissed me to." Therefore when he journeyed to England in the fall of 1688, he went as one without official ties. During his absence, however, the Andros regime was overthrown and the old Charter government re-established. His return home, therefore, meant return to office, and when the Court of Assistants reconvened in December, 1689, he once more sat in his familiar place.[9]

But the government was as weak as the eighty-seven-year-old Bradstreet at its head. Like him, it was waiting to die. The Charter struggle had been abandoned by the colony's agents in England in favor of getting whatever they could for Massachusetts as a royal province.

"Dolefull Witchcraft"

When, in the spring of 1692, Governor Phips arrived to establish the new government, he found the province "miserably harassed with a most Horrible witchcraft or Possession of Devills which had broke in upon severall Townes, some scores of poor people were taken with preternaturall torments [;] some scalded with brimstone [;] some had pins stuck in their flesh [;] others hurried into the fire and water [;] and some dragged out of their houses and carried over the tops of trees and hills for many Miles together."[1]

In earlier years an occasional unfortunate had been brought to the gallows in the colony for "entring hellish Contracts with infernal Spirits," but those suffering "preternatural torments" at Salem (principally eight teen-age girls) were making accusations by the score. Hearings and examinations had begun at the end of February under Magistrates Corwin and Hathorne of Salem with occasional help from a visiting colleague (Sewall, for example, came to Salem on April 11 and found it "awful to see how the afflicted persons were agitated"), and when Phips arrived three months later he found jails "thronging" with the accused, many of them having "lyen long . . . at this hot season of the year." Something had to be done, and since there were "no Judicatores . . . yet established," Phips established an emergency Court of Oyer and Terminer (a court, that is, to hear and decide), named nine judges to sit on it (Sewall among them), and left on an expedition against the Indians in Maine.[2]

The work of this court in its five months of existence was summarized by Robert Calef, a merchant of Boston and its angry critic:

> And now Nineteen persons having been hang'd, and some prest to death, and Eight more condemned, in all Twenty and Eight, of which a third part were Members of some of the Churches in N. England, and more than half of them of a good Conversation in general, and not one clear'd; About Fifty having confessed themselves to be Witches [this being the only means of escaping the gallows], of which not one Executed; above an Hundred and Fifty in Prison [all later set free], and above Two Hundred more accused [most of them later declared guiltless by the courts, the few judged guilty being pardoned by Phips], the Special Commission of Oyer and Terminer comes to a period.[3]

The details of this summer of "Dolefull Witchcraft," though grisly and often fantastic, are as charged with drama as anything in our history. Witness, for example, this exchange between the judges and Susanne Martin, a woman whose wit and independent spirit brought her under the imputation of witchcraft and would shortly cost her her life:

> Magistrate. "Pray what ails these people?" (that is, the afflicted).
> Martin. "I don't know."
> Magistrate. "But what do you think ails them?"

Martin. "I do not desire to spend my judgment upon it."

Magistrate. "Don't you think they are bewitched?"

Martin. "No. I do not think they are."

Magistrate. "Tell us your thoughts about them, then."

Martin. "No, my thoughts are my own when they are in, but when they are out they are another's. Their master—"

Magistrate. "Their master! Who do you think is their master?"

Martin. "If they be dealing in the black art, you may know as well as I."

Magistrate. "Well, what have you done toward this?"

Martin. "Nothing at all."

Magistrate. "Why, 'tis you or your appearance." (The fatal spectral evidence, against which a defendant was powerless.)

Martin. "I can't help it."

Magistrate. "Is it not your master? How comes your appearance to hurt these?"

Martin. "How do I know? He that appeared in the shape of Samuel, a glorified saint, may appear in any one's shape."[4]

Susanne Martin was one of five led to Gallows Hill on July 19 and hanged.

Still more obstinate was Giles Corey, whose story Sewall briefly tells: "Monday. Sept. 19, 1692. About noon, at Salem, Giles Corey was press'd to death for standing Mute [the "peine forte et dure" for one who refused to be tried]; much pains was used with him two days, one after another . . . but all in vain." Next day Sewall was startled to learn that "about 18 years agoe, he [Corey] was suspected to have stamp'd and press'd a man to death, but was cleared. Twas not remembered till Anne Putnam was told of it by said Corey's Spectre the Sabbath-day night before the Execution." A popular ballad of the time ran as follows:

Giles Corey was a Wizzard strong,
  A stubborn Wretch was he,
And fitt was he to hang on high
  Upon the Locust Tree.

"Giles Corey," said the Magistrate,
  "What has thou heare to pleade
To these that now accuse thy Soule
  Of Crimes and horrid Deed?"

Giles Corey—he said not a worde,
  No single Worde spoke he;
"Giles Corey," Sayth the Magistrate,
  "We'll press it out of thee."

They got them then a heavy Beam,
  They laid it on his Breast.
They loaded it with heavie Stones,
  And hard upon him prest.

"More Weight," now said this wretched Man,
  "More Weight," again he cryed,
And he did no Confession make,
  But wickedly he dyed.

Corey made his end on September 16, and six days later his wife, a woman whose very blamelessness of life caused her to be "cried out upon," was hung:

> Dame Corey lived but six Dayes more,
>   But six Dayes more lived she,
> For she was hanged at Gallows Hill
>   Upon the Locust Tree.[5]

So the march of victims continues, with a variety of fearsome but fascinating detail—Sarah Good being told at the gallows by Sewall's friend Nicholas Noyes that she was a witch and knew it, replying, "You are a Liar. I am no more a

Witch than you are a Wizzard, and if you take away my Life, God will give you Blood to drink"; this same Nicholas Noyes piously declaring after the execution on September 22, "What a sad thing it is to see Eight Firebrands of Hell hanging there"; Mary Easty, one of the "Firebrands," a mild, meek woman, mother of seven, petitioning the court, not for herself, "for I know I must die . . . but if it be possible, that no more innocent blood be shed, which cannot be avoided in the way . . . you go in"; George Jacobs being testified against by his granddaughter, who too late acknowledged herself a liar; Rebeccah Nurse being found innocent by the jury, the court refusing the verdict, and the jury finally bringing in the desired judgment; Bridget Bishop dying while protesting her innocence (as they all did) and her accuser confessing his guilt on his deathbed years later; John Willard, a deputy of the court in making arrests, becoming convinced of the innocence of the accused and being himself therefore "cried out upon," arrested, tried, condemned, and hanged.[6]

The Salem story has often been told, but not by Sewall. The diary offers no "secret history." Instead, its author seems bemused. On July 20, for example, the day after five supposed witches were hanged, he wrote to his London agent: "Wells [Maine] beat off the Enemy [French and Indians]. His Excellency [Phips] is going in person to beat up their Quarters. Are perplexed by witchcrafts; six persons have already been condemned and executed at Salem. Tis a very dry time." On August 4 he notes being at Salem but says nothing of the fact that his friend and Harvard schoolfellow, the Reverend George Burroughs, was to go on trial next day under charge of "confederacy with the devil."[7]

Because of Sewall's relations with Burroughs, the case deserves special mention. Burroughs was graduated with the Harvard class of 1670, a year before Sewall. In 1680 he accepted a call to Salem but left after two years because of division in the parish inherited from the minister before him. From Salem he went to Casco (Portland), Maine, and from there to Wells. It was therefore as a respected clergyman that he stopped to dine with Sewall on November 18, 1685, and that, five years later, he addressed the Wednesday night meeting of the South Church Society, where Sewall heard him speak on the Beatitudes. On March 14, 1692, Sewall served as his banker, giving him twenty-six pounds in exchange for a note on his brother in London. Then, on April 30, he was complained against by "Captain Jonathan Walcot and Sergeant Thomas Putnam of Salem Village . . . for themselves, and also for severall of their Neighbours." John Partridge, "field Marshal," was promptly sent to apprehend and "convey him with all speed to Salem before the Magestrates there, to be Examened, he being suspected for a Confederacy with the devil." He was delivered to authority four days later and on May 9 was examined by four judges: William Stoughton, Chief Justice and one of God's angrier men at the trials; John Hathorne and Jonathan Corwin, Salem magistrates active in all the preliminary examinations; and Sewall, whose diary is silent.[8]

Burroughs' examination shows what was happening. Among other things, he denied "that his house . . . was haunted," but he had to admit "there were toads." At one point he was examined for the tell-tale "teats" (where Satan's imps might feed), but nothing was found "but what is natural." Proceedings had thus far been in private, "none of the Bewitched being present." When he was brought before them, immediately "many (if not all of the Bewitched) were greviously tortured," some to the point where "Authority ordered them to be taken away." Once, when Burroughs turned around, the malevolence of his gaze "knockt down all (or most), of the afflicted which stood behind him." Sufferers called upon to testify "all fell into fits." Asked what he thought of this, Burroughs said "it was an amazing and humbling Providence, but he understood nothing of it."[9]

Testimony presented was similarly fantastic. Susan Sheldon (one who "fell into fits") said that Burroughs' two dead wives had appeared to her "in their winding sheets, and said that man killed them." Susan Sheldon and Ann Putnam testified that Burroughs "brought the [Devil's] Book and would have them write," Sarah Bibber that he had "hurt her, tho she had not seen him personally before as she knew," Ann Putnam that she "saw the Apperishtion of a minister . . . and then presently he tould me that his name was George Burroughs." He had "'bewitched two wives to death," several children, and "a grate many souldiers." He was "above a witch he was a conjurer." She had seen the dead wives, looking "as pail as a white wall." Mercy Lewis: "[He] carried me to an exceeding high mountain and shewed me all the Kingdoms of the earth and tould me that he would give them all to me if I would writ in his book, and if I would not he would thro me down and brake my neck."

A special feature of the Burroughs testimony concerned feats of strength, one of the "more certain signs" of hellishness.[10] Samuel Webber said Burroughs "put his fingers into the Bung of a Barrell of Molases and lifted it up, and Carryed it Round," and Simon Willard had seen him "hold out [a] . . . gun with one hand" which he, Willard, couldn't sight with two. John Brown "testifyed about a bbl Cyder," and others "about his great Strength and the Gun."

A final example of evidence used is the deposition of Benjamin Hutchinson, which reveals all too clearly the sort of world Sewall was in at Salem. "Benjimin hushension," it reads,

> said that one ["on"] the 21st aprell 92. abegeral wiluams said that there was a lettell black menester that Lived at Casko bay he told me so and said that he had kild 3 wifes two for himself and one for mister Losen and that he had made nine Weches in this place and said that he could hold out the hevest gun that is in Casko bay with one hand which no man can . . . [undecipherable] hold out with both hands that this is about a 11

a clock an I ask her where about this lettel man stood
said she Just where the Cart wheell went along I had
a 3 graned irne fork in my hand and I thru it where
she said he stud and she presently fell in a letel feet
["fit"] and when it was over Said She you have toren
his coot for I herd it tare wher abouts said I one
["on"] won side said she, then we come into the house
. . . [undecipherable] Ingersall and I went into the
great roome and abigle come in and said ther he stands
I said wher wher and presently draed my rapyer but
he emmedetly was gon as she said then said she ther
is a gray catt then I said wher abouts doth she stand
ther said she thar then I struck with my rapyer than she
fell in a fitt and when it was over she said you kild hur
and immedatly Sary good com and carried hur away,
this was about 12 a clock. The same day after lectorr
["lecture"] in the said Ingersalls chamber abigaill williams mary walcat said that goody hobs of topsell bitt
mary walcot by the foot then both falling into a fit as
soone as it was over the said william hobs and his wife
goe both of them a longe the table the said hucheson
tooke his rapier stabed gooddy hobs one the side as
abigaill williams and mary walcot said the said abigaill
and mar[y] said the roome was full of them then the
said hucheson & Ely putnam stabed with their raperres
at a ventor ["venture"] then said mary and abigell you
have killed a greet black woman of Stonintown and
an Indian that come with her for the flore is all covered
with blood then the said mary and abigaill looked out of
dores and said the[y] saw a greet company of them one
a hill & there was three of them lay dead the black
woman and the indian and one more that the[y] knew
not. This being about. 4. a clock in the afternoon.

Such evidence caused Cotton Mather, symbol of clerical
interest at the trials, to wish he "had never known the name
of this man." Convinced that Burroughs "had the promise
of being a King in Satans Kingdom, now going to be Erected,"
the Hutchinson testimony was a gun in Mather's hands.[11]

But the gun had unexpected recoil, for when it became clear that lies and delusion, not toads and little black men, were the moving agents, and that the only real sufferers were the "witches," clerical authority was suddenly thrown in doubt. Salem, in short, gave bitter encouragement to the next century's unclerical, more enlightened spirit.

With five others, Burroughs came to trial on August 5— a trial only in name of course, the defendants' guilt being assumed. Review of evidence, addition of anything new, and deliberation by the jury were quickly gotten through. Five of the six were condemned, Elizabeth Proctor being let off because she was pregnant.[12] Sewall's diary entry for the day (he was on the bench) concerns "news of the desolation at Jamaica" caused by an earthquake. Not a word of the man he had known so long, now about to hang.

Robert Calef describes Burroughs' execution:

Mr. Burroughs was carried in a cart with the others, through the streets of Salem to Execution; when he was upon the Ladder, he made a Speech for the clearing of his Innocency, with such Solemn and Serious Expressions, as were to the Admiration of all present; his Prayer (which he concluded by repeating the Lord's Prayer [supposedly a hard thing for a witch to do]) was so well worded, and uttered with such composedness, and such (at least seeming) fervency of Spirit as was very affecting, and drew Tears from many (so that it seemed to some, that the Spectators would hinder the Execution). The accusers said the black Man stood and dictated to him; as soon as he was turned off, Mr. Cotton Mather, being mounted upon a Horse, addressed himself to the People, partly to possess the People of his guilt; saying that the Devil has often been transformed into an Angel of Light; and this did somewhat appease the People, and the Execution went on; when he was cut down, he was dragged by the Halter to a Hole, or Grave, between the Rocks, about two foot deep, his Shirt and Breeches being pulled off, and an old

73

pair of Trousers of One Executed put on his lower parts, he was so put in, together with Willard and Carryer, one of his Hands and his Chin and a Foot of one [of] them being left uncovered.[13]

Here, by comparison, is Sewall: "This day George Burrough, John Willard, John Proctor, Martha Carrier and George Jacobs were executed at Salem, a very great number of Spectators being present. Mr. Cotton Mather was there, Mr. Sims, Hale, Noyes, Chiever, &c. All of them said they were innocent, Carrier and all. Mr. Mather says they all died by a Righteous Sentence. Mr. Burrough by his Speech, Prayer, protestation of his Innocence, did much move unthinking persons, which occasions their speaking hardly concerning his being executed." In the margin Sewall later wrote "Dolefull Witchcraft," token of his recognition that "unthinking" was a word less suited to those moved by Burroughs' protestations than to such as Cotton Mather and himself.

That the business had indeed been doleful everyone soon recognized. As the number of accusations grew to include more and more persons of good reputation and upright life, including the wife of the governor, even Mather saw that "many unsearchable cheats were interwoven into the . . . business" and that, while there were undoubtedly witches, "a good name, obtained by a good life, should not be lost by meer spectral accusations." The Special Court of Oyer and Terminer was disbanded in October, and when the new, regularly constituted Superior Court met on January 3, "they cleared the accused as fast as they tried them . . . and the land had peace restored unto it." When asked by the jury what account should be taken of spectral evidence, the court answered "As much as Chips in Wort"—of less than no worth.[14]

Peace to the land was not peace to some of its people. Innocent men had hanged, and a man like Sewall would find himself, in Whittier's words, remembering

When he sat on the bench of the witchcraft courts,
With the laws of Moses and Hale's Reports,
And spake, in the name of both, the word
That gave the witch's neck to the cord.

One can imagine his unhappiness when, on August 12, 1696, Mr. Melyen, "upon a slight occasion," spoke to him "very smartly about the Salem Witchcraft: in discourse he said, if a man should take Beacon hill on's back, carry it away; and then bring it and set it in its place again, he should not make any thing of that," referring to evidence used against Burroughs. A month later, at a "day of prayer in the East end of the Town-House," the Governor, his Council, and members of the Assembly attending, Mr. Morton preached and "Spake smartly at last about the Salem Witchcrafts, and that no order had been suffer'd to come forth by Authority to ask Gods pardon."[15]

If Sewall's conscience had slept, these words brought it awake, for when, shortly after, he had his son Sam recite some verses from the twelfth chapter of Matthew, the seventh verse ("If ye had known what this meaneth, I will have mercy and not sacrifice, ye would not have condemned the guiltless") "did awfully bring to mind the Salem Tragedie." And when January 14, 1696/7, was made a day of solemn fasting and prayer for what might have been done amiss "in the late tragedy, raised among us by Satan and his instruments, through the awful judgment of God," Sewall determined to bring before the congregation at South Church a statement confessing his guilt and asking their prayers. As Mr. Willard, the pastor, passed where he sat, Sewall handed him a note, "standing up at the reading of it, and bowing when finished." "Samuel Sewall," it read,

> sensible of the reiterated strokes of God upon himself
> and family; and being sensible, that as to the Guilt
> contracted upon the opening of the late Commission of

Oyer and Terminer at Salem (to which the order for this Day relates) he is, upon many accounts, more concerned than any that he knows of, Desires to take the Blame and shame of it, Asking pardon of men, And especially desiring prayers that God, who has an Unlimited Authority, would pardon that sin and all other of his sins; personal and Relative: And according to his infinite Benignity, and Sovereignty, Not Visit the sin of him, or of any other, upon himself or any of his, nor upon the Land: But that He would powerfully defend him against all Temptations to Sin, for the future; and vouchsafe him the efficacious, saving Conduct of his Word and Spirit.

Much has been made of this act and in some ways it truly was unique. On the other hand, while Sewall was alone among the judges in doing what he did, the Salem jurors asked public forgiveness in the same year, and several ministers did the same. Also, "putting up a bill" was common practice. Sewall had done it scores of times. Moreover, when he did it for the witchcraft, it was on a day of public humiliation for the whole colony. This is not to say that Sewall's act does not deserve our admiration, if only for its freedom from false humility and morbid self-abasement.

If history shows anything, it shows that men act under force of circumstance and within the limits of their knowledge. The Puritan "knew" the Bible to be a divine report of literal truth and hence a sufficient lamp for men's feet. And the Bible said, "Thou shalt not suffer a witch to live." True, it didn't say what a witch was, but God's wish was plain, and everyone "knew" witches were somewhere about, busily pursuing the devil's business. Those who didn't "know" this were, said Cotton Mather, "sensual Sadducees" willing "to credit nothing but what they see and feel," a habit which, he rightly observed, "does much to settle men in Atheism." What was Sewall to do? To no one was "the forward spirit of Sadducism" more repellent or strange. Faced with stories of demon possession which, again to quote his friend Mather, "hundreds of the most sober people in [the] country . . . know . . . to be true," his course of action was set before he arrived in the Salem court.[16]

One thing he never did do was abandon belief in witches. What troubled him, along with the court and colony generally, was how to spot them. The Bible didn't say how to do it, and following the Old World's best authorities they had delivered justice to "unsearchable cheats." The situation was baffling, "raised," as the fast day order said, by "Satan and his instruments, through the awful judgment of God." One is tempted to use the word "tragic," but it doesn't strictly apply. For the Puritans knew that things were in the hands of God and that somehow they were being shaped to His ends. Their feeling was therefore not so much one of tragedy as of confusion and dismay—confusion because they found themselves somehow betrayed in a righteous cause, dismay because in this "awful judgment" God had expressed His displeasure. Their belief in God's providence and His invisible world remained unshaken, but after it there were no more examinations for "Devil's marks," no more "touch tests" or "spectral evidence." The invisible world remained, but attempts to demonstrate it in court would not again be made in Massachusetts.

It is easy to sit in judgment on the mistakes of history, scornfully holding up those who made them to the light of knowledge they did not possess. The Puritans are an attractive target for such abuse, especially those who played leading parts in the witchcraft delusion. It has been said of the judges that they "served, if they did not worship the Devil, and took him to be their God, whether they signed his Book or not," that had his Book been brought into court, the names of more than one of them "would have flared in the sapphire blaze."[17] But aside from the satisfaction one may derive from such judgments, voicing them would hardly seem a useful exercise. Better to recognize that every generation has its Salems, its search for witches—our own with the rest. The fact that Sewall and his colleagues proceeded wrongly and so caused innocent men to die is of no great importance in itself. More important is the fact that Salem's motivations and procedures are, with certain technical variations, as alive and destructive today as in the summer of 1692.

Provincial Councillor and Judge

The colony was not disposed to blame individual judges for the Salem affair, considering they had but shared in the common delusion. Chief Justice William Stoughton, for example, retained his post in the newly constituted Superior Court and later served as the colony's Lieutenant Governor for many years. Similarly, Sewall's commission as Superior Court judge was renewed by five royal governors during thirty-six years, when he resigned to "prepare for the entertainments of another world." The last ten of these years he served as Chief Justice, God having annointed him with these "fresh oyls."[1]

It is not possible to form an exact judgment of Sewall as a judge in these years because court records for the Province, like those for the Colony, give only verdicts, nothing of opinions or of reasoning employed. (The witchcraft records are a notable exception.) It has been said that he followed "a very respectable course of study" and "was altogether better read in the principles of the common law than any other judge on the bench." Perhaps so, but the evidence suggests otherwise. True, he mentions ordering legal works in considerable number, but his mastery of them is doubtful. If he indeed "followed a respectable course of study," it is remarkable that in all the records he kept during more than forty years in the highest courts of both Colony and Province, he should so seldom refer to legal authorities. It is probably not without significance that once when he went to visit Mr. Danforth, a judicial colleague, Danforth made him look on

top of the cupboard and tell what he saw. "I told him," says
Sewall, "I saw there a Law-book, Wingate on the Common
Law. He said he would lend it me. . . . Again when took
leave after prayer, He said he lent me that Book not to wrap
up but to read." It may be unfair to infer from this that
Sewall's legal reputation was a bit shaky. But the incident is
not alone in suggesting that he remained of the old mentality,
which is to say generally content that Scripture and his own
"right reason" were sufficient guides to right.[2]

To say this is not so much to belittle Sewall as to charac-
terize him. While the consequences of his approach to law
were sometimes unfortunate, the picture we are able to form
of him as a judge is, on the whole, attractive. When, after
thirty years on the bench, he expressed the hope that "as the
great Judge (for whose sake I was named) said, I may say,
Whose Ox have I taken?—and that Partiality or Bribery,
cannot be laid to my Charge,"[3] he only expressed what his
career had amply demonstrated—integrity, fairness, kindliness
("the Word" permitting), even liberality.

References to judicial positions he took are few but revealing. For example, his life-long concern for the Indian and
Negro found expression in a note to Addington Davenport,
a fellow judge on his way to the trial of Samuel Smith of
Sandwich for killing a Negro: "The poorest Boys and Girls
within this Province, such as are of the lowest condition;
whether they be English, or Indians, or Ethiopians, They have
the same Right to Religion and Life, that the Richest Heirs
have." Those who would deprive them of this right "attempt
the bombarding of HEAVEN; and the Shells they throw, will
fall down upon their own heads." On another occasion he
expressed opposition to the law of primogeniture as "contrary to . . . the Law of Nature and the Law of God." And
when Governor Dudley found his passage along Boston neck
blocked by the carts of Thomas Trowbridge and John Winchester—the latter telling him, "I am as good flesh and blood
as you; I will not give way; you may goe out of the way"—

and set upon them with his sword, calling them "divells" and "dirty dogs," Sewall defended the carters, got their bail lowered, saw to their writ of Habeas Corpus, and finally sat in the court which set them free.[4]

In the sermon he preached at Sewall's funeral, the Reverend Thomas Prince spoke of him as "solemn, patient, grave and fixed in his Attachment to the Laws of GOD; a Terror to the Children of Belial." One doubts that he was a "terror" to many, but as God's magisterial spokesman he may well have induced awe in someone like Mary Okelly of Yarmouth, when, indicted for adultery, she heard him speak about "the woman of Samaria," ending with a grave "Repent and amend." Similarly, Esther Rogers, judged guilty of murdering her two bastard children, doubtless felt her wickedness more keenly when she heard herself, "a great destroyer," compared with Esther of old, "a great saviour."[5]

It is mainly when the Puritan judge turns from determination of right to enforcement of righteousness that he becomes a grim and sometimes ridiculous figure. A sinner like Esther Rogers might (as happened with Elizabeth Negro) be sent by Sewall to Cotton Mather for prayers and then brought to the weekly lecture at South Church (as was Sarah Threeneedles) to "improve" that occasion. There she would be addressed by the eloquent Mather in these words:

> Be astonish'd, O congregation of God! Stand astonished at the horrible spectacle that is now before you. . . . Behold a young woman, but an old sinner, going this day to die before her time, for being wicked overmuch! Behold one just nineteen years old, and yet found ripe for the vengeance of a capital execution. Ah, miserable soul, with what a swift progress of sin and folly, has thou made haste unto the congregation of the dead! Behold a person, whose unchaste conversation appear'd by one base born child many months ago! God then gave her a space to repent, and she repented not; She repeated her whoredoms, and by an infatua-

tion from God upon her, she so managed the matter of her next base born, that she is found guilty of its murder. Thus the God whose eyes are like a flame of fire, is now casting her into a burning bed of tribulation. . . .

Behold, O young people, what it is to vex the Holy Spirit of God, by rebelling against him. This, this 'tis to be "given over of God!" And yet, after all this hardhearted wickedness, is it not possible for the grace of Heaven to be triumphantly victorious in converting and pardoning so unparallel'd a criminal? Be astonish'd, miserable Sarah, and let it now break that stony heart of thine to hear: it is possible! it is possible!

There would be "a very vast Assembly" of those seeking edification, and outside the streets would be filled with "such as could not get in." After Lecture she would be led to the place of execution and there prayed over again before being "turned off," as the saying went, "to general satisfaction." A critical member of Mather's congregation might have recalled that, a few years before, he learned one of his servant girls was with child and "turn'd her out of's house," apparently reserving to God the powers of forgiveness he so admired.[6]

War against sin was war against Satan, just as real as the Indian border wars and considerably more discouraging, for while the Indians declined, sin and wickedness increased. An English visitor to New England in 1686 observed that though many walked "in the steps of their pious fathers," others, outwardly pious, were "the most profligate and debauched wretches in the world." As usual, the chief source of trouble was "the sweet sin of Procreation." It needs only a glance into lower court records for the period to realize that Puritan fiat had not made the people of Massachusetts very different in this regard from those found anywhere else.[7]

As his diary shows, Sewall was no stranger to sexual offenses. But they were mostly outside his judicial province. Except for ones involving murder and occasionally adultery, they did not reach Superior Court, nor were they his concern as a Justice of the Peace. In the latter role his war against wickedness was more prosaic. "Lying," "galloping in the street," "striking," "travelling on the Lord's day," "swearing more than once," "breaking glass-windows," "drunkenness" (both men and women), "going disguised in the night & making a shout scaring folks," "carrying [a] box" on the Sabbath— such were the sins against which he labored.[8]

Embarassments suffered in performance of his duties as Justice of the Peace gave him as much pain as they now give amusement to readers of his diary. On a Saturday evening in February, 1714, for example (Sabbath observance having begun at sundown), his neighbor, a Mr. Colson, knocked at his door to tell him there were "disorders" at John Wallis' nearby tavern, and asked that he go there with Constable Howell and Mr. Bromfield, another magistrate. Sewall took Aeneas Salter, a servant, with him and started out. Arriving at the tavern—

> Found much Company. They refus'd to go away. Said were there to drink the Queen's Health, and they had many other Healths to drink. Call'd for more Drink: drank to me. . . . Said must and would stay upon that Solemn occasion. Mr. John Netmaker drank the Queen's Health to me. I told him I drank none; upon that he ceas'd. Mr. Brinley put on his Hat to affront me. I made him take it off. I threaten'd to send some of them to prison; that did not move them. They said they could but pay their Fine, and doing that they might stay. I told them if they had not a care, they would be guilty of a Riot. Mr. Bromfield spake of raising a number of Men to Quell them, and was in some heat, ready to run into Street. But I did not like that. Not having Pen and Ink, I went to take their Names with my Pensil, and not knowing how to Spell their Names, they themselves of their own Accord writ them. Mr. Netmaker,

reproaching the Province, said they had not made one good Law.

At last I address'd my self to Mr. Banister. I told him he had been longest an Inhabitant and Freeholder, I expected he should set a good Example in departing thence. Upon this he invited them to his own House, and away they went; and we, after them, went away. The Clock in the room struck a pretty while before they departed. I went directly home, and found it 25. Minutes past Ten at Night when I entred my own House.

Next Monday morning:

Mr. Bromfield comes to me, and we give the Names of the Offenders at John Wallis's Tavern last Satterday night, to Henry Howell, Constable, with Direction to take the Fines of as many as would pay; and warn them that refus'd to pay, to appear before us at 3. p.m. that day. Many of them pay'd. The rest appear'd; and Andrew Simpson, Ensign, Alexander Gordon, Chirurgeon, Francis Brinley, Gent. and John Netmaker, Gent., were sentenc'd to pay a Fine of 5^s each of them, for their Breach of the Law Entituled, An Act for the better Observation, and Keeping the Lord's Day. They all Appeal'd, and Mr. Thomas Banister was bound with each of them in a Bond of 20^s upon Condition that they should prosecute their Appeal to effect.

Capt. John Bromsal, and Mr. Thomas Clark were dismiss'd without being Fined. The first was Master of a Ship just ready to sail, Mr. Clark a stranger of New York, who had carried it very civilly, Mr. Jekyl's Brother-in-Law.

John Netmaker was fin'd 5^s for profane cursing; saying to Colson, the Constable's Assistant, God damn ye; because the said Colson refus'd to drink the Queen's Health. This he said presently. Then Mr. Bromfield and I demanded of the said Netmaker to become bound in a Bond of Twenty pounds, with two Sureties in Ten pounds a-piece to Answer at the next General Session of the Peace for Suffolk, his Contempt of Her Majesties Government of this Province and vilifying the same at the house of John Wallis, Innholder in Boston, last Satterday night. Mr. Banister declin'd being bound; and none else offer'd (To imbarass the Affair as I conceiv'd). Upon this Mr. Netmaker was dismiss'd, giving his Word to Appear on Tuesday, at 10. a.m. that he might have Time to provide Sureties.

Next day:

Mr. Bromfield and I waited till past 11. and dismiss'd the Constables Howell and Fenno, supposing No body would come. Constable met Mr. Netmaker at the door, and came back again with him: He came all alone. Mr. Bromfield and I spent much time with him to bring him to some Acknowledgment of his Error, but all in vain. Offer'd not so much as his own Bond: which constrain'd us to Write a Mittimus, and send him to Prison. Angry words had pass'd between him and Const. Howell; he Threatn'd Const. Howell what he would do to him; or his Servants for him. For this reason I dismiss'd Constable Howell; sent for Mr. John Winchcomb, and gave him the Mittimus, out of respect to Mr. Netmaker; and he took it kindly. This about ¼ past 12. at Noon by my Clock. Went into Town; Mr. William Pain spake with me near the Townhouse; express'd himself concern'd that Mr. Netmaker was in prison; he would pay his Fine that he might be releas'd, I told him there was no Fine.

After a Council meeting on the same day, when it was "late and Duskish" and members present were sitting "round a little Fire," Sewall happened to sit next to General Nicholson, lately arrived from England—

He apply'd himself to me and Mr. Bromfield, ask'd whether did not know that he was here with the Broad

84

Seal of England? I answer'd, Yes! Ask'd whether did not know that Mr. Netmaker was his Secretary? I answer'd, Tis generally so receiv'd. Then with a Roaring Noise the General said, I demand JUSTICE against Mr. Sewall and Bromfield for sending my Secretary to prison without acquainting me with it! And hastily rose up, and went down and walk'd the Exchange, where he was so furiously Loud, that the Noise was plainly heard in the Council-Chamber, the door being shut.

Governor Dudley urged Netmaker's discharge and finally, after the "Mittimus" was sent for and "read by Candle-Light," got it on the grounds that the order was too general, the Council reluctantly voting its approval.

It was hard for a man who knew what God intended a magistrate to be, and who remembered the respect once accorded him on the streets of Boston, to feel that now (without his ever really admitting it) he was being made ridiculous. Sometimes it was a local person in whom he met with "refractory Carriage," but more often it was a "stranger" like Mr. Netmaker. Two New York merchants, for example, had violated the law against travelling on the Sabbath. One of them turned out to be Richard Gerrish, about whom there was "a smell of Relation," while the other, Peter La Blond, was the son of one of Sewall's neighbors. Feeling "in a strait," he prayed God to direct and decided that if the two culprits would sign a statement acknowledging their offense and promising not to let it happen again, he would drop the matter. This offer "they rejected with Disdain," Mr. La Blond paid the two pounds fine, and they went their way.[9]

Much more distressing was the trouble caused by his own Pastor, Ebenezer Pemberton, when he, Sewall, fined John Banister and Aaron Suckey for publishing what he considered "villanous Libels" against the Mathers.[10] Being at Sewall's for dinner, Mr. Pemberton, with extraordinary Vehemency said, (capering with his feet) If the Mathers order'd it, I would shoot him thorow. I told him he was in a passion. He said he was not in a Passion. I said, it was so much the worse. He said the Fire from the Altar was equal impartial. Upbraiding me, very plainly, as I understood it, with Partiality. . . . I was surpris'd to see my self insulted with such extraordinary Fierceness, by my Pastor, just when I had been vindicating two worthy Embassadors of Christ (his own usual Phrase).

After dinner, walking with several others to the Council chamber, the testy pastor again upbraided him. Sewall was "griev'd" and said,

What in the Street! He answer'd, No body hears. But Mr. Sergeant heard so much that he turn'd back to still us. Mr. Pemberton told me that Capt. Martin . . . had abus'd him, yet I took no notice of it: I answer'd, you never laid it before me. He said, You knew it. I said, I knew it not. (For every Rumor is not ground sufficient for a Justice of peace to proceed upon; and Mr. Pemberton never spake word of it to me before). He said Capt. Martin call'd him Rascal in the Street.

So the business continued, Sewall protesting and the angry minister refusing to be mollified. Finally Sewall learned what was really bothering the man—Martin had been invited in his place to dine with the Superior Court. "These things," Sewall concludes, "made me pray Earnestly . . . that God would vouchsafe to be my Shepherd, and perform for me what is mention'd in the 23. Psalm, that He would not leave me behind in my Stragglings; but brings me safely to his Heavenly Fold."

Pemberton was not yet done. In the afternoon service of the next Lord's day, he asked the congregation to join in singing the first five verses of the fifty-eighth psalm, which, in the Tate and Brady version, runs:

Speak, O ye Judges of the Earth
   if just your Sentence be:
Or must not Innocence appeal
   to Heav'n from your Decree?

Your wicked Hearts and Judgments are
   alike by Malice sway'd;
Your griping Hands, by weighty Brides,
   to Violence betrayed.

To Virtue, strangers from the Womb
   their Infant Steps went wrong:
They prattled Slander, and in Lyes
   employ'd their lisping Tongue.

No Serpent of Parch'd Afric's Breed
   doth ranker Poison bear;
The drowsy Adder will as soon
   unlock his sullen Ear.

Unmov'd by good Advice, and deaf
   as Adders they remain;
For whom the skilful Charmer's Voice
   can no attention gain.

"I think," wrote Sewall, "if I had been in his place and had been kindly and tenderly affectioned, I should not have done it. . . . Another Psalm might have suited his Subject as well as . . . this. Tis certain, one may make Libels of David's Psalms; and if a person be abused, there is no Remedy: I desire to leave it to God who can and will Judge Righteously."

Despite such tribulations, Sewall loved the judicial role and was grateful each time a governor renewed his commission. In 1715 he sought and gained the office of Judge of Probate for Suffolk County, a fairly lucrative post to which he devoted Tuesday mornings when not on the Circuit, and which, like the funerals he loved to attend, constantly reminded him of man's mortality. "May I be ready to follow!" he would write after proving a will; "Fit me for my change!" In 1718 he wrote Governor Shute saying that if his Excellency could find it "convenient" to nominate him for the post of Chief Justice of the Superior Court, he would be very "sensible" of his Excellency's favor and his own "further Obligations to Gratitude." The Governor found it convenient, and Sewall was sworn in on April 25, 1718.[11]

That he should have liked being a Superior Court Justice is easy to understand. It was a worthy occupation, the nearest thing in his life to a "calling." It also brought status, the meager pay being compensated for by pomp: "Augt. 16. [1698; judges Winthrop, Cooke, and Sewall on their way to Springfield] To Quaboag with a guard of 20 Men under Cornet Brown. Between Worcester and Quaboag we were greatly wet with Rain; wet to the skin. Got thither before twas dark. A guard of 20 from Springfield met us there, and saluted us with their trumpets as we alighted." Another time, at Plymouth, there was a volley by soldiers and "Huzzas, at [their] entrance into Town." On the way from Newbury to Portsmouth there was "a Guard of Six men from Newbury, [which was] met with 12 from New Hampshire." Once, approaching Bristol, they were met by the sheriff and judges of the court of common pleas. And there was much agreeable dining—at the Black Horse and the Peacock on the way to Bristol, the Three Cranes in Charlestown, and the "Blew Bell" in Salem, to name a few of the "baiting places."[12]

It was pleasant to distribute sermons and sweetmeats, renew acquaintances along the way, ride through the countryside listening to swallows "proclaim the Spring," and engage one's colleagues in argument. One Friday evening, for example, Sewall and the Attorney of the Province, Paul Dudley, "had Discourse about the Body."

Mr. Dudley maintained the Belly should not be raised, because he knew no use of it. I maintained the Contrary, because Christ saw no Corruption: Saints shall be conformed to Him. The Creator in his infinite Wisdom will

know what use to make of them. D. What use of Tast-
ing, Smelling? S. 'Tis possible the Bodies of the Saints
may have a Fragrancy attending them. D. Voice is
Laborious. S. As much Labour as you please, the more
the better, so it be without Toil, as in Heaven it will
be. I dare not part with my Belly. Christ has redeemed
it, and there is danger of your breaking in further upon
me, and cutting off my Hand or foot. Wee'l continue
this Action to the next term. This morning it comes to
my mind I cant believe the blessed Womb which bore
our Saviour, will always be buried.[13]

In court the next Monday were the usual cases—defaulted
payment for "50. Barrels of Mackarell," a debt for "Shoos,"
charges against Samuel Hedge, an Eastham Innholder, for
"thrust[ing] Amos Simpson backward over a Threshold upon
rought Stones all his Length whereby his Skull was broken,"
several cases of "trespass and ejectment" (disputes over land
boundaries appear in the records by the hundreds), and one
against Joshua Handing "for Increasing and Altering Province
Bills."[14]

Examining volume after stout volume of the Superior
Court records for the years when Sewall was a member, one
is finally amazed at the stamina of the man. For almost forty
years, to the age of seventy-six (three years before he died),
he toured the province, county town to county town—Salem,
Charlestown, Plymouth, Kittery, Ipswich, Cambridge, Bristol,
and Boston. Winter and summer he travelled, generally by
horseback, sometimes by water, often in the last years by
calash and coach, never missing a meeting of court "for more
than Twenty years together."

Surprisingly little is known about travel in colonial America,
but we do know that only a narrow coastal strip was settled
and that immediately bordering lay the forest, trackless save
for Indian trails, silent and illimitable. Even a well-travelled
path, like that from Boston to Plymouth, could be lost after
a fall of snow:

March, 27. [1710.] Am much disheartened by the Snow
on the ground, and that which was falling, there being
a dismal face of Winter. Yet the Sun breaking out, I
stood along about 10. [a.] m. Everything look'd so wild
with Snow on the Ground and Trees; that was in pain
lest I should Wander: But it pleas'd God graciously to
direct, so that I got well to D. Jacobs, and then call'd
his Tenant Riply to guid us over the Rocky Swamps to
Curtis's. Din'd at Bairstow's; from thence had the under-
Sheriff Briant. At Cook's the Sheriff met me. Mr. J.
Cotton, Otis and others with him. Got to Rickard's
about Sun-set.

Frequently Sewall travelled with his "pilot," some local
person who knew the path, and in later years he was generally accompanied by a servant, such as the faithful Scipio, a
Negro. If meal time found them on the road, they might stop
to eat in the woods; thirsty, they would fill a bottle from a
stream and drink. Sewall was many times thrown from his
horse, but always "through the goodness of God" he "had
no harm."[15]

Off the circuit, Sewall's most imporant work was in the
Governor's Council, where again he was the constant attender
to duty ("the most constant" he confided to his diary when
Governor Dudley once chided him for being late). Here again
were pleasant dignities of office: "Splendid Treat[s]" by
various Governors; dining at the Exchange Tavern, the
Crown Coffee House, the Dolphin, and the Green Dragon;
standing with the Governor in "the Gallery" of the Townhouse, "many Auditors below" and the "Serjeants in red
Cloaths with Horlberts [halberts]," to hear an act of Parliament published "by Beat of Drum, and Sound of Trumpet";
calling for pipes when the day's work was done.[16]

Sewall's politics in this job are interesting to watch. He was
generally "for upholding the Government, whether in or out
of it." Given his choice, he would wish to be in, but in or
out he desired stability. His first affection was for things as

they were in the old days, but lacking that he supported the
status quo. Governors in whose Councils he sat were addressed, without exception, in terms of felicitation and obedient service. Governor Phips had known John Hull and so
was invited home for reminiscence and a glass of brandy.
The Earl of Bellomont he found "very satisfactory." The
sending to Massachusetts of Governor Dudley he pronounced
"a very fair First-Fruit" of God's goodness in placing Queen
Anne on the throne. Dudley quarreled with almost everyone, and Sewall more than once found him a trial, but never
did he permit a breach in their relations. When Dudley was
at last relieved of his post, Sewall called on him, drank to
him, and offered his "humble service."[17]

So it went. When news came that Samuel Shute was to
be Governor, Sewall heard it with "great Joy," wanted Shute
to "make haste in coming," and considered that his "Qualifications commend him to the Embraces of all that are of his
acquaintance." When Shute returned to England and William
Dummer took over as acting Governor, Sewall rose at the
installation ceremony to compliment him on his fitness to
govern "the People you Have to do with . . . a part of the
Israel of God," and to promise that "they that sit at this Board,
will yield their Faithfull Advice to your Honour, according
to the Duty of their Place." When "Infirmities of Age" prevented his greeting Governor Burnet in person—the last under
whom he served—he wrote a letter expressing his hope for
Burnet's safe and speedy arrival and sent it to the new governor on his way up from Bristol.[18]

Part of all this was the politician watching his fences. Part
was simple good nature. If, however, a question of right or
wrong was involved, Sewall was guided by more than politics
or the desire to please. When Dudley was charged with
"Trading, or allowing a Trade with Her Majesty's Enemies,
the French, and Indians in their Interest" and badgered his
Council into a vote of vindication, Sewall investigated, decided that all was not "as white as Chalk, as clear as the

Driven snow," and reversed himself in a broadside giving the reasons. This action, characteristically honorable, was also free of any wish to antagonize. He dined with Dudley the day after the broadside appeared, "drank to his Excellency, and presented [his] duty to him." But he stood firm, saying "pleasantly" to Col. Townsend, who suggested that he withdraw the paper and put it in his pocket, "I could as easily put [you] in my Pocket."[19]

Except for his conservative vote in favor of a bill, passed in 1693, which restricted a town's representatives in the House of Deputies to residents and freeholders of the town,* the balance sheet of Sewall's known positions is liberal and humane. He opposed Dudley's attempt to disallow the House of Deputies' election of its Speaker; he regarded a bill "against fornication, or Marriage of White men with Negros or Indians" as "an Oppression provoking to God" and "got the Indians out of the Bill, and some mitigation for them [the Negroes] left in it"; he tried to prevent "Indians and Negros being Rated with Horses and Hogs, but could not prevail; he spoke, also without success, against a bill for making counterfeiting a capital crime, saying that it were best to go slow in passing "a sanguinary Law" of this kind.[20]

Paper money, issued to pay expenses of the province in expeditions against the French and Indians, provoked controversy through many years of Sewall's service on the Council. The matter has been seized on to show that in "the usual class alignment" attending the controversy, "the wealthy opposing the issues, and the poor generally favoring them," Sewall's position was clear—"He vigorously opposed every issue." The situation was not so simple, and the statement that Sewall opposed every issue is false. "I was," he says, "at making of the first Bills of Credit in the year 1690," and when an issue of fifty thousand pounds was proposed in 1714, he wrote in his diary: "Chief-Justice [Wait Winthrop]

---

* The bill was aimed at Boston's comparatively liberal influence in the government.

said twas contrary to the Statute of Mortmain [inalienable ownership]. I answer'd, twas quite on the other side, for this was all for the Publick benefit." Shortly after this he was "busy in signing Bills," a job he performed as a member of the committee appointed to see to their manufacture.[21]

In 1712 he opposed a bill "for forcing the Bills of Credit to be accepted in all payments for the future" as containing in it the possibility that the government might "make a vast Quantity . . . and leave them with us in Exchange for our Estates." They had such a bill in Barbados and men there were "ready to knock one another in the head." A "better expedient" (he does not say a desirable one) would be "to oblige Creditors to take Wheat, Indian Corn, Salt, Iron, Wool at a moderat valuation, as twas of old: Then there would be *quid pro Quo*." When an issue of five thousand pounds was proposed in 1716, he again stood opposed, this time because the General Court refused to levy taxes in the amount originally agreed on "for drawing them into the Treasury again." Feeling that such a refusal would "tend . . . greatly to weaken the publick Credit," and finding himself alone in his opposition (where, one might ask, was "the usual class alignment"?), resolved "to Sign no more Bills." When a thirty thousand pound issue was proposed in 1724, he again stood with those in favor of drawing it in again at a hard rather than an easy rate, remarking that inflation was "the Cause of much Oppression in the Province: And I dare not have a Hand in adding to the heavy Weight of this Oppression." God, he observed, is sympathetic toward the oppressed, "He bottles the[ir] Tears . . . and enters them fairly in his Book of Records. Let us imitate our Maker, in shewing our Sympathy with them, and our syncere and just desire to help them. Many of the Oppressed are the Pastors of our Congregations."[22]

Was this a pious veil for class interest? If it be liberal to favor cheap money because it will help debtors, what is it to desire a tax program that will ease the effects of inflation on the man of small, relatively fixed income? At what point does a man cease being a liberal because he desires inflation and becomes one because, like Sewall, he desires measures that will bring it under control? That he was in many ways profoundly conservative is certainly true; but it is also true that, like most men, he resists the divisions of history written in black and white.

Militia Captain

As a Justice of the Peace, Sewall's most persistent concern was the "ward on the Neck at the Line of Defence between Boston & Roxbury"—hours for keeping the gate shut, the number on watch, etc. His opinion on these matters was sought less as a Justice of the Peace than as a military officer of long experience.

The New England Puritan was quite literally a soldier of the Lord. The enemy was the devil, and the battle was hard. Indians were his active agents, who in their "pagan Powaws . . . raise[d] their masters, in the shapes of Bears and Snakes and Fires." So were the French with their "bawdy bloudy Cross." The militant spirit of the colony's first years shows in Edward Johnson's *Wonder Working Providence* (1654), where New England was reminded that

> the time is at hand wherin Anti Christ will muster up all his Forces, and make war with the People of God. . . . See then you store your selves with all sorts of weapons for war, furbrish up your Swords . . . incourage every Souldier-like Spirit among you, for the Lord Christ intends to atchieve greater matters by this little handful then the World is aware of. . . . You are called to fight the Battails of your Lord Christ; who must raigne till hee hath put all his enemies under his Feet [;] never yet did any Souldier rejoyce in dividing the Spoyle after Victory, as all the Souldiers of Christ shall, to see his judgement executed upon the great Whore,

and withall the Lambs bride prepared for him, who
come skipping over & trampling down the great Moun-
taines of the Earth.[1]

This was not just rhetoric. The Boston of 1660 described
by the visiting Samuel Maverick was notable in its facilities
to worship God, do business, and make war—

> The wholl Towne is an island except two Hundred
> paces of land at one place on the Sout[h] side. . . . It
> hath two handsome Churches in it, a handsome market
> place, and in the midst of it a Statehouse. In the Towne
> are fouer full compañys of foote and a Troope of
> horse[.] On the Southeast side of the Towne on a little
> Hill there is a Fort, and under it a Batterie[,] both
> having a dozen of Gunns or more in them, and on the
> Northeast side of the Towne there is a Battery of 6
> Gunns commanding the Rode and the entrance of
> Charles River. and on the tope of the Hill above the
> Towne and in the stra[i]ts are severall good Gunns,
> The Towne is full of good shopps well furnished with
> all kind of Merchandize and many Artificers, and
> Trad'smen of all sorts.[2]

The town's military base was the "train-band," patterned
after those which had long existed in London. In 1537 Henry
VIII issued a charter to one of these companies and set apart
a ground for its exercises known as "the Artillery Garden."
Since some members of the first Boston train band were also
members of this "Ancient and Honourable Artillery Company," they applied to the General Court for a charter which
would permit the Boston company to function like that in
London. The charter was granted in 1638, along with a thousand acres of land "to be improved . . . for providing neces-
saries."[3]

In 1644 a colony-wide militia was organized which required
eight training days a year from all but "timerous persons."

Officers were to be chosen by a vote of the soldiers in the respective companies, a Sergeant Major for each county by vote of the officers, and a Major General, in charge of the four counties, by annual vote of the General Court. This system remained in effect until Andros' arrival in 1686. Under it the Ancient and Honorable Artillery Company retained its earlier, separate identity, so that a man like Sewall could be active both in it and his company of militia.[4]

One of history's common distortions is that by which some periods come to be known as "unexciting." Such a period is the one between the "exciting" time of New England's first settlements and the later one, also "exciting," of the Revolution. Such phrases as "old Colony days" and "Provincial New England" suggest a sleepy haze, sermons on dead issues, and drowsing summer afternoons—in a word, dullness and peace.

To some extent this impression is justified. Compared with the years which preceded it and those which followed, the period was quiet. But a fair question to ask is what the historian means by "exciting"—exciting to participants in the events about which he writes or exciting to him and his audience because of later developments? If, from the standpoint of participants, it is presumed that bloody Indian attacks followed by equally bloody reprisals, razing of towns, the threat of pirates, hangings, scalpings, ravishments, and organized slaughter generally—if such things are exciting, then the years when Sewall lived were exciting.

In 1678, the year he entered the Boston scene and began drilling with the South Company, Edward Randolph wrote to the government in London that the town's troops of horse were "all well mounted and compleatly armed with back, breast, headpiece, buffe coat, sword, carbine and pistols, each troop distinguished by their coats." Foot soldiers were "very well furnished with swords, muskets, and bandaliers. . . . The late wars have hardened their infantry, made them good firemen, and taught them the ready use of armes"—the "late wars" being the long struggle against the Indians under their

King Philip.[5] From this time on, indeed beginning with news of engagements in the war against Philip, news of bloody events runs like a red thread through Sewall's pages.*

Because the threat of war hung over New England during most of his adult life, one can appreciate his exclaiming on a tour of Boston's fortifications—"The Lord keep the City!" One can understand how a man whose interest was more in saving Indians' souls than in obtaining their scalps could write after Philip's defeat: "As to our enemies, God hath, in a great measure, given us to see our desire on them. Most Ring leaders in the late Massacre have themselves had blood to drink, ending their lives by Bullets and Halters"; and how, in 1690, a year that brought reports of women "ripp'd up" and children having "their Brains dash'd out," he could send to friends in England "4 Ind. Scalps in Barrals marked with ink S.S."[6]

The picture was not, however, one of unrelieved grimness. Boston was relatively safe, and despite "presses" of men to go against the enemy and frequent news of disasters on the frontier, its training days mixed duty and pleasure. In the year of the Deerfield massacre (1704), for example, Sarah Kemble Knight witnessed a training day in Boston and wrote: "On training dayes The Youth divert themselves by Shooting at the Target . . . [and] hee that hitts neerest the white has some yards of Red Ribbin presented him, which being tied to his hatt band, the two ends streeming down his back, he is Led away in Triumph, with great applause, as the winners of the Olympiack Games."[7]

An Ensign in the South Company in 1681, Sewall was elected Captain in 1683 following the death of John Hull, its previous commander. That year the General Court, "Upon complaint of Leftenant Frary, that [the] . . . company is under much discouragement, by reason of the removing of Mr. Sewall . . . to command another company," decided he

* King Philip was the name given by the English to the Indian leader, Chief of the Wampanoags.

should be "captaine of that company as formerly."[8] This he remained till shortly before Andros' arrival, when the proposal to put the red cross back in the company colors caused him to resign. At the training on August 30, 1686, he appeared only to take his leave, giving each soldier a copy of John Cotton's *Gods Promise to His Plantation* and twenty shillings to the company as a whole "for a Treat." A few days later, on his way home from delivering up his commission, he was asked to the home of Capt. Hill and there surprised with "a good Supper. Capt. Hutchinson, Townsend, Savage, Wing and sundry others to the number of 14 or 15, were there. After Supper sung the 46th Ps."

Sewall was a popular officer. On the first training day after his return from England, for example, he went into the field with the South Company, exercised them in "a few Distances, Facings, Doublings," and "thanked them for their Respect in mentioning me when in England, warning the Company in my name; and told them the place I was in required more Time and Strength than I had, so took leave of them." Despite such protests, it was not until 1693 that he could note concerning orders for the South Company: "Words run, *late under the Command of Capt. Samuel Sewall*." He remained in the Ancient and Honorable Artillery Company, and in 1701 was elected its Captain.[9]

The cause of Sewall's being liked is suggested by a speech he made on being elected Captain of the Artillery Company. They had, he said, "mistaken a sorry pruning Hook for a Military Spear," but he promised to do his dutiful best, and asked everyone to his house for "bread, Beer, wine[, and] Silli-bub."* It is likewise suggested in his once giving a silver cup "to him who made the best Shott," saying that since at a previous training he had called on them to shoot and had not himself "hit the Butt," he gave it "in Token of the value [he] had for that virtue in others, which I my self could not attain

---

* A drink in which wine, cider, or the like was mixed with milk or cream.

to." Also, unlike most other officers, he never used corporal punishment.[10]

Perhaps it was this unwillingness to be "sanguinary" that kept him from the field of battle. It is true that as a judge he shared in much legalized mayhem, but otherwise he was the most peaceable of men. The one time that he notes doing anyone bodily harm was when his four-year-old son Joseph hit his sister on the head with a brass doorknob. For this, "and for his playing at Prayer-time, and eating when Return Thanks," Sewall "whipd him pretty smartly."[11] Ordinarily he much preferred to "have discourse." As a magistrate he was never "a striker" and disliked those who were. Twice when "pressed in His Majesties name to appear at the Townhouse compleat in Arms," in 1688 and again in 1690, he hired others to take his place.

The closest he got to combat was when Governor Dudley ordered him and two others to "search for and seize" some pirates at Marblehead. Arriving at Salem, the group enlisted the services of Sewall's brother Stephen, who, with the help of forty-two volunteers and "the singular all-powerfull gracious Providence of God," effected the capture. Samuel had returned to Boston, where he later witnessed the pirates' execution.[12]

Rather than fight pirates, Sewall for many years collected money and arranged for ransom of "poor Captives in Algeer or Sally." In 1690, when the French and Indians destroyed Schenectady and ravaged town after town in New Hampshire and in Maine, Sewall, as already noted, hired a substitute to take his place among those going out to fight; he himself set out for New York to meet with representatives of other colonies to make plans for "subdueing of the Comon Enemy." Returning home, he accepted a commission to be Connecticut's agent in handling money raised for relief of New Hampshire and Maine, laying it out for such things as salt, rye, Indian corn, pork, and nails. In 1697 he did this job again, declaring himself "gratified and honoured" to take part in so worthy a design. Connecticut's show of brotherly love confirmed his belief that the people of New England were "Cousen German to the Citizens of the New Jerusalem."[13]

A suitable ending to this recital of Sewall's military activities is his description of an Artillery training on October 6, 1701, the year he became Captain of the company:

> Very pleasant fair Wether; Artillery trains in the Afternoon. March with the Company to the Elms; Go to prayer, March down and Shoot at a Mark. Mr. Cushing I think was the first that hit it, Mr. Gerrish twice, Mr. Fitch, Chauncy, and the Ensign of the Officers. By far the most missed, as I did for the first. Were much contented with the exercise. Led them to the Trees agen, perform'd some facings and Doublings. Drew them together. . . . I inform'd the Company I was told the Company's Halberds &c. were borrowed; I understood the Leading staff was so, and therefore ask'd their Acceptance of a Half-Pike, which they very kindly did; I deliver'd it to Mr. Gibbs for their Use.
>
> They would needs give me a Volley, in token of their Respect on this occasion. The Pike will, I suppose, stand me in fourty shillings, being headed and shod with Silver.

The pike's silver ferrule still exists and bears this inscription:

Agmen Massachusetts
est in tutelam Sponsae
AGNI Uxoris.
1701
Ex dono Honorabalis
SAMUELIS SEWALL Armigeri

Which is to say: "The Massachusetts Company is for the protection of the Bride, the wife of the Lamb. 1701. By gift of the Honorable Samuel Sewall, Esquire." The motto sentence, joining Mars, Christ, and the Church, was most apt for a Puritan military organization.

CHAPTER FIVE

Writer

Humanitarian

Next to his diary, the work by Sewall which most interests the modern reader is *The Selling of Joseph*, an anti-slavery tract brought out in 1700. He explains how he came to write it:

Fourth-day, June, 19. 1700. . . . Having been long and much dissatisfied with the Trade of fetching Negros from Guinea; at last I had a strong Inclination to Write something about it; but it wore off. At last reading Bayne, Ephes. [Paul Baynes, *Commentary on the First Chapter of the Ephesians* (1618)] about servants, who mentions Blackamoors; I began to be uneasy that I had so long neglected doing any thing. When I was thus thinking, in came Brother Belknap to shew me a Petition he intended to present to the General Court for the freeing a Negro and his wife, who were unjustly held in Bondage. And there is a Motion by a Boston Committee to get a Law that all Importers of Negros shal pay 40ˢ per head, to discourage the bringing of them. And Mr. C. Mather resolves to publish a sheet to exhort Masters to labour their Conversion. Which makes me hope that I was call'd of God to Write this Apology for them; Let his Blessing accompany the same.

"Drawn up in haste" for presentation to the Council and General Court, *The Selling of Joseph* still speaks with compelling force. If ever its author touched greatness it was here, and no judgment of him or his Puritan heritage should forget its pages. "Forasmuch as Liberty," it begins,

> is in real value next unto Life: None ought to part with it, or deprive others of it. . . . It is most certain that all Men, as they are the Sons of Adam, are Coheirs; and have equal Right unto Liberty, and all other outward Comforts of Life. GOD hath . . . made of One Blood, all Nations of Men. . . . So that Originally, and Naturally, there is no such thing as Slavery. Joseph was rightfully no more a Slave to his Brethren, than they were to him: and they had no more Authority to Sell him, than they had to Slay him. And if they had nothing to do to Sell him; the Ishmaelites bargaining with them, and paying down Twenty pieces of Silver, could not make a Title. . . . For he that shall in this case plead Alteration of Property, seems to have forfeited a great part of his own claim to Humanity. There is no proportion between Twenty Pieces of Silver, and LIBERTY. . . .
>
> And seeing GOD hath said, He that Stealeth a Man and Selleth him, or if he be found in his hand, he shall surely be put to Death . . . What louder Cry can there be made of that Celebrated Warning,
>
> Caveat Emptor!

Whittier had this tract in mind when he wrote:

> Honor and praise to the Puritan
> Who the halting steps of his age outran,
> And, seeing the infinite worth of man
> In the priceless gift the Father gave,
> In the infinite love that stooped to save,
> Dared not brand his brother a slave.

Unlike most of Whittier's lines on Sewall, these are precisely right. *The Selling of Joseph* stands almost alone in pre-revolutionary America. True, there had been scattered protests ever since slavery's start in the New World, notably from

Mennonites and Quakers, but Sewall's was the first from a Puritan, and after it a generation passed before Elihu Coleman, a Quaker of Nantucket, wrote "A Testimony against that Anti-Christian Practice of making Slaves of Men." Then nothing appeared until the Revolution.[1]

Certainly few Puritans were, to use Sewall's word, "uneasy" over slavery. From Massachusetts' earliest years Indian captives had been handled like any other plunder of war. Similarly, trade in Negroes, of little importance in the first years but rapidly developing by the turn of the century, was a matter of relative indifference to someone like Cotton Mather, who, presented with a Negro by members of his congregation, "rejoiced in Heaven's Smile." His pious pleasure suggests the Newport elder who gave thanks "that an overruling Providence had been pleased to bring to this land of freedom another cargo of benighted heathen to enjoy the blessing of a gospel dispensation."[2]

For taking a stand against "this wicked practice of Slavery" Sewall got many "Frowns and hard Words."[3] One angry reaction came from John Saffin, a slave-holding Superior Court colleague. Saffin's ire was aroused not so much by what Sewall had written as by his support of Saffin's slave Adam's desire to be free. Saffin's pamphlet, titled *A Brief and Candid Answer to A Late Printed Sheet, Entituled, The Selling of Joseph* (1701), shows the hypocritical piety and malignity of spirit which Sewall faced. Saffin argues that the case of Joseph and that of Negro slaves are not comparable because selling Negroes to live "among Christians" clearly improves their condition; that to argue against slavery on the ground that all men are sons of Adam is to favor banishing degree altogether, something he is sure Sewall does not want; that the colony's laws against man-stealing do not apply to "strangers"; and so on. At the end of his piece Saffin abandons argument for simple abuse:

> Cowardly and cruel are those Blacks Innate,
> Prone to Revenge, Imp[s] of inveterate hate.

He that exasperates them, soon espies
Mischief and murder in their very eyes.
Libidinous, Deceitful, False and Rude,
The Spume Issue of Ingratitude.
The Premises consider'd, all may tell,
How near good Joseph they are parallel.

Had Sewall possessed the spirit of a true crusader, he would not have let matters rest here. But he possessed no such spirit, thinking it best not to "trouble the Province with any Reply." In the winter of 1705, however, a bill providing for what he regarded as "extraordinary penalties" for inter-racial marriages caused him again to take a stand. Feeling its passage would be "an Oppression provoking to God," he had printed for distribution an article in the *Athenian Oracle,* an English publication, which roughly restated his earlier arguments. He followed this with a piece for the Boston *News-Letter* of June 12, 1706, in which he argued that from a practical military and economic standpoint the colony would do better to import white servants. After this he wrote no more but continued to oppose such legislation and to express privately his dislike for the slave traffic.[4]

Another racial minority to whose welfare Sewall devoted himself was the Indian. Before considering his activities in this regard, however, the reader should understand the state of Indian affairs in the first years of the Massachusetts settlement.

Like all colonizing charters of the time, that for Massachusetts Bay announced that to "wynn . . . the natives of the country, to the knowledg and obedience of the only true God and Saviour of mankinde" was "the principall ende of [the] . . . plantation," and members of the Court of Assistants swore when they took office to work for advancement of the Gospel in New England. Not till 1646, however, was significant work begun, when John Eliot and three others "went unto the Indians inhabiting within our bounds, with desire to make known the things of their peace to them." Their first effort took place at an Indian village near Eliot's Roxbury pastorate in a wigwam crowded with men, women, and children. (The place seemed to Eliot a "darke and gloomy habitation of filthiness and uncleane spirits.") First there was prayer, then an hour and a quarter of sermon, then questions to see whether it was possible "to screw, by variety of means, something or other of God into them." After three hours of this the missionaries "asked them if they were weary, and they answered, 'no.' "[5] Not all were so receptive. When Eliot sought to evangelize King Philip, that haughty leader took hold of a button on Eliot's coat and said he "cared no more for his Gospel than for that Button." Another told Experience Mayhew, missionary at Nantucket, to "go and make the English good first."[6]

Among some tribes, however, the work was surprisingly successful. In 1651 Eliot founded the first town of "praying Indians" at Natick, eighteen miles from Roxbury, where he applied the theocratic postulates of his *Christian Commonwealth*. Other such towns were quickly established, until by the time of King Philip's War (1675–76) there were fourteen in the region of the Bay with others at Nantucket, Martha's Vineyard, and Plymouth. Also, the famous Indian Bible, a twelve-hundred page translation into Algonkian by the tireless Eliot, had been printed at the Cambridge press and two hundred copies distributed.[7]

Such undertakings needed more money than the colony could afford. The decade of the forties, moreover, when the Indian work first began, was a time of financial crisis in Massachusetts, and money for any cause was in short supply. Edward Winslow, sent to England to seek financial aid, saw in the colony's need a chance to serve not only God but Massachusetts and proposed that a missionary society be organized to raise funds for converting the Indians. Thanks to a series of promotional pamphlets by Eliot and others, the idea caught on, collections were begun, and the London corporation charted for the undertaking soon had investments yielding a thousand pounds a year.[8]

To supervise distribution of money sent to New England, the corporation, named the Society for the Propagation of the Gospel of Jesus Christ in New England and Adjacent Parts, appointed commissioners in the field who met from time to time and made reports to London. One of these was Sewall. First appointed in 1699, he soon succeeded William Stoughton as Secretary and Treasurer, a post he held for twenty-five years, calling meetings, preparing the annual accounts, making journeys of inspection to reservation lands held by the society, and doling out money and supplies.[9] The money was considerable. In 1701, for example, Sewall noted the arrival of six hundred pounds in bills of exchange. Money went to merchants for supplies, to outlying preachers, to settlers who lived near the Indians and kept an eye on their affairs, and to students of the Indian language. If God was well served, so was the Bay.[10]

After Eliot's death in 1690, the work fell off. Sickness had made disastrous inroads at Martha's Vineyard, and everywhere the praying Indians were being brutalized by the white man's rum. Some in the colony's southern parts were relatively undefiled, but the number of communicants "according to the most strict order of the Congregational way" was small. Sewall's first mention of the work, in a letter to a relative in England written while Eliot was yet alive, expressed disappointment: "As to the Design of Converting them, we in N. E. may sorrowfully sing the 127. Psalm. Except the Lord build the House, they Labour in vain that build. . . . Beseech Him to put his Hand to that work, and not in a great measure as it were to stand and look on."[11]

It is against this background that Sewall's *Phaenomena* (1697) and what he called its "appendix," *Proposals Touching the Accomplishment of Prophecies* (1713), should be viewed. Taken out of context, they seem fantastic. In context, however, they do not; for their aim, beyond showing how America "stands fair for being made the Seat of the Divine Metropolis," was a practical program for making that prospect possible.

Since, as everyone knew, Christ would not return until the Gospel had been preached to all the world, something had to be done about the "sorrowfull Decay and Languishing of the Work" among the Indians. "What say you?" Sewall asked his readers, "Do you so love Christ, as to say . . . *Come Lord Jesus! Come quickly!* Are you in good earnest? . . . Desire then, Pray and Labour that the Gospel may be preached in all the World; in this Indian End of it. For till then, Christ himself tells you, He will not, He cannot come. The Door is, as it were, shut against Him. . . . For Love, or Shame, Get Up! and open the Door!" The cost would not be small, but "Truth is a Kind of Gold that cannot be bought too dear."[12]

There was also the possiblity, as Eliot and others had long believed, that the Indians were descendants of the lost tribes of Israel and that showing them kindness might be "shew[ing] Kindness to Israelites unawares," a fact which led Sewall to declare, quoting Roger Williams:

Boast not proud English, of they birth and blood:
Thy brother Indian is by birth as good.

If things were as they should be, the Indians, "instead of being branded for Slaves with hot Irons in the Face, and arms; and driven by scores in mortal Chains . . . [would] wear the Name of God in their foreheads, and . . . be delivered unto the glorious Liberty of the Children of God."[13]

The present-day reader, encountering speculation about America being the "Seat of the Divine Metropolis" and Indians being descendants of the lost tribes of Israel, wonders whether to smile or yawn. He should remember that all transcendental beliefs are in some sense "fantastic"; that some of the most fantastic have figured in man's greatest accomplishments; and that in the absence of a better means of evaluation, one must look to results. Sewall's belief, for example, led, among other things, to an enlightened Indian policy. In his public capacity he opposed legislation directed against them. Privately he interested himself in their education and well-being, laying out land to that purpose from his Narragansett holdings and providing funds for a meeting house at Sandwich on Cape Cod.[14]

In addition to his routine duties as executive secretary for the Society for the Propagation of the Gospel, Sewall made several trips to its more remote holdings, such as the island of Arrowsick off the coast of Maine. One result was that when, in 1721, a resolution was passed for sending an expedition to Maine to put down Indian uprisings there, he brought out his *Memorial to the Kennebeck Indians,* recalling his journey and declaring that the fault lay less with the Indians than the English. The Indians had wanted a line drawn, showing "a great Reluctancy against Erecting Forts higher up the [Kennebec] River; and against the arrival of a Multitude of New Inhabitants; lest they should prove unable heartily to embrace them. . . . But no Proposals for fixing Boundaries, were offered to them." Such a course he thought as unreasonable as it was dishonorable. "Boundaries are necessary for the preservation of Honesty and Peace among those that border one upon another," and failure to establish them must suggest to the Indians that the English were bent on their destruction. Therefore, Sewall concluded, "It is Necessary to state and settle plain and lasting Bounds between the English, and the Indians; that so the Natives may have a certain and establish'd Enjoyment of their Own Country: and that the English may have *Deus Nobiscum* legibly embroidered in their Banners."[15]

In short, Sewall's position on the Indian, as on the Negro, was positive and humane. His failure lay in not providing the leadership needed for his policies to be effective. But then few men have altered the course of empire by consideration of right.

Poet

On New Year's Day morning, 1701, while it was yet dark, four trumpeters appeared on Boston Common. They had

been hired by Sewall (at a cost of five pieces of eight) to
assist him in greeting the new century. After sounding a
blast on their horns, they retired to his home, where they
continued their "levets" until sunrise. Then one of the bell-
men of Boston who was present recited these verses:

> Once more! our God vouchsafe to shine:
> Correct the Coldness of our Clime.
> Make haste with thy Impartial Light,
> And terminate this long dark night.

> Give the poor Indians Eyes to see
> The Light of Life: and set them free.
> So Men shall God in Christ adore,
> And worship Idols vain, no more.

> So Asia, and Africa,
> Europa, with America;
> All Four, in Consort join'd, shall Sing
> New Songs of Praise to Christ our King.

Their author was Sewall, a ready maker of Latin and English verse. If this surprises us, one reason is that his poetry
is forgotten. Another is that the writing of poetry is not part
of our working stereotype of the New England Puritan. The
oblivion into which the great body of early New England
verse has fallen has caused us to forget its existence. True,
such names as Michael Wigglesworth, Benjamin Thompson,
and Edward Taylor are not altogether strange, but we find
it hard to believe, for example, that Harvard in its first years
produced more practicing poets in proportion to the number
of students than at any time since, or that at least seventeen
recognized poets were writing in New England at the same
time as Sewall.[1]

Generally speaking, their poems deserve to be forgotten. We
should not, however, forget that they were written. Boston was
a community of lively literary interest, a fact which makes the
emergence from it of a writer like Franklin something more
than a cultural freak.

Most Puritan poetry is not to present-day taste. For one thing, much of it is in Latin, the worth of which few feel impelled to judge. For another, the greater part consists of "shadie lamentations" on someone's demise. Any kind of occasional verse is difficult, but the poet who uses it to edify his reader, as the Puritan felt obliged to do, has foredoomed himself to failure. So, we should add, it seems to us. Consider, for example, Sewall's poem titled "A small Vial of Tears brought from the Funeral of JOHN WINTHROP, a very goodly Child" (1711):

> In loving, lovely, Darling John,
> Winthrop and Dudley Met in One:
> Such Harmony of Charming Features
> Rarely appears in Mortal Creatures.
> But Oh—! What, meet to part so soon!
> Must we Resign this Budding Boon?
> We must: We will! CHRIST'S Will is done;
> Our wills shall make an Unison.
> JESUS will call John from the Grave,
> From Sin, Eternally to Save.

Agreeable enough in its opening, the poem dies at the point of exhortation. So, we should note again, it seems to us. It did not to Sewall's audience. For them, it was in exhortation that a poem justified itself. Like the other arts, poetry's highest aim was not to please but to strengthen the cause of God in New England. Beauty was not its own excuse for being but a handmaiden of the good. The poet's aim, as Wigglesworth declared, was "to set forth truth and win men's souls to bliss."[2] If we do not now approve that aim, we ought not to be contemptuous of it or of efforts for its accomplishment. Just as it is unfair to judge belief in witches by the knowledge of another age, so is it unfair to apply modern standards to Puritan poetry. To say this is not to urge its re-evaluation, only that we not allow aesthetic considerations to prevent our understanding those for whom it speaks.

Early New England poetry, however infelicitous it now seems, tells us much about its creators.

Though death was Sewall's commonest poetic theme, he did write about other things. When Samuel Willard, for example, after a siege of illness returned to his pulpit in South Church on Thanksgiving Day, 1700, Sewall circulated a broadside for the occasion, and when the Reverend John Sparhawk had a son born to him, Sewall wrote saying:

> Hath G. who freely gave you his own Son,
> Freely bestowed on you, one of your own?
> You certainly can justly do no less
> Than thankfull to own, yours to be his. . . .

On the occasion of "the drying up of that Ancient River, THE RIVER MERRYMAK," he wrote thirty-six lines which so pleased him that he ordered three hundred copies for distribution. Reading it, one is reminded of "the wonderful one-hoss shay." Like it, the Merrimack enjoyed a "pleasant, steady course" and "hop'd for Ages to endure." But,

> At length, an Ambushment was laid
> Near Powwaw Hill, when none afraid;
> And unawares, at one Huge Sup,
> Hydropick Hampshire Drunk it Up!

The poem cannot stop here. Lines for uplift are needed. Therefore,

> Look to thy self! Wadchuset Hill;
> And Bold Menadnuck, Fear same Ill!
> Envy'd Earth knows no certain Bound;
> In HEAV'N alone, CONTENT is found.[3]

Such was the kind of verse Sewall brought into print. The fact that it is as good as that by such other writers as John Wilson, Anna Hayden, Samuel Torrey, Samuel Danforth,

William Adams, Thomas Wally, and Joshua Moody is doubtless sufficient indication why all are forgotten.

Considerably better are verses which did not get beyond his diary or letters. One doubts that their brevity evinces what one writer has termed "a classic terseness and restraint" so much as shortness of wind, but they are better than most pieces he had published. When, for example, Tom Child, a local painter, died, Sewall noted the fact in his diary and added:

> Tom Child had often painted Death,
> But never to the Life, before:
> Doing it now, he's out of Breath;
> He paints it once, and paints no more.

On the death of his wife in 1717 he wrote to his friend Jeremiah Dummer telling what had happened and ending:

> What signify these Locks, and Bolts, and Bars?
> My Treasures gone, and with it all my Fears.

After the death of his fellow councillor and judge, Isaac Addington, he wrote:

> Isaac's withdrawn; my laughter's done
> In Council now, I see not Addington.[4]

Slight as they are, such lines afford welcome relief to the reader of Sewall's pages. One is pleased to encounter the diary entry for May 11, 1698: "As I lay in my bed in the morn [thinking of the hard winter behind], this verse came into my mind,

> To Horses, Swine, Net-Cattell, Sheep and Deer,
> Ninety and Seven prov'd a Mortal year."

Or that for April 9, 1726: "Mrs. Mary Coney died somewhat suddenly on Tuesday morning . . . and was inter'd in one

of the new Tombs in the South-burying place; Bearers, Sam.
Sewall, John Clark esqr; Sam. Brown esqr, Thomas Fitch
esqr; Sa. Checkley esqr. Capt. John Ballantine. . . . Three
Sams being Bearers together on the right side, occasion'd
my binding all the Bearers up together in this band,

> Three Sams, two Johns, and one good Tom
> Bore Prudent Mary to her Tomb."

Such lines hardly deserve printing for themselves, but they
suit the diary. In such artless trivia lies much of its fascination.

Diarist

Sewall is less important for what he was than for what he lets
us know about the world in which he lived. In the diary we
stand face to face with more than half a century of New England life—from the winter of 1674, when he was still at
Harvard, to the fall of 1729, a few months before he died. As
with any good diary, its character cannot be adequately shown
by excerpts. It should be approached entire, with something
of the same patience that went into its writing. Some of it
is dull and more is trivial, but the reader who meets its demands enters, almost imperceptibly, the world in which
Sewall lived.

No other diary of that introspective, diary-keeping time—
and literally hundreds survive—sets forth the scene in detail
so quick with life. Only Cotton Mather's compares with it
in interest, and Mather has his eyes so fixed beyond the
Jordon that he largely ignores New England. Not Sewall. No
one serves better to dispel the sense of unreality—along with
the uncritical disparagement and the equally uncritical praise
—that gathers about the time in which he wrote. Lieutenant
Governor Stoughton is seen "Carting Ears of Corn from
the upper Barn." Cotton Mather, fishing in Spy Pond, "falls
into the Water, the boat being ticklish, but receives no hurt."
Sewall gallops across Boston Common on a runaway horse,

his hat jammed under his arm, catching a "great cold in [his] ear thereby," and friends stop to chat while he builds a chicken coop in the yard. In such detail legend can hardly survive.[1]

The diary's power to evoke reality might be endlessly illustrated. Telling of a mid-week meeting of the South Church Society, Mrs. Noyes being among those present, Sewall writes: "I went away a little before her but she overtook me near the New Meetinghouse; I saw the Glimpse of her Light and call'd to her; spake a few words and parted; feeling in my self a peculiar displeasure that our way lay no further together." The Council meeting late, he notes "twas dark, and the Candle was brought in." After the funeral of Thomas Graves, Mr. Morton, being short of breath, "sat upon the Tomb in the burying-place, and said, for ought he knew he should be next." Meeting Madam Dudley's coach on the causeway of the salt works, he "saw no person; the Coach passing by suddenly in the Dusk."[2]

These passages strike a somewhat gloomy note, and rightly so. The diary, like the clothes its author frequently ordered for himself, is "sad-colored." Its funerals are innumerable, as are its author's visits to the sick and dying. On his way to Cambridge court he stopped to see Increase Mather dying of "the stone." Mather "was agonizing and Crying out, Pity me! Pity me!" "I told him," says Sewall, "God pity'd him, to which he assented and seem'd pacify'd." Dame Walker, whom Sewall had attended with his prayers, "had an odd Conceit all the last night of her life that she was in Travail; and though she ceas'd groaning and gave attention to me when at prayer; yet one of the last words I heard her say, was, My child is dead within me; which were indeed some of the very last." The dying Mr. Baily cried out, "I am even gon, even gon! . . . In his Paroxism said, Cutting, Cutting, Cutting all to pieces." When Sewall visited him again several weeks later, he heard him say: "I long to be at home; why tarry thy chariot wheels?" Finally: "New Pains: Cryes out, My

Head! my Head! what shall I doe?" Visiting the ancient schoolmaster, Ezekiel Cheever, he was received "with abundance of Affection, taking me by the Hand several times. He said, The Afflictions of God's people, God by them did as a Goldsmith, Knock, knock, knock; knock, knock, knock, to finish the plate."[3]

On Thursday, November 9, 1682, Sewall attended the marriage of Daniel Quinsey to Anne Shepard—

> Many Persons present, almost Capt. Brattle's great Hall full. . . . Mr. Willard begun with Prayer. Mr. Tho. Shepard concluded. . . . A good Space after, when had eaten Cake and drunk Wine and Beer plentifully, we were called into the Hall again to Sing. In Singing Time Mrs. Brattle goes out being ill; Most of the Company goes away, thinking it a qualm or some Fit; But she grows worse, speaks not a word, and so dyes away in her chair, I holding her feet (for she had slipt down). At length out of the Kitching [sic] we carry the chair and Her in it, into the Wedding Hall; and after a while lay the Corps of the dead Aunt in the Bride-Bed: So that now the strangeness and horror of the thing filled the (just now) joyous House with Ejulation: The Bridegroom and Bride lye at Mr. Airs, son in law to the deceased, going away like Persons put to flight in Battel.

In such passages the diary almost merits the name of literature. Written in haste, crude, ungrammatical, it has a virtue to which such matters are not only subordinate but a positive help—it lives. We do not ask for more. We do not want a polished style and can do without deep thought. We want the face of life, which Sewall gives us.

His manner is ordinarily downright. He could shape a period but declared himself "somewhat disgusted" by Cotton Mather's use of phrases like "sweet sented hands of Christ, Lord High Treasurer of Aetheopia, [and] Ribband of Humility." He preferred homely expressions, for which he had a considerable gift. What could be better than the angry Reverend Mr. Pemberton upbraiding Sewall "with extraordinary Vehemency (capering with his feet)," or the equally troublesome General Nicholson, a Church of England man who partook of the Lord's Supper on Saturday and "was this Lord's Day Rummagin and Chittering with wheelbarrows &c., to get aboard at the long Wharf," or the funeral of Governor Dudley, where there "were very many people, spectators out of windows, on Fences and Trees, like Pigeons"? A fine of ten shillings for Boston rioters he thought "too small a Plaister for so great a Sore." The dying Mr. Morton, he says, "earnestly streach'd out his flaming hand to me." The diary abounds in such turns of phrase.[4]

Sewall has been called "a Puritan Pepys," and the epithet has more than alliteration to justify its use. As a reviewer in the *Nation* wrote when the diary first appeared in print,

> Gov. Joseph Dudley does not fill the place of Charles II; nor was "Boston's greatest Fire," whereby on November 27, 1676, "about fifty Landlords were despoyled of their Housing" . . . equal in interest to the London fire of September ten years previous; nor are the futile expeditions of Queen Anne's War like the naval engagements of Van Tromp and De Ruyter. This, however, is merely saying that Judge Sewall did not have the incidents to describe which fell in the way of Secretary Pepys. So far, however, as glimpses of life and manners are covered—the revival of a buried past with its lights and shadows—Sewall is hardly inferior to Pepys. It is the touch of nature again; and, though the nature and social existence revealed may not be inviting, it is none the less genuine. It is like an engraving of Hogarth or a chapter of Fielding.[5]

CHAPTER SIX

Private Life and Last Years

The High Street House

The home of John Hull was in Boston's south end on the east side of High Street (now Washington) a few doors south of Mylne (now Summer) Street. Somewhat less than a mile to the south were the fortifications on the Neck, and not quite half a mile to the north stood the Townhouse, half way to which was Old South Church. A few hundred yards to the rear lay Boston Common. Begun by John Hull's father, the house had first been a simple rectangular structure with a chimney at one end. The son built an addition on the chimney's far side and a kitchen to the rear. At the front were stairs to the upper floor and a hall to the street. The second story overhung the first.[1]

It was in this house that on February 28, 1675/6, Sewall married Hannah Hull, in "the Old Hall" rather than the newer "Little Hall" which John Hull had added. " 'T was then all in one," wrote Sewall, "a very large Room." Dividing it into several rooms was part of the alterations which Sewall began in 1693. When completed five years later, they had transformed the house into one of the "stately Edifices" on High Street admired by Ned Ward on his arrival from England at the close of the century. Some of these homes, he reckoned, cost their owners "two or three Thousand Pounds the raising."[2]

Plans for the remodelling made Sewall uneasy; they seemed to "bespeak a Grandure . . . beyond [his] estate," something he had so far "purposely avoided." His pastor, Mr. Willard, assured him that the plans seemed necessary and meet, but Sewall hesitated. Then a fire in the kitchen chimney ("by the good Providence of God, no harm done . . . and we sat merrily to dinner on the Westfield Pork that was snatch'd from the fire") so frightened old lady Hull that she decided they were "called to remove." This was on March 22, 1692/3. On April 26 the kitchen was torn down and work began.[3]

Built across the front of the old residence, the addition was "comfortable" (Sewall's word), even "stately" (Ward's). Great changes had taken place in the fifty years since Hull's father first erected his simple dwelling. In place of shingles for the roof there were sheets of lead from England. In place of clapboard siding there was cut stone, also from England, and brickwork. Larger casements made the rooms pleasantly airy and light. Just one thing was lacking, God's sure approval. On the afternoon of April 29, 1695, there was, says Sewall,

> a very extraordinary Storm of Hail, so that the ground was made white with it, as with the blossoms when fallen; 'twas as bigg as pistoll and Musquet Bullets; It broke of the Glass of the new House about 480 Quarrels [squares] of the Front. . . . Mr. Cotton Mather dined with us, and was with me in the new Kitchen when this was; He had just been mentioning that more Ministers Houses than others proportionably had been smitten with Lightening; enquiring what the meaning of God should be in it. Many Hail-Stones broke throw the Glass and flew to the middle of the Room, or farther: People afterward Gazed upon the House to see its Ruins. I got Mr. Mather to pray with us after this awfull Providence; He told God He had broken the brittle part of our house, and prayd that we might be ready for the time when our Clay-Tabernacles should be broken. Twas a sorrowfull thing to me to see the house so far undon again before twas finished.

When at last it was completed, Sewall's friends stopped by to approve the result. Ninety-two-year-old Simon Bradstreet wished him joy of it, "drank a glass or two of wine, eat some fruit, took a pipe of Tobacco in the new Hall." "Cousin Quincey," who came with others to dine, was especially pleased with the painted shutters and "in pleasancy said he thought he had got into Paradise." A row of poplars stood "in the Foreyard, to shade the windows from the Western sun," and "Cherubim's Heads" adorned the front gate. An orchard and garden occupied a part of the spacious grounds at the rear.[4]

But all this lay far in the future when twenty-three-year-old Sewall and his eighteen-year-old bride first began their married life in the High Street house.

The Marriage Relation

Just what the arrangements were between the Hulls and the younger couple Sewall does not say. In fact, he says little about his married life generally. Rarely, for example, does he mention conversation with his wife. One almost thinks of her as permanently retired to an upper chamber for the purpose of child bearing, something she did with fearsome regularity for twenty-five years, after which she did "leave off." We do not know whether or not as a bride she was really as plump as Hawthorne makes her in his pine-tree shilling story, but by the time she had borne thirteen of her fourteen children (seven sons and seven daughters) she was so stout that she could no longer be sure whether she was "with child or no." In one of his few references to the subject, Sewall wrote *"Uxor praegnans est,"* a three-word description of his marriage.[1]

Occasionally we learn of Hannah's being taken to some neighboring town—Dorchester, Sherborn, Braintree, Cambridge—to attend a lecture, visit a friend, or just "take the Aer," and once she emerges as the writer of a letter to Love Fowle in Bermuda, wife of one of her husband's business associates there. Mrs. Fowle had sent her a gift of unidentified edibles which somehow disappeared before they reached Boston, and Hannah asks her "to prevent the Inconveniece of being so deceived for the future, by forbareing to give yourself the trouble of sending." She is "glad to hear of gods blessing" Mrs. Fowle with children, speaks of her own recent loss of two, and hopes that her friend will benefit by the Lord's "various wayes of Providence." The letter suggests a person of mild temper and conventional piety.[2]

In a book titled *The British Apollo: Containing about Two Thousand Answers to Curious Questions* (London, 1711) Sewall found it asked: "Is there now, or will there be at the Resurrection, any Females in Heaven, Since there seems to be no need of them there?" His answer was an indignant affirmative ("God is their Father, & therefore Heaven is their Country: Ubi Pater Ibi Patria"). Woman's place in the earthly present, however, was equally plain: "Amongst all the Ornaments wherewith the Chaste Mother is enriched, there is none more constantly worn, or more adorning than that of the Peremptory desire of her Husband's Presence. This causes her to record the time of his departure, keep an exact reckoning of his absence; and with frequent Calculations and Enquiries, to long and look for the appointed Season of his Expected Return"[3]—an attitude typically medieval and Paulistic. Woman was the weaker vessel, her husband's legal vassal, on whom the virtues of service and silence were enjoined. For the Puritan, this did not sanction abuse or tyranny: Solomon had called his wife his crown, and crowns should not be trampled. Neither did it necessarily mean a lack of tenderness and affection as the well-known correspondence between John and Margaret Winthrop beautifully testifies.

We learn most of Sewall as a husband in the journal he kept on his English journey. Several times he notes "dreamed of my Wife," which made him "very heavy." Eating food she had prepared for him, he finds "the remembrance of [her] is ready to cut me to the heart." He rejoices in letters from "my dear Wife" and writes to ask that he be remembered to "our dear Quaternion. S.H.E.J."—Samuel, Hannah, Elizabeth, and Joseph, their four children then living. He approves Nicholas Noyes' saying at the wedding of one of his Salem nieces that "Love was the Sugar to sweeten every Condition in the married Relation" and disapproved of humor that made light of it.[4]

Sewall's diary has none of the adventure below stairs which enlivens the diary of Pepys. In fact, during the more than forty years of his marriage, he makes but one reference to another woman's attractiveness. Visiting in Southampton on his English journey, he saw "a young Maid, comely enough, whom some allot for my Cousin."[5] The courtships of his old age are another story.

Hannah Sewall's last years were filled with pain. As Sewall wrote to Increase Mather, "She has brought forth fourteen Children, and is depress'd with chronical Infirmities and Diseases." In October, 1717, she was "seised with a Vehement Cold, which began to abate . . . but upon the 15.th of that Month, it return'd with much greater force. Her Pains grew intolerable, and she Expired upon the 19.th, on Saturday a little before sun-set. . . ."

"She is now no longer mine," wrote Sewall, "but is joyned to the Spirits of Just Men made perfect." In a letter to Gurdon Saltonstall expressing thanks for his "obliging and Refreshing Sympathy," he found that he could "hardly write for tears." His wife was, he said, "my most Constant Lover, my most laborious Nurse, a most tender Mother."

On October 23 Hannah was buried, with the Governor and General Court attending. John Danforth had a poem for the occasion:

> She was too Sparkling for Plebeian Eyes,
> Heaven Bless'd SEWALL with this Noble Prize;
> Plac'd in the Chrystal Sphere of Chastest Love,
> She Flow'r'd a Race, Devote to Heav'n above.

Full of Contentment and Devoid of Strife,
In Golden Characters She wrote her life.
. . . .
Wisdom, with an Inheritance, She had:
Her Charities did make her Neighbours Glad.

Then, addressing the bereaved Sewall:

Behold! Our Samuel to the Utmost Try'd:
CHRIST's Alsufficient Grace, Ne're yet Deny'd.
. . . .
JESUS Remains: You cannot be Undone;
Excessive Grief, Saints well may Blush to own.
Long may you Stay, to Bless the Church & State!
Kind Heav'n, We Hope, will large Years longer wait.
Strong Consolations from the OMNIPOTENT,
Let Fill your Heart, in your thus Emptied Tent![6]

Puritan Father

The lot of the Puritan child, like that of its mother, was not easy. An immediate concern for both was survival. Of Sewall's fourteen children, just six lived to maturity, a rate of mortality which, though high, was not unusual. (Of these six, incidentally, just three outlived the father. Cotton Mather had sixteen children and survived all but one.)

The story which the diary tells has an appalling fascination. Hannah Sewall's first "groaning" (Sam had prepared a batch of "groaning beer" several weeks before) was on the first of April, 1677:

About Two of the Clock at night I waked and perceived my wife ill: asked her to call Mother [Hull]. She said I should goe to prayer, then she would tell me. Then I rose, lighted a Candle at Father's fire, that had been raked up from Saturday night, kindled a Fire in the chamber, and after 5 when our folks up, went

and gave Mother warning. She came and bad me call
the Midwife, Goodwife Weeden, which I did. But my
Wives Pains went away in great measure after she was
up; toward night came on again, and about a quarter
of an hour after ten at night, April 2, Father and I
sitting in the great Hall, heard the child cry, whereas
we were afraid 'twould have been 12 before she would
have been brought to Bed. Went home with the Midwife about 2 o'clock, carrying her Stool, whoes parts
were included in a Bagg. Met with the Watch at Mr.
Rocks Brew house, who had us stand, enquired what
we were. I told the Woman's occupation, so they bad
God bless our labours, and let us pass. The first Woman
the Child sucked was Bridget Davenport.

April 3. Cousin Flint came to us. She said we ought
to lay scarlet on the Child's head for that it had received
some harm. Nurse Hurd watches. April 4. Clear cold
weather. Goodwife Ellis watches. April 7, Saturday,
first laboured to cause the child suck his mother, which
he scarce did at all. In the afternoon my Wife set up,
and he sucked the right Breast bravely.

Next day the child was baptized with the name of his
grandfather Hull. Then on June 17 he had a convulsion. "He
was asleep in the Cradle, and suddenly started, trembled, his
fingers contracted, his eyes starting and being distorted." Two
days later another. Shortly after this Sewall's diary breaks off
with the start of the lost second volume. In John Hull's, however, the entry for September 19, 1678, says that after "about
seventeen sore fits" the child died.

Sewall's next three children, born in quick succession,
survived—Samuel, June 11, 1678; Hannah, February 3, 1679;
Elizabeth, December 29, 1681. Sam suffered convulsions, however, and was taken to Newbury "to see if change of air would
help him," and Hannah's life was filled with illness and
disaster. She falls from the cupboard and breaks her head
open, "vomits and hath Qualms," "droops" with the measles,
is run over by a horse, "has the Small Pocks very favourably,"

suffers a convulsion, breaks both knee pans tumbling down stairs, and dies at last with a "noxious Humour flowing from her Legg."[1]

The next three children died in infancy: little Hull Sewall ("Hullie") when not quite two, after a year of convulsions ("Wave upon Wave"); Henry at a year (December 20, 1685, falls ill; two days later, "makes no noise save by a kind of snoring as it breathed, and as it were slept. Read the 16th of the first Chron. in the family. Having read to my Wife and Nurse out of John: the fourteenth Chapter fell now in course, which I read and went to Prayer: by that time had done, could hear little Breathing, and so about Sunrise, or little after he fell asleep, I hope in Jesus, and that Mansion was ready for him in the Father's House. Died in Nurse Hill's lap"); Stephen at six months. (Coming from his funeral, the other children "cryed much . . . so that could hardly quiet them. It seems they look'd into Tomb, and Sam said he saw a great Coffin there, his Grandfathers.")[2]

The next child lived, but the next three died—two at about a month and the third at two years ("after a sickly painfull life"). The next was stillborn, and the last one lived. Six left out of fourteen—two sons, Sam and Joseph, and four daughters, Hannah, Betty, Mary, and Judith.[3]

With such a winnowing in progress, one shares Sewall's relief when he returns from a trip and finds the family alive and well ("Laus Deo!"), or when, after a spell of sickness, he writes, "Good night, all Hands." The diary is edged in black, illness and death on almost every page. With Sewall forever in demand as a "bearer," funeral going was a steady occupation. In his last years hardly a week passed that he did not attend at least one. Sometimes he got to two in the same day.

Family illness and death were but the first of many problems for "father Sewall." The children who lived had to be fed and clothed, educated, settled in their callings, and, if possible, married—all according to their place on earth and, one hoped, in heaven.

Sewall's devotion to these parental tasks is partly explained in a letter he wrote his friend Bridget Usher. "The Fruit of the Womb," he observed, "is a Reward, the Reward of the LORD. And therefore when Parents lay up for, and lay out upon their Children, it is a most convenient Expression of their Gratitude to GOD the Giver of them." When the Reverend Nathaniel Stone wrote asking, "Children are Blessings: but are they so, as depraved?", Sewall replied that parents should nonetheless be grateful, because all children are of the "Good Providence of God." "A good man is happy, if but in the Tenth Generation, any of his descendants become the Children of God." His fourteenth child was greeted with the same satisfaction as the first. When the thirteenth was still-born, Sewall prayed that God "would make up our Loss . . . pleading with Him as the Institutor of Marriage."[4]

Sewall was a kind parent, more given to prayer than to the rod of birch ("Birch breaketh no bones"), but affection did not blind him to signs of unregeneracy, as when young Sam (age ten) played hooky from his writing school, or Joseph (age four) hit his sister Betty. "When I first went in," says Sewall, called by mother Hull, "he sought to shadow and hide himself from me behind the head of the Cradle: which gave me the sorrowfull remembrance of Adam's carriage."[5]

Such signs meant, for one thing, that the child must be given useful employment (if someone didn't find work for him, Satan would). Thus Joseph at two years and eight months was sent "to Capt. Townsend's Mother's [reading school], his Cousin Jane [Tappan] accompanying him, carried his Horn-Book." Similarly, when Hannah and Betty were five and seven, Sewall sent to England for curtains and counterpanes on which they might "work and [thus] keep . . . out of Idleness."[6]

Steps must also be taken for the child's conversion. Eager watch was kept for, in Cotton Mather's words, "examples of children in whom the fear of God was remarkably budding before they died." A good time for doing this was at family devotions, led by the father and participated in by the children, sometimes with harrowing results. January 10, 1689: "It falls to my Daughter Elizabeth's Share to read the 24. of Isaiah, which she doth with many Tears not being very well, and the Contents of the Chapter, and Sympathy with her draw Tears from me also." Betty was then eight years old. May 3, 1696: "Betty [now fifteen] can hardly read her chapter for weeping; tells me she is afraid she is gon back, does not taste that sweetness in reading the Word which once shee did; fears that what was once upon her is worn off. I said what I could to her, and in the evening pray'd with her alone." One night after dinner, a few months later, she "burst out into an amazing cry" because

> she was afraid she should goe to Hell, her Sins were not pardon'd. She was first wounded by my reading a Sermon of Mr. Norton's. . . . And those words in the Sermon . . . Ye shall seek me and shall die in your sins, ran in her mind, and terrified her greatly. And . . . she read out of Mr. Cotton Mather—Why hath Satan filled thy heart, which increas'd her Fear. Her Mother ask'd her whether she pray'd. She answer'd, Yes; but feared her prayers were not heard because her Sins not pardon'd. [Mr. Willard, minister of the South Church, being sent for] . . . he discoursed with Betty who could not give a distinct account, but was confused as his phrase was. . . . Mr. Willard pray'd excellently. The Lord bring Light and Comfort out of this dark and Dreadful Cloud, and Grant that Christ's being formed in my dear child, may be the issue of these painfull pangs.[7]

Betty was not alone. When Richard Dummer, "a flourishing youth of 9 years old" died of smallpox, Sewall told his ten-year-old son Sam of it and "what need he had to prepare for Death, and therefore to endeavour really to pray when he said over the Lord's Prayer." Sam "seem'd not much to mind, eating an Apple; but when he came to say, Our father, he burst out into a bitter Cry, and when I askt what was the matter and he could speak, he . . . said he was afraid he should die. I pray'd with him, and read Scriptures comforting against death, as, O death where is thy sting, &c. 'twas at noon." Sewall often hoped that his children might learn to "speak the Jews Language and to forget that of Ashdod." The schooling was not easy.[8]

Other parts of the Puritan child's upbringing were equally trying. For example, a common means of avoiding too much "cockering" (pampering) was to leave children with friends and relatives. Thus, on October 12, 1693, thirteen-year-old Hannah was left with Sewall's sister Longfellow at Rowley, though on coming away Sewall had "much adoe to pacify my dear daughter, she weeping and pleading to go with me." The two boys, Sam and Joseph (ages fifteen and five), were at Newton that same fall. When Sam had been there two years before and Sewall came to visit him, the boy "could hardly speak . . . his affections were so mov'd, having not seen me for above a fortnight."

And marriage, as Betty learned when she reached the mature age of seventeen, might mean simply a determination to wed (often with sharp parental prodding) followed by choice of a suitable mate (a "good Match" in which she might be "equally yoked"), a choice which might or might not be hers to make.

Captain Tuthill having expressed an interest in her (to the father, not to her), Sewall made enquiries to learn whether he "had any blot." Finding the man's reputation good, Sewall invited him to call:

[January 4, 1698/9.] About 11 m. [morning] Daughter Elizabeth reads to me the second of Genesis in course. In the evening between seven and eight Capt. Zech. Tuthill speaks with her.

. . . .

[January 7(?)] At night Capt. Tuthill comes to speak with Betty, who hid her self all alone in the coach for several hours till he was gon, so that we sought at several houses, till at last came in of her self, and look'd very wild.

January 9. . . . Speaks with her in my presence.

January 10, at night sent Mr. Tuthill away, because company was here, and told him [I] was willing to know her mind better.

. . . .

Friday, January 20. Capt. Brown and Turner break-fast here: Betty came in afterward, and serv'd Almonds and Raisings, and fill'd a Glass of Wine to us; and it fell to her to drink to Capt. Turner. She went out of the way at first, after I had spoke to her to fill wine: which surpris'd me: and I contrived that of the Raisins on purpose to mend the matter.

Such behavior made poor Betty the special object of her father's prayers, and when, a few months later, she refused Grove Hirst as well, Sewall asked that "the Lord [would] sanctify . . . Afflictions." When Hirst proved persistent, Sewall wrote Betty, then visiting at Braintree:

ELISABETH,—Mr. Hirst waits on you once more to see if you can bid him welcom. It ought to be seriously considered, that your drawing back from him after all that has passed between you, will be to your Prejudice; and will tend to discourage persons of worth from making their Court to you. And you had need well to consider whether you be able to bear his final Leaving of you, howsoever it may seem gratefull to you at present. When persons come toward us, we are apt to look upon their Undesirable Circumstances mostly; and thereupon to shun them. But when persons retire from us for good and all, we are in danger of looking only on that which is desirable in them, to our woful Disquiet. Whereas tis the property of a good Balance to turn where the most weight is, though there be some

128

also in the other Scale. I do not see but the Match is well liked by judicious persons, and such as are your Cordial Friends, and mine also.

Yet notwithstanding, if you find in yourself an immovable, incurable Aversion from him, and cannot love, and honour, and obey him, I shall say no more, nor give you any further trouble in this matter. It had better be off than on. So praying God to pardon us, and pity our Undeserving, and to direct and strengthen and settle you in making a right Judgment, and giving a right Answer, I take leave, who am, Dear Child,

your loving father.[9]

While the parents got together at home, Grove set out for Braintree. Whether because of his wooing or Sewall's letter we do not know, but a year later the young couple was married in the parlor of Sewall's new house. Cotton Mather presided, and Sewall led in singing Psalm 128, accidentally setting the wrong tune. The bride, sufferer of so many embarassments and fears, now became a mother, soon and often. At thirty-four she died, having borne eight children, five of whom were then living. "I am just a-going," her father heard her say, "Call Mr. Hirst," After this, says Sewall, "She Moan'd lower and lower till she dyed, about Midnight."[10]

The courtships and marriages of Sewall's children, all watched over by their conscientious father, are novels in the rough. Take Mary. Her "marriage to Christ" had cost Sewall "considerable Agony and . . . many Tears," and he must have turned with some relief to the more tangible business of arranging her marriage on earth. When she was eighteen a suitor appeared in Sam Gerrish, Boston bookseller and son of a country clergyman, the Reverend Joseph Gerrish. That Mary should look favorably upon him was at first disliked by her parents, there being "various and uncertain reports" about Gerrish paying court to Sarah Coney. Finally Sewall wrote the boy's father demanding "the naked Truth . . . whether the way be now fairly open for an Address of that

kind, upon assurance of agreeable entertainment." Receiving
a satisfactory reply, he left word at Gerrish's shop that he
would like to see him that night after prayer meeting.[11]

[February 18, 1708/9.] He came and I bid him well-
com to my house as to what his father writt about. So
late hardly fit then to see my daughter, appointed him
to come on Tuesday, invited him to Supper; I observ'd
he drunk to Mary in the third place. Febr. 23. When I
came from the Meeting at Mr. Stephens's I found him
in the Chamber, Mr. Hirst and wife here. It seems he
ask'd to speak with Mary below, whether it were best
to frequent my House before his father came to Town:
I said that were the best introduction; but he was well-
com to come before, and bid him come on Friday night.
Febr. 24. Mr. Hirst tells me Mr. Gerrish courted Mr.
Conney's daughter: I told him I knew it, and was uneasy. In the evening daughter [Betty] Hirst came hether,
I suppose to tell that Mr. Gerrish had courted Mr.
Coney's daughter: and if she should have Mr. Stoddard,
she would mend her market. Friday, Febr. 25. Madam
Winthrop, Oliver, and Mico visit my wife. In the
evening S. Gerrish comes not; we expected him, Mary
dress'd her self: It was a painfull disgracefull dis-
appointment. Febr. 26. Satterday, Sam Gerrish goes to
Wenham unknown to me, till Lords-day night Capt.
Greenleaf told me of it. He was not seen by us till
Wednesday March 2, David [a servant] saw him.

March, 11th S. Gerrish calls here. . . . March, 14. The
Reverend Mr. Joseph Gerrish comes to our house in
the evening. Dines with us March 15th. . . . At night
his Son comes, and Mary goes to him. Mr. Gerrish goes
home on Wednesday. His son comes and is entertain'd
then also.

Friday-night. [March 18.] S. Gerrish comes. Tells
Mary except Satterday and Lord's-day nights intends to

wait on her every night; unless some extraordinary thing happen.

Satterday, March 19. I call at S. Gerishes shop; he was not within: but came in presently: I desired him to Bind me a Psalm-Book in Calv's Leather.

In August they were married, and on November 10 of the following year Mary gave birth to a daughter. Then—

November 15. Came home [from court], fair Wether, and not very Cold. Enquired of Mr. Gerrish as I came along concerning his Wife: He said she was something disorder'd; but I apprehended no danger, and . . . went not to see her that night.

November 16. Thanksgiving. My wife sent my daughter Gerrish part of our Dinner, which as I understood she eat of pleasantly. But twas a Cold Day and she was remov'd off her Bed on to the Palat Bed in the morning. After the Evening Exercise my wife and I, rode up in the Coach: My daughter ask'd me to pray with her, which I did; pray'd that God would give her the Spirit of Adoption to call Him Father. Then I went away with Mr. Hirst to his House, leaving my wife with my daughter Gerrish, till she call'd to go home. After our coming home, the northern Chimney of the New house fell a-fire and blazed out extreamly; which made a great Uproar, as is usual. An hour or two after midnight Mr. Gerrish call'd me up acquainting us of the extream illness of his wife; All the family were alarm'd, and gather'd into our Bed-Chamber. When I came there, to my great Surprise my Daughter could not speak to me. They had try'd to call up Mr. Wadsworth [minister of South Church]; but could not make the family hear. I sent for Mr. Mayhew, who came and pray'd very well with her.

Sewall's reader knows what a minister's appearance at such a time means and is not surprised that at "four a clock after

Midnight my dear child expired, being but Nineteen years, and twenty days old." Next day was the funeral, for which John Danforth prepared on elegy in honor of her who had thus suddenly "Entred on the Celebration of Triumphant Hallelujahs." That spring the child followed its mother to the grave, thus ending the sad chronicle of Sewall's Mary.

One thing had not been arranged before she died, namely her marriage portion, a standard piece of unsentimental business. Three months after the funeral Sewall met with the Gerrishes to talk terms, arguing for five hundred and fifty pounds while they held out for six. Finally they split the difference, with Sewall throwing in the young couple's unpaid rent on his Cotton Hill house. A last wry detail is that Sam Gerrish married Sarah Coney on May 8, 1712. Sewall was there, set the tune for a psalm, and enjoyed the refreshments very much (sack-posset and cake).

Judith, the only Sewall daughter who outlived her father, married at age nineteen the Reverend William Cooper after five months of "noble" correspondence, sleigh riding, and gift giving. Sewall presided at the wedding, which as a magistrate was his right, and spoke these words:

> Sir, Madam [addressing Simeon Stoddard and his wife, mother of the groom by a previous marriage], The great Honour you have conferr'd on the Bridegroom and the Bride, by being present at this Solemnity, does very Conveniently supersede any further enquiry after your Consent. And the part I am desired to take in this Wedding, renders the way of my giving my Consent very Compendious: There's no manner of room left for that previous Question, Who giveth this Woman to be married to this Man?
>
> Dear Child, you give me your Hand for one moment, and the Bridegroom forever. Spouse, You Accept and receive this Woman now given you &c.

Joseph Sewall, now a pastor at South Church, "pray'd before the Wedding, and Mr. Colman [of the Brattle Street Church, whose assistant Mr. Cooper was to be] after. Sung the 115. Psalm from the 9. verse to the end, in the New-Hall, [to] St David's, which I set[.] There we had our Cake, and Sack-posset."[12]

With his last daughter about to be married, Sewall sent to a cousin in England, Samuel Storke, a list of things to buy—an approximate inventory of the girl's "movables." "To be Bought," it begins,

Curtains and Vallens for a Bed, with a Counterpane, Head-Cloth and Tester, of good yellow waterd worsted camlet [note added: "Send also of the same Camlet and Trimming, as may be enough to make Cushions for the Chamber Chairs"], with Trimming, well made: and Bases, if it be the fashion.

A good fine large Chintz Quilt well made.

A True Looking Glass of black Walnut Frame of the newest Fashion (if the Fashion be good), as good as can be bought for five or six pounds.

A second Looking Glass as good as can be bought for four or five pounds, same kind of frame.

A Duzzen of good black Walnut Chairs, fine Cane, with a Couch. A Duzzen of Cane Chairs of a different figure, and a great Chair, for a Chamber; all black Walnut.

One Bell-mettal Skillet of two Quarts: one ditto one Quart.

One good large Warming Pan bottom and Cover fit for an Iron handle.

Four pair of strong Iron Dogs with Brass heads, about five or six shillings a pair.

A Brass Hearth for a Chamber, with Dogs, Shovel, Tongs and Fender of the newest Fashion. (the Fire is to ly upon Iron).

A strong Brass Mortar, that will hold about a Quart, with a Pestle.

Two pair of large Brass sliding Candlesticks, about four shillings a pair.

Two pair of large Brass Candlesticks, not sliding, of the newest Fashion, about five or six shillings a pair.

Four Brass Snuffers, with stands.

Six small strong Brass Chafing-dishes, about four Shillings a-piece.

One Brass basting Ladle; one larger Brass Ladle.

One pair of Chamber Bellows with Brass Noses.

One small Hair Broom sutable to the Bellows.

One Duzzen of large hard-mettal Pewter Plates, new Fashion weighing about fourteen pounds.

One Duzzen hard-mettal Pewter Porringers.

Four Duzzen of small Glass Salt-cellars, of white glass, Smooth, not wrought, and without a foot.

And if there be any Money over, send a piece of fine Cambrick, and a Ream of good Writing Paper.

A Duzzen of good Ivory-hafted Knives and Forks.[13]

We last hear of Judith as the mother of five, living in her father's house at Cotton Hill and receiving help from him in "Disbursements."[14]

Joseph Sewall appears to have been a pious mediocrity whose habit of shedding tears at prayer gained him the name of "the weeping Apostle." That he was long a popular minister of South Church, so well thought of that at thirty-six he was chosen President of Harvard (he "gave them a denyall"), shows what had happened to the "right New England spirit."[15]

To Sewall, however, he gave endless satisfaction and joy—from the time when, at the age of three, he said, "News from Heaven, the French [are] come" ("No body has been tampering with him as I could learn"), to the time when he stood in the pulpit of Old South Church and preached from Psalm 73:28: "But it is good for me to draw near unto God." He "stood a little above an hour," notes Sewall, and "Before we went out of the seat, Major General [Winthrop] congratulated me on account of my son; said he had done Pie et Docte."[16]

To all his children Sewall was kind and generous, but

especially to Joseph—taking him out to see the military companies marching on the common, delighting in his childish boasting ("If this Country stand when I am a man [he was six], I'll drive . . . [the French] all out"), buying him cakes, thinking his teachers not properly sympathetic, buying him gold buttons when he entered the ministry, refusing to eat when he was ill ("I refrain going to Dinner; because of my Son's incapacity to feed, I refus'd to Feast"), giving him an allowance of thirty pounds a year after his marriage, and at the time of his ordination reacting with extreme sensitivity to any sign of indifference from other ministers ("I could not perceive that in either of his prayers he [Cotton Mather] did one jot mention the Building the South-church has in Hand in Settling another Minister." "Hear nothing particular in Mr. Wadsworth's Prayer, only *for this Flock.*" "Could not perceive that Mr. Bridge pray'd for my Son." "Could not discern that Mr. Pemberton pray'd for my son.")[17]

Joseph's courtship of Elizabeth Walley in the summer of his ordination (1713) was of truly clerical propriety. So far as one can learn, initiative lay more with the father than the son and found expression in gifts such as "Dr. C. Mather's Treatise against Antinominianism, just come out" and "Mr. Walter of CHRIST, very well bound in Calvs Leather." On the couple's wedding night, Sewall notes, "Daughter Sewall [the bride] came in the Coach with my Wife, who invited her to come in and lodge here with her Husband; but she refus'd, and said she had promis'd to go to her Sister Wainwright's, and did so." One is not altogether surprised that only two children came of this marriage.

The story of Joseph's older brother, Sam, is in quite a different key. Though sufficiently pious, Sam suffered from a liking for taverns and serving maids. His father warned him against the first, and as for the second, many years later Sam's wife, Rebecca, angrily told his mother that "if it were not for her, no Maid could be able to dwell at their house."[18]

Also, Sam was much troubled by "unsettledness." Having

at age sixteen neither the desire nor the aptitude for Harvard, he had to be settled in some respectable but "ordinary calling." First he went to live and work with a shopkeeper named Perry, but after about three months he came home with "sore and swoln feet" caused by the cold (it was January and Perry "had no coles"). A bit later he returned home for good, Sewall's Negro servant Bastian being sent to fetch his things.[19]

After six months of idleness—during which Sewall had special sessions of prayer for help in "Sam's being to be placed out"—he went to work at the shop of Sam Checkley. But a few months later he found he could not sleep one night because his father's brother Stephen, down from Salem, had been

speaking to him of removing to some other place, mentioning Mr. Usher's. I put him to get up a little wood, and he even fainted, at which Brother [Stephen] was much startled, and advis'd to remove him forthwith and place him somewhere else, or send him to Salem and he would doe the best he could for him. . . .

He [Sam] mention'd to me Mr. Wadsworth's Sermon against Idleness, which was an Affliction to him. He said his [work with Checkley] was an idle Calling, and that he did more at home than there, take one day with another. And he mention'd Mr. Stoddard's words to me, that should place him with a good Master, and where had fullness of Imployment. It seems Sam. overheard him, and now alledged these words against his being where he was because of his idleness. Mention'd also the difficulty of the imployment by reason of the numerousness of Goods and hard to distinguish them, many not being marked; whereas Books, the price of them was set down, and so could sell them readily. I spoke to Capt. Checkly again and again, and he gave me no encouragement that his being there would be to Sam's profit; and Mrs. Checkly always discouraging.

Mr. Willard's Sermon from those Words, What doest thou here Elijah? was an Occasion to hasten the Removal.

Feb. 10. [1695/6] Secund-day. I went to Mr. Willard
to ask whether had best keep him at home to day. He
said, No: but tell Capt. Checkly first; but when I
came back, Sam was weeping and much discompos'd,
and loth to goe because it was a little later than usual,
so I thought twas hardly fit for him to go in that Case,
and went to Capt. Checkly and told him how it was,
and thank'd him for his kindness to Sam. Capt. Checkly
desired Sam. might come to their house and not be
strange there, for which I thank'd him very kindly. He
presented his Service to my wife, and I to his who was
in her Chamber. Capt. Checkly gave me Sam's Copy-
Book that lay in the drawer.

Just before I got thether, I met Mr. Grafford who told
me that Mumford said I was a knave. The good Lord
give me Truth in the inward parts, and finally give
Rest unto my dear Son, and put him into some Calling
wherein He will accept of him to Serve him.

The patient father now found Sam a place with Mr. Wilkins, a bookseller, and the last we hear of him as a young
man he had sold "some of the Joy of Faith and some of Dr.
Goodwin's 3d volum," books on which the prices were
doubtless plainly marked.[20]

The summer he turned twenty-two (1702) Sam began
courting Rebecca Dudley, daughter of the irascible Governor.
The match was liked by parents on both sides, and that fall
the marriage took place in Sewall's dining room. After some
bickering, a property settlement was reached by which Sam,
who now wished to be a farmer, got the Sewall lands at
Muddy River (Brookline) with the understanding that Dudley would there build a house for the couple.

A few years pass and we learn that Sam is "melancholy."
Sewall asks the wife "what might be cause of my Son's
Indisposition, are you so kindly affectioned one toward another
as you should be?" She: "I do my Duty." Following this
exchange, Sam went home with his father and a week passed
before friends got the couple together again.[21]

The story continues in scattered diary entries:

Febr. 27. [1712/13, after a meeting of the Council at Governor Dudley's house] I slipt into [the] Kitchen . . . sat with Madam Dudley alone a pretty while; She said nothing to me; I gave her my Silk-Hand-kerchief, which I bought last Satterday for my daughter [Rebecca], but was prevented giving it to her, she being just gon before I got home. Yet this occasion brought her not to speak. . . .

Febr. 28. Amos Gates comes to Town, and says my Son is better.

. . . .

April 28. . . . I saw Samuel; It is yet dark wether at Brooklin.

. . . .

[October 5.] I goe to Brooklin, meet my daughter Sewall going to Roxbury with Hannah [an only child, two others having died], to dine with her Brother Winthrop. Sam and I dined alone. Daughter return'd before I came away. I propounded to her that Mr. Walter [the young couple's minister] might be desired to come to them and pray with them. She seem'd not to like the notion, said she knew not wherefore she should be call'd before a Minister! I urg'd him as the fittest moderator; the Governor or I might be thought partial. She pleaded her performance of Duty, and how much she had born. Mr. Hirst came in and smok'd a pipe and we came away together.

. . . .

[October 30.] Sam. and his Wife dine here, go home together in the Calash. William Ilsly rode and pass'd by them. My son warn'd him not to lodge at his house; Daughter said she had as much to doe with the house as he. Ilsly lodg'd there. Sam. grew so ill on Satterday, that instead of going to Roxbury [for services on Sunday] he was fain between Meetings to take his Horse, and come hither; to the surprise of his Mother, who was at home. Lord save him and us!

. . . .

November 2. Sam. is somthing better, yet full of pain; He told me with Tears that these sorrows (arising from discord between him and his wife) would bring him to his Grave. I said he must endeavour to be able to say, O Death, where is thy sting? O Grave, where is thy victory?

At this point Sewall falls silent, not mentioning, for example, that Sam again returned to his parents in the winter of 1715, this time for several years.[22] On October 16, 1716, Sewall

Went a foot to Roxbury [where the Dudleys lived]. Governor Dudley was gon to his Mill. Staid till he came home. I acquainted him what my Business was; He and Madam Dudley both, reckon'd up the Offenses of my Son; and He the Vertues of his Daughter. And alone, mention'd to me the hainous faults of my wife, who the very first word ask'd my daughter why she married my Son except she lov'd him? I saw no possibility of my Son's return; and therefore asked, that he would make some Proposals, and so left it. Madam Dudley had given me Beer as I chose; G: Dudley would have me drink a Glass of very good Wine; and made a faint of having the Horses put in, to draw me; but with all said how many hundred times he had walked over the Neck. I told him I should have a pleasant journey; and so it prov'd; for coming over with Mrs. Pierpoint, whose maiden name was Gore, had diverting discourse all the way. Met Mr. Walter in his Calash with his wife returning home, were very glad to see one another, he stopping his Calash. 'Twas quite night before we got to our house.

On December 20 a bastard child was born. Then, on August 29, 1717, after a Thursday lecture—

Note, As I came out of the Meetinghouse, Mr. Eliot's youth told me Governor Dudley would speak with me. ... I said, I think it will be best after Dinner; and went accordingly, after a little Waiting on some Probat business, which I thought not of. Governor Dudley mention'd Christ's pardoning Mary Magdalen; and God hates putting away; but did not insert *sine causa.* . . . I said my Son had all along insisted that Caution should be given, that the infant lately born should not be chargeable to his Estate. Governor Dudley no ways came into it; but said 'twas best as 'twas, No body knew whose twas.

Finally, on February 28, 1717/18:

My Son Samuel Sewall and his Wife sign and Seal the Writings in order to my Son's going home. Governor Dudley and I witnesses, Mr. Sam. Lynde took the Acknowledgment. I drank to my Daughter in a Glass of Canary. Governor Dudley took me into the Old Hall and gave me 100. in Three-pound Bills of Credit, new ones, for my Son; told me on Monday, he would perform all that he had promised to Mr. Walter. Sam agreed to go home next Monday, his wife sending the Horse for him.

After this we hear no more of strife at Muddy River. Divorce, though permissable in such a case, had apparently not been considered. Instead, the remedy was what Henry Smith, a Puritan preacher in England, described as "hold [ing] their noses together till weariness make them leave struggling; like two spaniels which are coupled in a chain, at last they learn to go together because they may not go asunder."[23] Obviously it was not meet that Governor Dudley's daughter should join her unchaste sisters at the whipping post. Of the fate of the bastard child we hear no word.

The Observance of Religion

Today Sewall's religious concerns mainly amuse and amaze us. How, we ask ourselves, could a reasonably intelligent man be so preoccupied with dress, for example, a matter so far removed from religion's ostensible concern, man's relation to his God? The answer is that it wasn't removed from that concern but was its lively symbol. As Thomas Cartwright, a Puritan leader in England, declared, such things as the cap, tippet, and surplice were "marks of popish abominations . . . hurtful monuments of idolatry, grieving the godly who hold everything connected with Antichrist in detestation, tending to draw weak brethren back to Rome."[1] This so-called Vestiarian controversy gave Puritanism its name, and in it, loosely speaking, the movement may be said to have had its start.

Only by remembering its symbolic relevance can one view Sewall's life-long war on periwigs, to take another example, as other than absurd. The Puritans' aversion had originally been to long hair, which earned them the name of Roundheads. As late as 1675, Massachusetts' authorities inveighed against long hair as "this ill custome" and saw reverses suffered in King Philip's War as a punishment for the growing acceptance of it and other sins of pride.[2] Even Sewall wore his hair shoulder length, though he did occasionally get it trimmed.

With regard to wigs, however, he remained adamant. When old and partly bald, he wore a skull cap for protection against drafts, and when Colonel Townsend twitted him, saying he should get a wig, Sewall replied that the skull cap was his "chief ornament."[3] As usual in such matters, he stood increasingly alone. On March 19, 1690/1, no less a person than Cotton Mather

> Said one sign of a hypocrit was for a man to strain
> at a Gnat and swallow a Camel . . . to be zealous against

141

an innocent fashion, taken up and used by the best of men; and yet make no Conscience of being guilty of great Immoralities. Tis supposed means wearing of Perriwigs: said would deny themselves in any thing but parting with an opportunity to do God service; that so might not offend good Christians. Meaning, I suppose, was fain to wear a Perriwig for his health. I expected not to hear a vindication of Perriwigs in Boston Pulpit by Mr. Mather.

Other men of God also surrendered to fashion and visited Mr. Farnham, Boston's "peruke-king"—Pemberton, Wadsworth, Charles Chauncy, even Sewall's son-in-law, William Cooper. Faced with such wholesale defection, Sewall thought of Ezekiel Cheever, the town's ancient schoolmaster: "A rare Instance of Piety, Health, Strength, Serviceableness. The Wellfare of the Province was much upon his Spirit. He abominated Perriwigs."[4]

Mostly Sewall kept silent, but now and then he made his thoughts known. When, for example, Josiah Willard, son of his pastor, cut off his "very full head of hair," Sewall went to see him—

Told his Mother what I came about, and she call'd him. I enquired of him what Extremity had forced him to put off his own hair, and put on a Wigg? He answered, none at all. But said that his Hair was streight, and that it parted behinde. Seem'd to argue that men might as well shave their hair off their head, as off their face. I answered men were men before they had hair on their faces, (half of mankind have never any). God seems to have ordain'd our Hair as a Test, to see whether we can bring our minds to be content to be at his finding; or whether we would be our own Carvers, Lords, and come no more to Him. . . . He seem'd to say would leave off his Wigg when his hair was grown. I spake to his Father of it a day or two after; He thank'd me that had discoursed his Son, and told me that when his hair was grown to cover his ears, he promis'd to leave off his Wigg. If he had known of it, would have forbidden him. His Mother heard him talk of it; but was afraid positively to forbid him; lest he should do it, and so be more faulty.[5]

Some months later Sewall dramatized his protest by absenting himself from Mr. Willard's congregation and going instead to Mr. Coleman at the Brattle Street Church, where "people were much gratified by my giving them my Company, Several considerable persons expres'd themselves so."[6] And he surprised at least one backsliding friend into thought: "In the morning [January 16, 1703/4] walk'd with Major Walley, Capt. Timothy Clark, Mr. Calef, constable Franklin, to visit disorderly poor; Met at my house. Capt Clark took up his Wigg: I said would have him consider that one place; The Bricks are fallen &c. But here men *cut down* the sycamores. He seem'd startled."

Holiday keeping was another great concern. A cardinal point in the Puritan creed was elimination of all church festivals as smelling of Rome. Only the Sabbath should be kept. So we find Sewall, two centuries after the battle was joined, writing: "Yesterday [August 17, 1708] the Governor committed Mr. Holyoke's Almanack to me; and looking it over this morning, I blotted against February 14.th *Valentine;* March 25. *Annunciation of the B. Virgin;* Apr. 24, *Easter;* September 29. *Michaelmas;* December 25 *Christmas."* On April 1 of the same year he sent a letter of protest to Boston's schoolmasters, Ezekiel Cheever and Nathaniel Williams:

If men are accountable for every idle word; what a Reckoning will they have, that keep up stated Times, to promote Lying and Folly! What an abuse is it of precious Time; what a Profanation! What an Affront to the Divine Bestower of it! I have heard a child of Six years old say within these 2 or 3 days; That one must tell a man his Shoes were unbuckled (when they were indeed buckled) and then he would stoop down to buckle them; and then he was an April Fool.

Pray Gentlemen, if you think it convenient, as I hope you will, Insinuat into your Scholars, the defiling and provoking nature of such a Foolish practice; and take them off from it.

Eleven years later:

In the morning I dehorted Sam. Hirst and Grindal Rawson from playing Idle Tricks because 'twas the first of April; They were the greatest fools that did so. N. E. Men came hither to avoid anniversary days, the keeping of them. . . . How displeasing must it be to God, the giver of our Time, to keep anniversary days to play the fool with ourselves and others.

The chief target was Christmas. In 1659 the General Court passed a law that whoever kept the day "by forbearing to labor, feasting or any other way" should be fined five shillings. Charles II's commissioners demanded that it be repealed as against the laws of England. In 1681, with the charter threatened, it was "left out," and in 1685, with the charter lost, it was formally annulled.[7]

But not for Sewall, to whom nothing gave more satisfaction than observing on each Christmas day that business went on pretty much "as formerly." On December 25, 1685, for example, the year the law against Christmas observance was annulled, he noted that "Carts come to Town and Shops open as is usual. Some somehow observe the day; but are vexed I believe that the Body of the People prophane it, and blessed be God no Authority yet to compell them to keep it." The next Sunday he heard Mr. Allen preach against observance: "Called it Anti-christian Heresie: Spoke against the Name. Canker began in the Tongue." On Christmas day, 1686, Governor Andros, who had arrived five days before, held special services in the Townhouse, "a Red-Coat going on his right hand and Capt. George on his left." Nevertheless, "shops open . . . generally and persons about their occasions. Some, but few, Carts at Town with wood."

The question of observing Christmas by adjourning the General Court came up in 1722. Governor Shute, a Church of England man and so in favor of the idea, took Sewall aside in the Council chamber and asked what he thought. Sewall said he "would consider of it." Next day he consulted with Cotton Mather, who felt the matter should be put to a vote of the Council and House of Representatives. On December 21,

> The Governour took me to the window . . . and spake to me again about adjourning the Court to next Wednesday. I spake against it; and propounded that the Governour would take a Vote for it. . . . His Excellency went to the Board again, and said much for this adjourning; All kept Christmas but we; I suggested K. James the first . . . how he boasted what a pure church he had; and they did not keep Yule nor Pasch.
>
> Mr. Dudley ask'd if the Scots kept Christmas. His Excellency protested, he believ'd they did not. Governour said they adjourn'd for the Commencement and Artillery [training day]. But then 'tis by Agreement. Col. Taylor spake so loud and boisterously for Adjourning, that 'twas hard for any to put in a word. . . . I said the Dissenters came a great way for their Liberties and now the [Episcopal] Church had theirs, yet they could not be contented, except they might Tread all others down.

Dudley went ahead and adjourned the Court. On Christmas day Sewall therefore chose not to go to Roxbury Lecture, which might savor of observance. Instead, he visited his "old friend and Carpenter, Peter Weare, but found him gon to h[eaven]. He expired about one a-clock in the Morning. He was quiet, minded his own business, eat his own Bread, was *antiquis moribus, prisca fide,* about 73. years old."

Like Peter Weare, Sewall stood for things as they were in the old days, whether with regard to wearing wigs, observing Christmas, taking oaths (the hand should be lifted up, not laid on the Bible: man "must Swear by his Creator, not Creature"), dancing around Maypoles (in 1687 one was set up at Charlestown by sailors from an English frigate; when it was cut down a bigger one appeared in its place with "a Garland upon it"), naming days (so that "in stead of Tuesday, Thursday, and Satterday in every Week, it might be said, Third, fifth and seventh," a change for which Sewall strove hard; but he "could not prevail, hardly one in the Council" being willing to second him), or saying "*Saint* Luke, and *Saint* James &c." ("not Scriptural . . . absurd and partial to [say] *Saint* Matthew &c. and Not to say *Saint* Moses, *Saint* Samuel &c. And if we said *Saint* we must goe thorough, and keep the Holydays appointed for them").[8]

The new provincial government meant many more "strangers" in Boston—Royal governors, soldiers of the King, minor government officials—men far different from Sewall. Under their influence, life in the community rapidly changed. Roisterers appeared in the streets at night ("singing as they come . . . inflamed with Drink. . . . Such high-handed wickedness has hardly been heard of before in Boston"); celebrators of the Queen's birthday desecrated the Sabbath ("Made a great Fire in the Evening [Saturday], many Hussas." "Down Sabbath, Up Saint George"); pranksters marched in the streets on Shrove Tuesday playing their outlandish tricks (a man appeared with "a Cock at his back, with a Bell in's hand . . . severall follow him blindfold, and under pretence of striking him on's cock, with great cart-whips strike passengers [in passing vehicles]"); duellers paraded through the town ("one array'd in white, the other in red . . . with naked Swords advanced," the victor appearing later "accompanyed with a Drumm and about 7. drawn Swords, Shouting . . . in a kind of Tryumph"); and a room at the Castle Tavern was fixed up "for a man to shew Tricks in" ("It seems the Room is fitted with Seats")—abomination after abomination.[9]

In the spring of 1714 there was talk of having "a Play acted in the Council-Chamber," which caused Sewall to write Isaac Addington, Secretary of State: "As much as in me lyes, I do forbid it. The Romans were very fond of their Plays: but I never heard they were so far set upon them, as to turn their Senat-House into a Play-House. . . . Let not Christian Boston goe beyond Heathen Rome in the practice of shamefull Vanities." The performance never took place. Some things, however, he could do nothing about. The organist of King's Chapel, Edward Enstone, became a dancing master with approval of his church and so could not be touched. Neither could Governor Shute, who patronized horse racing and staged balls that lasted far into the morning.[10]

Opposition of men like Sewall to many things enjoyed by the unregenerate has fostered the notion that their's was a joyless existence, and from our point of view perhaps it was. But satisfactions are where men find them. The founders of Massachusetts crossed the ocean in pursuit of what they deemed the good life, and, careless of hardship, found it in their Wilderness Zion.

That they really did find it Sewall's pages amply testify. Though not of the first generation, he remembered its "primitive glories"; and though he himself exemplified the colony's growing secular interest, he exemplified more that was faithful to the spirit of its founders. Prayer and fasting, reading Scripture, singing psalms, going to meeting, communing with other "New English Christians"—these were, for him, ingredients of the good life. And it *was* a good life. Sewall's diary lives because its author found it so.

Take the matter of sermons. Looking through the little books in which Sewall kept careful notes of those he heard (in the Puritan tradition of "writing after the preacher"), one is struck by their seeming flatness. But they didn't seem flat

147

to Sewall, who, more often than not, was "much refresh'd" by them. Expressions such as "Spake well," "Made good work of it," "Preached excellently" appear a thousand times in the diary, and when illness forced him to miss a sermon he felt badly used. The idea that he might as well "read a good book at home" caused him to cry, "Fy for Shame! The presenting our selves before GOD in the solemn Assembly cannot be dispensed with." When, in 1721, Mr. Prince announced but one service for Thanksgiving Day, Sewall was disturbed that "so great an Alteration should . . . have been made; without the Knowledge and Agreement of the Councillours and other Justices in Town, met together for that purpose!" For him "twas the privilege we in Boston had, that might have two."[11]

Wednesday evening of each week the South Church Society met, with Sewall in faithful attendance through more than half a century. The nature of these meetings is suggested by the following:

Novem. 27, 1676. . . . This day at even went to a private meeting held at Mr. Nath. William's. Emaus Smith spake well to Script. Philip 2.3. latter part. Smith spake more to my satisfaction than before. Note, The first Conference meeting that ever I was at, was at our House, Aug. 30, '76 at which Anna Quinsey was standing against the Closet door next the Entry. Mr. Smith spake to Ps. 119.9. The next was Oct. 18, at Mrs. Olivers: Capt. Henchman spake well to Heb. 6. 18.

The Wednesday following I was at Sandwich.

The 3ᵈ at Mr. Hill's. Goodm. Heedan and my Father [Hull] spake to Heb. 3.12. Nov. 1.

The 4ᵗʰ. Nov. 15, at Mr. Wings where Mr. Willard spake well to that proper place, Malach, 3, 16.

The 5ᵗʰ. at Mrs. Tappins, where Mr. Sanford and Mr. Noyes spake to 1 Peter, 5.7. Nov. 22. Mr. Fox prayed after. 6ᵗʰ, Nov. 29, at Mrs. Aldens, where Mr. Williams and Wing spake to Heb. 5.7. Dec. 6. no meeting because of the ensuing Fast. The 7th. at Mr. Williams's mentioned first.

When, in later years, Josiah Franklin was Wednesday night host, a youthful member of the audience would be his son Benjamin, enjoying the privilege of sitting quite still at meeting.

Thursday afternoon brought the weekly lecture. From the first years of the colony, Lecture day had been a popular institution, and though its hold was weakening at the turn of the century, Madam Knight found that on her 1704 visit Boston people still diverted themselves in "Lecture days and Training days mostly."[12] On Lecture days, she says, there was "Riding from town to town," a custom illustrated many times in Sewall's diary:

> Friday [December 23, 1687] goe to Charlestown Lecture. . . .
> Wednesday, Jan. 4. Rode to Cambridge-Lecture, Mr. John Bayly preached from Ephes. 2.1.
> Visited Aunt Mitchell and Cousin Fissenden, where I dined in Company of him, his wife and father Chany. Very cold day, yet got home comfortably.
> Tuesday, Jan. 10th. 1687/8. Carried Mother Hull on my Horse to Roxbury-Lecture, where Mr. Moodey preached from John 15.6. shewing, that not abiding in, or apostatizing from Christ, is a ruinating evil. Mr. Stoughton, the President, and Unkle Quinsey there. A very pleasant comfortable day. . . .
> Thorsday, Jan. 12. . . . Mr. Allen preaches the Lecture.

With Lecture days thus staggered in the Boston area, an enthusiast like Sewall could attend one almost at will. On his travels through outlying districts he often stayed over to hear a lecture. Thus, on a visit to Newbury in 1686 he stopped at Salem, where he "lodged 2 nights for the sake of Mr. Noyes's

Lecture, who preached excellently of Humility, from the woman's washing Christ's feet."[13]

A final type of service took place on days of public fasting and prayer. The following declaration by the General Court on May 27, 1685, shows their character:

> This Court having taken into their serious considera-
> tion, that in respect of afflictive Sicknesses in many
> Places, and some Threatenings of Scarcity as to our
> necessary food, and upon other Accounts also, we are
> under solemn Frowns of the Divine Providence; being
> likewise sensible, that the People of God in other parts
> of the World are in a low Estate,
> Do therefore appoint the Sixteenth day of July next,
> to be set apart as a Day of publick *Humiliation* by
> Fasting and Prayer throughout the Colony, exhorting
> all who are the Lord's Remembrancers, to give Him no
> rest, till Isai. 62.7. He establish and make Jerusalem a
> Praise in the Earth: And do hereby prohibit the In-
> habitants of this Jurisdiction all servile Labour upon
> the said Day.[14]

Five years earlier, Jaspar Danckaerts visited Boston and attended a fast-day service. "We went into the church," wrote that Dutch traveller, "where, in the first place, a minister made a prayer in the pulpit, of full two hours in length; after which an old minister delivered a sermon an hour long, and after that a prayer was made, and some verses sung out of the Psalms. In the afternoon three or four hours were consumed with nothing except Prayers, three ministers relieving each other alternately; when one was tired another went up into the pulpit." Sewall, after such a marathon, would note in his diary "twas a good day."[15]

His endurance, or, better perhaps, the measure of his con-
tent in this kind of exercise, is wonderfully shown by an entry in which he sets down a petition for one of his own private days of fasting and prayer:

The appointment of a Judge for the Super. Court being to be made upon next Fifth day, Febr. 12, I pray'd God to Accept me in keeping a privat day of Prayer with Fasting for That and other Important Matters: I kept it upon the Third day Febr. 10. 1707/8 in the upper Chamber at the North-East end of the House, fastening the Shutters next the Street.———Perfect what is lacking in my Faith, and in the faith of my dear Yokefellow. Convert my children; especially Samuel and Hannah; Provide Rest and Settlement for Hannah: Recover Mary, Save Judith, Elisabeth and Joseph: Requite the Labour of Love of my Kinswoman Jane Tappin, Give her health, find out Rest for her. Make David a man after thy own heart, Let Susan live and be baptised with the Holy Ghost, and with fire.* Relations. Steer the Government in this difficult time, when the Governour and many others are at so much Variance: Direct, incline, overrule on the Council-day fifth-day, Febr. 12. as to the special Work of it in filling the Super. Court with Justices; or any other thing of like nature; as Plimouth infer[ior] Court. Bless the Company for propagation of the Gospel, especiall[y] Governour Ashurst &c. Revive the Business of Religion at Natick and accept and bless John Neesnumin who went thither last week for that end. Mr. Rawson at Nantucket. Bless the South Church in preserving and spiriting our Pastor; in directing unto suitable Supply, and making the Church unanimous: Save the Town, College; Province from Invasion of Enemies, open, Secret, and from false Brethren: Defend the Purity of Worship. Save Connecticut, bless their New Governour: Save the Reformation under N. York Government. Reform all the European Plantations in America; Spanish, Portuguese, English, French, Dutch; Save this New World, that where Sin hath abounded, Grace may Superabound; that CHRIST who is stronger, would bind the strong man and spoil his house; and order the Word to be given,

---

* David and Susan were servants.

Babylon is fallen.———Save our Queen, lengthen out
her Life and Reign. Save France, make the Proud helper
stoop [Job 9:13], Save all Europe; Save Asia, Africa,
Europe and America.

He ends by remarking that "these were general heads of my
Meditation and prayer; and through the bounteous Grace of
GOD, I had a very Comfortable day of it."

Sewall obviously found these sessions satisfying, or, to use
his word, "comfortable." But more important was their
practical object of winning God's aid. For He could if He
wished, heal the sick, end a drouth, or rout the Indians. Proof
was in the frequency with which He did these things. That
He often did not was proof, on the other hand, of His sup-
plicants' unworthiness. Another proof was in the result of
prayer's neglect. One morning, for example, when Sewall
"went . . . out without private prayer," his horse ran away
and he "took great cold in [his] ear." Another time, while
staying over night at Plymouth—"I pray'd not with my
Servant being weary; seeing no Chamber-pot calld for one:
A little before day I usd it in the Bed, and the bottom came
out, and all the water run upon me. I was amazed, not knowing the bottom was out till I felt it in the bed. The Trouble
& Disgrace of it did afflict me. As soon as it was Light, I calld
up my man & he made a fire & warmd me a clean sheet & I
put it on, & was comfortable. How unexpectedly man may be
Exposd! There is no Security but in God, who is to be sought
by Prayer."[16]

This was but one of innumerable occasions where Sewall
discerned either a potent moral or the portentous working of
God's busy hand. Thus, on January 13, 1676/7:

Giving my chickens meat, it came to my mind that I
gave them nothing save Indian corn and water, and
yet they eat it and thrived very well, and that that food
was necessary for them, how mean soever, which much

affected me and convinced what need I stood in of spiritual food, and that I should not nauseat daily duties of Prayer, &c.

. . . .

June 15. [1689.] Being at Mrs. Calvin's alone in a Chamber, while they were getting ready dinner, I, as I walked about, began to crave a Blessing, and when went about it remembered my Cloaths I had bought just before, and it came into my mind that it was most material to ask a blessing on my Person: so I mentally pray'd God to bless my Flesh, Bones, Blood and Spirits, Meat, Drink, and Apparel. And at Dinner, paring the Crust of my Bread, I cut my Thumb, and spilt some of my Blood, which word I very unusually, or never before, have used in prayer to my present remembrance.

. . . .

Tuesday, Jan. 12, 1691/2. . . . This night [blank] Hamlen, formerly Plats, before that, Crabtree, a middle-aged woman, through some displeasure at her Son whom she beat, sat not down to Supper with Her Husband and a Stranger at Table: when they had done, she took away, and in the Room where she set it, took a piece of grisly meat of a Shoulder of Mutton into her mouth which got into the top of the Larynx and stopt it fast, so she was presently choak'd. Tho. Pemberton and others found it so when they opened her Throat. She gave a stamp with her foot and put her finger in her mouth: but Pemberton not at home, and di'd immediately. What need have all to Acknowledge God in whose Hand their breath is, &c.

. . . .

Satterday, Feb. 27. [1691/2.] Between 4. and 5. *mane,* we are startled at the roaring of a Beast, which I conjectur'd to be an Ox broken loose from a Butcher, running along the street, but proved to be our own Cow bitten by a dog, so that were forc'd to kill her; though calved but Jan 4.th and gives plenty of Milk. Happy are they, who have God for their Spring and Brest of Supplies.

. . . .

January 1. 6.th day 1696/7 One with a Trumpet sounds a Levet [blast] at our window just about break of day, bids me good morrow and wishes health and hapiness to attend me. I was awake before, and my wife, so we heard him: but went not to the window, nor spake a word. The Lord fit me for his coming in whatsoever way it be.

. . . .

[February 10, 1696/7.] Goodw. Duen putting on a Rugg and going into our house much scares the children; so that come running to me throw the old Hall, with a very amazing Cry. I was sawing wood; and much surpris'd. Wife came and all. The Lord save me and his people from astonishing, suddain, desolating Judgments; pardon all my folly and perverting my way, and help me to walk with a right foot.

. . . .

[October 1, 1697.] Jer. Balchar's sons came for us to go to [Hogg] Island. My Wife, through Indisposition, could not goe: But I carried Sam. Hannah, Elisa, Joseph, Mary and Jane Tapan: I prevail'd with Mr. Willard to goe, He carried Simon, Elisabeth, William, Margaret, and Elisa Tyng: Had a very comfortable Passage thither and home again; though against Tide: Had first Butter, Honey, Curds and Cream. For Dinner, very good Rost Lamb, Turkey, Fowls, Applepy, After Dinner sung the 121 Psalm. Note. A Glass of spirits my Wife sent stood upon a Joint-Stool which, Simon W. jogging, it fell down and broke all to shivers: I said twas a lively Emblem of our Fragility and Mortality.

. . . .

Third-Day, July, 25. 1699. . . . When I came home Sam, Hannah and Joanna being gon to Dorchester with Madam Usher to the Lecture, I found the House empty and Lock'd. Taking the key I came in and made a shift to find a solitary Dinner of bak'd Pigeons and a piece of Cake. How Happy I were, if I could once become Wise as a Serpent and harmless as a Dove!

[October 1, 1709.] Bait at Dedham. I got to Mr. Belcher's, where I drink warm chockelat, and no Beer; find my self much refresh'd by it after great Sweating to day, and yesterday. Got home to Dinner about One. *Laus Deo*. My Horse went very hard, which made me strain hard on my Stirrup and contract a Lameness on my Left Hip. . . . If I might with Jacob prevail with GOD for his Blessing; and be surnamed Israel, how happy should I be! though I should go limping.

Satterday, June, 6. [1713.] The Rain-water grievously runs into my son Joseph's Chamber from the Window above. As went out to the Barber's I observ'd the water to run trickling down a grate pace from the Coving. I went on the Roof, and found the Spout next Salter's stop'd, but could not free it with my Stick. Boston [a Negro servant] went up, and found his pole too big, which I warn'd him of Before; came down a Spit, and clear'd the Leaden-throat, by thrusting out a Trap-Ball that stuck there. Thus a small matter greatly incommodes us; and when God pleases, tis easily remov'd.

October 25. [1713.] In the Night after 12. Susan comes, and knocks at our chamber door, said she could not sleep, was afraid she should dye. Which amaz'd my wife and me. We let her in, blew up the Fire, wrapt her warm, and went to bed again. She sat there till near day, and then return'd; and was well in the morning. *Laus Deo*. I was the more startled because I had spilt a whole Vineyard Cann of water just before we went to Bed: and made that Reflection that our Lives would shortly be spilt.

Citations have been made numerous to show the constancy of the habit they illustrate. One can almost say that for Sewall everything was a sign of something else. Rainbows were good omens, a "Token that CHRIST remembers his Covenant for his beloved Jews," and repeatedly he noted their appearance. In them God was trying to "speak . . . to New-England," and he lamented that it had not "ears to hear." When an inverted rainbow appeared, however, he soberly recorded the speculation of his friend Mr. Lee that God was "shooting at sombody."[17]

Showers were propitious. Thunder and lightning, on the other hand, showed that God was in one of His blacker moods and sent him to his knees ("I humbly and Thankfully bless God that we saw the quick and powerfull fire; heard the Terrible Voice, and yet we live!"). On and on—small pox, severe cold, loss of cattle, all were "Tokens of [God's] Anger"; when two ministers died in one week Sewall hoped that it "be not portentous . . . *Deus avertat omen";* worms in the barley meant God was trying to waken New England by "his stroaks."[18]

In thus regarding events, Sewall ran true to Puritan form. In Samuel Mather's life of his father Cotton, he says that "when he [Cotton] washed his hands, he must think of clean hands, as well as pure heart, that belong to the citizens of Zion. . . . And when he did so mean an action as paring his nails, he thought how he might lay aside all superfluity of naughtiness." From the Puritan point of view this made excellent sense. John Cotton saw all nature as "a mappe and shaddow," in which there are "numberless Lessons of Morality, which by the Help of the Analogy between the Natural and Spiritual World . . . we may learn." At the Synod meeting in 1648, from which came the famous Cambridge Platform, a snake entered at the door and was crushed by an elder from Braintree. Governor Winthrop saw the incident as "being so remarkable, and nothing falling out but by Divine providence, it is out of doubt the Lord discovered something of his mind in it. The serpent is the devil; the synod, the representatives of the Churches of Christ in New England."[19]

If this way of thinking now seems strange, we should remember that Winthrop's remark found expression in Hawthorne and that Emerson's "correspondence" was not learned from Swedenborg. The idealism of New England's renaissance was rooted in traditions two hundred years old.

But if we grant that Sewall's religious life was somehow satisfying, even "sweet," it is still hard not to feel that his was a grim existence. A too-demanding God, an ever-scheming Satan, children crying out for fear of being damned, a brutal scheme of election and reprobation, ominous portents on every side, witches riding the midnight air—these are not elements of a happy life. But all were present in "merrie" Old England just as much as in her "sad" New England offspring. The Puritan was not original in his beliefs; what he desired was their more rigorous application. This meant a good deal, but it did not mean he ceased to be human. If, like Sewall, a man was blessed with good digestion, a good wife, good food and drink, and the respect of his fellows, the doctrine of reprobation held few terrors.

Nor should we forget that Puritan doctrine, though harsh enough, was considerably less so than that of John Calvin with which it is so often equated. Under the Puritan's "covenant theology" God was absolute but not arbitrary. A man who honestly submitted himself, repenting of his sins, would not be turned away. God had placed himself under a covenant, according to which the man who did his necessary part had little to fear.

The nearest thing to a crisis in Sewall's spiritual life came at the time of his joining Old South Church, when for several months he was distressed by thoughts of unworthiness ("Troubled that I could love Xt. no more"); but the elders encouraged him, and when he confessed his doubts to his minister, Mr. Thatcher, he was told that such "stirring up . . . was of God" and to come ahead. So on March 30, 1677, he stood "together with Gilbert Cole, [and] was admitted . . . making a Solemn covenant to take the L. Jehovah for our God, and to walk in Brotherly Love and Watchfulness of Edification. Goodm. Cole first spake, then I, then the Relations of the Women were read: as we spake so were we admitted; then all together covenanted. Prayed before, and after."[20]

Once he became a church member, Sewall's experience is best described by his favorite word "comfortable." True, there were times when he felt himself "Listless as to Spiritual Good," less "constantly and effectually inquisitive about the Way to Heaven" than he should have been—even one of the elect was not immediately made perfect—but his position was sure, and if, having sinned, he earnestly prayed for help and forgiveness, he had done his part and God would do his. Thus he writes: "I pray'd this morn that God would give me a pardon of my Sins under the Broad Seal of Heaven; and through God's goodness have receiv'd some Refreshment and Light; I hope I doe thirst after Christ; and sensible of my own folly . . . that I value Him no more, and am so backward to be married by Him." It was quite unthinkable that the God so addressed would deal hardly with His busy and conscientious servant, one whose place was in the "fore-seat" of His New England Israel.[21]

If Sewall ever brooded on the threat of hell he did not record the fact, as he did at various times his anticipation of heaven. Thus on January 26, 1696/7:

I lodged at Charlestown. at Mrs. Shepards, who tells me Mr. Harvard built that house. I lay in the chamber next the street. As I lay awake past midnight, In my Meditation, I was affected to consider how long agoe God had made provision for my comfortable Lodging that night; seeing that was Mr. Harvards house: And that led me to think of Heaven the House not made with hands, which God for many Thousands of years has been storing with the richest furniture (saints that are from time to time placed there), and that I had some hopes of being entertain'd in that Magnificent Convenient Palace, every way fitted and furnished. These thoughts were very refreshing to me.

Nor did his pleasures lie entirely beyond the Jordan. For the Puritan, despite his distrust of the flesh, was no ascetic who fled to the wilderness in refuge from the world. The only wilderness he ever fled to was New England, and there he quickly made himself as comfortable as possible, so that by the start of the eighteenth century, as a writer of the time declared, "a Gentleman from London would almost think himself at home at Boston when he observes the Numbers of People, their Houses, their Furniture, their Tables, their Dress and Conversation, which perhaps is as splendid and showy, as that of the most considerable Tradesman in London."[22]

One of the houses here referred to was Sewall's own place on High Street. He doesn't say much of how it was furnished, but its inhabitants clearly did not dress in accord with the idea that any color was all right so long as it was black. Among the items of clothes Sewall ordered from England, many, it is true, were of a "grave" or "sad" color (by which he meant brown, not black). Others, however, were "Silk Stockings, pink colored," "Serviceable Silk for our Daughter, colourd with two kinds of Red; or Red and White," "Three yards of Silver Net," "Red and White Flowerd silk enough to make a Woman Suit," flowered damask (some "Green and White" and some "Blue and White" with "Silk laces for trimming the petit coats to be made of [it]"), silk in "Orange, blew, red, white colours," and "Checquered Galoom" (trimming tape).

Such things were for the women. For himself there was "good black Broad-Cloth" for "Coat[,] Jacket and Breeches with Trimming Buttons of Hair &c. to make it up," "an end of coloured Broadcloth to make my self a suit," "Holland for shirting," and "good black Silk Mens Stockings." One of the boys got "a red Coat [with] . . . blew facing for the sleeves."[23] The undoctrinal motive for some of these purchases shows in a letter to an English cousin asking him to "bye me a pattern of good silk to make my Wife a Gown.

She has great Credit by that she bougt in pater noster row."[24]

Another source of pleasure was alcoholic beverages, the Puritan attitude toward which was expressed in Increase Mather's saying that "Wine is from God, but the Drunkard is from the Devil." Sewall was "grieved" to see that his friend Nathaniel Saltonstall had imbibed so freely that his "head and hand were rendered less usefull than at other times," and wrote him a letter gently asking him to watch his step ("Don't furnish your Enemies with Arms"). He never thought to object to drink itself, so obviously one of God's better tokens of love for His human creatures. Later evangelicalism, not Puritanism, fathered the attitude which made drink wicked in and of itself.[25]

Sewall's own enjoyment of alcoholic beverages was grateful and life-long. Rarely a wedding without its "Sack-Posset"— or funeral. When he went to a barn raising at Hogg Island he "carried over a Jugg of Madera of Ten Quarts," and at a church raising at Charlestown he sat watching in a nearby shop with "a Cool Tankard." A "noble Treat," of which he enjoyed many score, was not complete without "good Drinks," and when none appeared he specially noted the fact: "Mr. Bedford invited Mr. Brattle and me to dinner to Mr. Dracot's. Had a dish of Fowls and Bacon with Livers: A Dish of Salt Fish, and a Piece of Mutton reaching from the neck a pretty way of the back, the Ribs reaching equally from the back bone, Cheese and fruit: no Wine."[26]

As the description of this dinner suggests, Sewall's attitude toward food can scarcely be called austere. Excessive drinking meant drunkenness, something to be deplored; but for excessive eating, short of foundering oneself, there was no yardstick. For Sewall at least, it meant no more than a gradual increase in girth. A short man, he weighed 193 pounds at the age of fifty and nineteen years later a comfortable 228. He enjoyed many a "sumtuous feast" with untroubled conscience. A man's weight was in the hands of God, who, Sewall prayed, would "add, or take away from this our corporeal weight, so as shall be most advantagious for our Spiritual Growth."[27]

So, with unalloyed satisfaction, he notes the times he sat down to "a good fat tender Goose," "a very good Minc'd Py," "applepy," "Strawberries and Cream," "Venison Pasty, Cake and cheese," "Green pease," "Fry'd Lamb and Partridge," "a good Frigusee of Fowls," and, of course, the ever-present cake and wine. Because he had a sweet tooth, the roomy pockets of his outer garments were filled with pleasant dainties: "Balls of Chockalett" (a favorite item), figs, currants, "Banbury Cakes,"* and oranges.[28]

We learn of these things through Sewall's presents to nieces and nephews, grandchildren, ailing friends, or simply persons on whom he called. At other times gifts took the form of money—usually only a shilling or two but more in case of need—and often of sermons and religious tracts. Because of his own fondness for them, it gave him particular pleasure to make presents of the Psalms. Thus, at the wedding of a niece at Salem: "After the Sack-Posset, &c. Sung the 45th. Psalm from the 8th verse to the end, five staves. I set it to Windsor Tune, I had a very good Turky-Leather Psalm-Book which I look'd in while Mr. Noyes Read: and then I gave it to the Bridegroom saying, 'I give you this Psalm-Book in order to your perpetuating this Song: and I would have you pray that it may be an Introduction to our Singing with the Choir above.' "[29]

The Puritan's dislike of music (by which was meant instrumental music, "singing" being the word otherwise used) has been misunderstood. What he was opposed to was instrumental music in church, partly because he found it nowhere mentioned in the Bible and partly because—as with part and antiphonal singing—it distracted from the business at hand, which was to praise God.

* Banbury was a town in England famous for its cakes and Puritanism, where, the saying went, a cat was hung on Monday "for killing of a mouse on Sunday."

When Sewall went to a service at St. Mary's in London, he was displeased with the booming of the organ and felt that the "justling out [of] the Institution of Singing Psalms by the organ, is [a thing] that can never be answered to the great master of Religious ceremonies." Yet he was "a lover of Musick to a fault"—outside the church. On his trip to England he enjoyed a "Consort of Musick" at Covent Garden, was privately played to at Oxford Inn by "Three Musicians . . . two Harps and a Violin," and liked the work of some bell ringers. At home he bought his wife a set of virginals, went to his "Cousin Porter's" at Salem to "See and Hear the Dulcimer," and was played to on various occasions by local musicians.[30]

The result of congregational singing without accompaniment and even, as in the Bay Psalm Book, without notes, was generally bad. As an anonymous versifier at Salem declared (in lines on the back of a pew),

> Could poor David but for once
> To Salem church repair,
> And hear his Psalms thus warbled out,
> Good Lord how he would swear.[31]

Sewall's experience suggests that things were much the same in Boston.

With his liking for music and having a good voice (an admirer called him "our Israel's Judge and Singer Sweet"), Sewall was a logical candidate for the office of precentor, whose job it was to "line out" the psalms. This meant singing the first line to establish pitch and tune, after which the congregation would join in, with the precentor working to keep it in the chosen path. Sewall made his first try at it on October 25, 1691, "Capt. Frary's voice failing him in his own Essay, by reason of his Palsie." Things went well and he thereafter held the post for twenty-four years. At gatherings outside the church he was also called on to "set the tune."[32]

With increasing age, he began to have voice difficulties. At Capt. Belchar's private thanksgiving for the preservation of his son he "intended Windsor, and fell into High-Dutch, and then essaying to set another Tune, went into a Key much too high. So I pray'd Mr. White to set it; which he did well, Litchf. Tune. The Lord humble me and Instruct me, that I should be occasion of any Interruption in the Worship of God. Had a very good Dinner at three Tables."[33]

On other occasions, especially in church, where the precentor role was most demanding, a selection would begin in one tune and end in another. February 6, 1714/15: "This day I set Windsor Tune, and the people at the 2^d going over run into Oxford, do what I could." February 2, 1717/18: "Lord's Day. In the Morning I set York Tune, and in the 2^d going over, the Gallery carried it irresistibly to St David's, which discouraged me very much. I spake earnestly to Mr. White to set it in the Afternoon, but he declines it. p.m. The Tune went well." Three weeks later:

Lord's Day, Feb. 23. Mr. Foxcroft preaches. I set York Tune, and the Congregation went out of it into St. David's in the very 2^d going over. They did the same 3 weeks before. This is the 2^d Sign. I think they began in the last Line of the first going over. This seems to me an intimation and call for me to resign the Praecentor's Place to a better Voice. I have through the divine Long-suffering and Favour done it for 24. years, and now God by his Providence seems to call me off; my voice being enfeebled. I spake to Mr. White earnestly to set it in the Afternoon; but he declin'd it. After the Exercise, I went to Mr. [Joseph] Sewall's, Thank'd Mr. Prince for his very good Discourse: and laid this matter before them, told them how long I had set the Tune; Mr. Prince said, Do it Six years longer. I persisted and said that Mr. White or Franklin [Ben's father] might do it very well. The Return of the Gallery where Mr. Franklin sat was a place very Convenient for it.

During the week he consulted the elders, who agreed he should step down, and warned Mr. White that the job was now his. Next Sabbath-day morning Mr. White "disabled himself, as if he had a Cold," but, says Sewall, "when the Psalm was appointed, I forbore to do it, and rose up and turn'd to him, and he set York Tune to a very good Key. I thank'd him for restoring York Tune to its Station with so much Authority and Honor. I was Glad; I saw twas Convenient that I had resign'd, being for the benefit of the Congregation."

Sewall's singing days were done, but when the "new way" of singing from notes was introduced, he gave it his support, attending the so-called "Singing Lectures" for instruction (he was happy to find the singing "extraordinarily Excellent, such as has hardly been heard before in Boston"), and at least once holding a meeting at his own house, where he "gave every one a Booke, so the singing was continued without reading between whiles. Gave 15 or 16. New Hall."[34]

Life for Sewall was obviously far from unrelievedly grim, though it was that often enough. If the point has been dealt with at length, the reason is partly the abundance of material to illustrate it. In fact, some which deserves at least passing notice has not been mentioned, such as that each spring he joyfully noted the passing of the "sad face of Winter" and the appearance of robins and swallows: "Swallows proclame the Spring"; "I saw Six Swallows together flying and chippering very rapturously"; "Singing of Birds is come"; "The Robbins cheerfully utter their Notes this morn." Now once more he could graft, plant, and prune, things he so loved to do.

When a writer describes the time in which Sewall lived as "bare and spiritless beyond description" and uses him as chief witness, he is either unfair or unperceptive. Few persons have enjoyed life more. Highly social, he loved to be with friends at dinner (once, in a somber mood, he refused an invitation "because," he said, "a feast is made for Laughter"), organize picnics, take part in shooting competitions, and attend "raisings." He liked to fish (brought from England "One Angling Rod"), swim ("healthfull and refreshing"), go nutting, and visit travelling shows. On his voyage to England he even entered a shipboard wager as to the day land would be sighted, which is surprising in view of the Puritan's dislike for lotteries as frivolous trials of providence. In London he attended concerts, took in the sights, even "plaid Nine Pins," a pastime which in Boston was punished by a five shilling fine.[35] The significance of such items, taken from voluminous records of half a century should not be exaggerated, but they do dispel some of the gloom that wants always to settle on the Puritan scene.

Finally, in estimating the effect of Sewall's religion on his life, one should remember a diary entry made during his visit to England: "Monday March 18, [1688/9.] Went and saw the Jews burying Place at Mile-End: Some Bodies were laid East and West; but now all are ordered to be laid North and South. Many Tombs. Engravings are Hebrew, Latin, Spanish, English, sometimes on the same stone. Part of the Ground is improv'd as a Garden. . . .———I told the keeper afterwards wisht might meet in Heaven: He answerd, and drink a Glass of Beer together, which we were then doing."

A Widower's Life

On the afternoon of October 19, 1717, Hannah Sewall breathed her last, "whereby," wrote the stricken husband, "the Chamber was fill'd with a Flood of Tears. God is Teaching me a new Lesson; to live a Widower's Life. Lord help me to Learn." Doubtless feeling that for a man sixty-five years of age such a lesson would not prove too difficult, the Lord withheld His helping hand. The result was that not four months had past before Sewall was "wandering in [his] mind whether to live a Single or a Married life" and noting the absence from meeting of Madam Winthrop, wife of his late colleague on the Superior Court.

It did not help when, as soon as he had visited her once or twice, people began to interfere. Cotton Mather sent him his "An Essay to do Good Unto the Widow" with a note saying Sewall had not yet done his full duty. On the other hand, Mrs. Willoughby "seem'd to hint persons had need be ware how they married again." The Rev. Mr. Walter at Roxbury said he had heard that Governor Dudley had "laid out" Madam Winthrop for him, and when Sewall objected that he "had been there but thrice, and twice upon Business: He [Walter] said, *Cave tertium.*" Mr. Walter's own recommendation was the Widow Ruggles. Mr. Leverett said that he and his wife thought Madam Brown was Sewall's best bet, though he had to admit there was much to recommend Madam Winthrop. Mr. Henchman "took occasion highly to Commend Madam Winthrop." Deacon Marion came to see Sewall, and "after a great deal of Discourse about his [own] Courtship—He told [me]," says Sewall, "the Olivers said they wish'd I would Court their Aunt [Madam Winthrop]. I said little, but said twas not five Moneths since I buried my dear Wife. Had said before 'twas hard to know whether best to marry again or no; whom to marry."

The subject of Sewall's old-age courtships may be studied for amusement, for disparagement, or for quaint and curious lore. Each approach is justified: the material is often amusing, much of it is unflattering to Sewall, and much of it, too, is quaint and curious. Another generally neglected aim of such study is understanding. The facts already given, for example, show that Sewall's early remarriage was not only a respected possibility, it was actively anticipated.

We know that the Puritan approach to marriage, as shown in arrangements Sewall made for his children, was matter-of-fact. Romantic sentiment was not presumed, and its absence commented in no way on the parties concerned. We know, too, that Sewall was now an old man, living in a house from which all his children had gone except the invalid Hannah. The idea of having a housekeeper was disagreeable to him; Puritan tradition called for a wife. As John Cotton declared, "Women are Creatures without which there is no comfortable Living for man: it is true of them what is wont to be said of Governments, That bad ones are better than none."[1]

For a man in Sewall's position a widow was preferable to a "thornback," which is to say a spinster. Furthermore, widows were in plentiful supply. During one of his calls on Madam Winthrop, for example, the two "had a pleasant discourse about 7 Single persons sitting in the Fore-seat [on the women's side of the aisle at South Church] . . . viz. Madam Rebekah Dudley, Catharine Winthrop, Bridget Usher, Deliverance Legg, Rebekah Loyd, Lydia Colman, Elizabeth Bellingham. She propounded one and another for me; but none would do, said Mrs. Loyd was about her Age [fifty-six]."[2] Making a marital bargain with one of these women meant no slur on the memory of his dead wife, of whom he continued to speak in most affectionate terms.

Sewall's first approaches to Madam Winthrop were broken off by the appearance of another prospect in Widow Denison, whose husband's funeral he attended on March 26, 1718. Next day: "Mr. Danforth gives the widow Denison a high Commendation for her Piety, Prudence, Diligence, Humility." A few days later she brought Sewall her husband's will for probate, and again he was reminded, this time by Mr. Dorr, that she was "one of the most dutifull Wives in the world." Mr. Boydell, "smiling," remarked that the will looked as if it had been written by Sewall. Sewall told him "yes, but there was not a tittle of it mine but the form."

Mr. Boydell's smiling was not without point, for when the widow came again on April 17, Sewall presented her with "a Widow's Book Bound, having writ her Name in it"— typical opening gesture. Then on June 3, a seemly two and a half months after Mr. Denison had been laid away, he journeyed to Roxbury, where the widow lived, and there took counsel with Mr. Walter, her Minister.

Talk with him about Mrs. D———n. He advises me not to see her then, lest should surprise her undress'd. Told him I came on purpose; yet finally submitted to his Advice. . . . Spake of her Coming to Town on Thorsday.

June, 5.th No body came, I writ to Mr. Walter.

June, 9. . . . Mrs. D———n came in the morning about 9 aclock, and I took her up into my Chamber and discoursed thorowly with her; She desired me to provide another and better Nurse. I gave her the two last News-Letters—told her I intended to visit her at her own house next Lecture-day. She said, 'twould be talked of. I answer'd, In such Cases, persons must run the Gantlet. Gave her Mr. Whiting's Oration for Abijah Walter, who brought her on horseback to Town. I think little or no Notice was taken of it.

. . . .

June, 17. Went to Roxbury Lecture, visited Mr. Walter. . . . Visited Governour Dudley, Mrs. Denison, gave her Dr. Mather's Sermons very well bound; told her we were in it invited to a Wedding. She gave me very good Curds.

. . . .

July, 7. . . . I give Mrs. Denison her Oath to the Inventory [of her late husband's estate]; gave her a Catalogue superscrib'd to her. Her Brother brought her. . . . At night, when all were gone to bed; Cousin Moodey went with me into the new Hall, read the history of Rebekah's Courtship, and pray'd with me respecting my Widowed Condition.

. . . .

July, 15. . . . Governour Warns a Council, which hinders my going to Roxbury Lecture, though had bespoke before.

. . . .

16. . . . Went to Woodell's and rode in his Coach to Meers's, from thence went and visited Mrs. Denison; Gave her K. George's effigies in Copper; and an Engl.

Crown of K. Charles 2.ᵈ 1677. Eat Curds with her; I craved a Blessing, and Returned Thanks; came home.

. . . .

25. 6. [Friday, July 25.] I go in the Hackny Coach to Roxbury. Call at Mr. Walter's who is not at home; nor Governour Dudley, nor his Lady. Visit Mrs. Denison: she invites me to eat. I give her two Cases with a knife and fork in each; one Turtle shell tackling; the other long, with Ivory handles, Squar'd cost 4ˢ 6ᵈ; Pound of Raisins with proportionable Almonds. . . . Came home by Day-light in the Coach, which staid for me at the Gray-Hound.

. . . .

August, 1. 6. . . . Visit Mrs. Denison. Madam Robers and Leverett much congratulated me upon my Courting her.

August 6. 4. Visited Mrs. Denison, Carried her, her Sister Weld, the Widow, and Mrs. Weld to her Brother Mr. Samuel Weld, where we were Courteously entertained. . . . Gave Mrs. Denison a Psalm-Book neatly bound in England with Turkey-Leather.

The next three months saw many visits and presents, much dining out with relatives and friends. Finally, on the first of November:

My Son from Brooklin being here I took his Horse, and visited Mrs. Denison. Sat in the Chamber next Major Bowls. I told her 'twas time now to finish our Business: Ask'd her what I should allow her; she not speaking; I told her I was willing to give her Two and Fifty pounds per annum during her life, if it should please God to take me out of the world before her. She answer'd she had better keep as she was, than give a Certainty for an uncertainty; She should pay dear for dwelling at Boston. I desired her to make proposals, but she made none. I had Thoughts of Publishment next Thorsday the 6th. But I now seem to be far from it.

May God, who has the pity of a Father, Direct and help me!

. . . .

Friday, 9.ʳ [November] 28. 1718. Having consulted with Mr. Walter after Lecture, he advised me to goe and speak with Mrs. Denison. I went this day in the Coach; had a fire made in the Chamber where I spake with her before, 9.ʳ the first: I enquired how she had done these 3 or 4 weeks; Afterwards I told her our Conversation had been such when I was with her last, that it seem'd to be a direction in Providence, not to proceed any further; She said, It must be what I pleas'd, or to that purpose. Afterward she seem'd to blame [me] that I had not told her so 9.ʳ 1. . . . . I repeated her words of 9.ʳ 1. She seem'd at first to start at the words of her paying dear, as if she had not spoken them. But she said she though twas Hard to part with *All*, and have nothing to bestow on her Kindred. I said, I did not intend any thing of the Movables, I intended all the personal Estate to be to her. She said I seem'd to be in a hurry on Satterday, 9.ʳ 1., which was the reason she gave me no proposals. Whereas I had ask'd her long before to give me proposals in Writing; and she up-braided me, That I who had never written her a Letter, should ask her to write. She asked me if I would drink, I told her Yes. She gave me Cider, Apples and a Glass of Wine: gathered together the little things I had given her, and offer'd them to me; but I would take none of them. Told her I wish'd her well, should be glad to hear of her welfare. She seem'd to say she should not again take in hand a thing of this nature. Thank'd me for what I had given her and Desired my Prayers. . . . Mr. Stoddard and his wife came in their Coach to see their Sister which broke off my Visit. Upon their asking me, I dismiss'd my Coach, and went with them to see Mr. Danforth, and came home by Moon-shine. Got home about 9. at night. *Laus Deo*.

My bowels yern towards Mrs. Denison; but I think God directs me in his Providence to desist.

Two days later,

In the evening . . . about 7 a-clock Mrs. Dorothy Denison comes in, her Cousin Weld coming first, saying she desired to speak with me in privat. I had a fire in the new Hall, and was at prayer; was very much startled that she should come so far a-foot in that exceeding Cold Season; She enter'd into discourse of what pass'd between us at Roxbury last Friday; I seem'd to be alter'd in my affection; ask'd pardon if she had affronted me. Seem'd to incline the Match should not break off, since I had kept her Company so long. Said Mr. Denison spake to her after his Signing the Will, that he would not [have] her put all out of her Hand and power, but reserve somewhat to bestow on his Friends that might want. I told her She might keep all. She excus'd, and said 'twas not such an all. I commended the estate. I could not observe that she made me any offer of any part all this while. She mention'd two Glass Bottles she had. I told her they were hers, and the other small things I had given her, only now they had not the same signification as before. I was much concern'd for her being in the Cold, would fetch her in a plate of somthing warm: (for I had not sup'd), she refus'd. However I Fetched a Tankard of Cider and drank to her. She desired that no body might know of her being here. I told her they should not. . . . She went away in the bitter Cold, no Moon being up, to my great pain. I Saluted her at parting.

Finally, on December 22—

Mrs. Dorothy Denison brings an additional Inventory. I give her her Oath; ask'd her Brother Brewer and her to dine with me: She said she needed not to eat;

Caus'd her to sit by the fire, and went with her to the door, at her going away. She said nothing to me, nor her Brother Brewer.

Three months later Providence again took a hand. On the first of April a messenger brought Sewall a package bearing his name. In it he found "a pair of very good white Kid's Leather Gloves, and a Gold Ring." The ring bore the motto *"Lex et Libertas"* and the initials "A.T." It was from his old friend Abigail Tilley, whom he had long known as a member of the Wednesday night prayer-meeting. Twice married, she was now again widowed. Apparently she was willing, and so was Sewall, who proposed on his third visit. "She express[d] her Unworthiness of such a thing with much Respect."

This was a good start, and after several pleasant weeks of the usual visits, congratulations from friends, and gifts (no talk about a property settlement), they were married on Thanksgiving Day, 1719,

between 6 and 7. Brother Moodey and I went to Mrs. Tilley's; and about 7, or 8, were married by Mr. J[oseph] Sewall, in the best room below stairs. Mr. Prince pray'd the 2.ᵈ time. Mr. Adams the Minister of Newington was there. Mr. Oliver and Mr. Timothy Clark Justices, and many more. Sung the 12, 13, 14, 15, and 16. verses of the 90ᵗʰ Psalm. Cous. S. Sewall [a nephew] set Low-dutch Tune in a very good Key, which made the Singing with a good number of Voices very agreeable. Distributed Cake. Mrs. Armitage introduced me into my Bride's Chamber after she was a-bed. I thank'd her that she had left her room in that Chamber to make way for me, and pray'd God to provide for her a better Lodging: So none saw us after I went to bed.* Quickly after our being

---

* The bridal chamber was often the scene of prayers and drinking of healths.

a-bed my Bride grew so very bad she was fain to sit up in her bed; I rose to get her Petit Coats about her. I was exceedingly amaz'd, fearing lest she should have dy'd. Through the favour of God she recover'd in some considerable time of her Fit of the Tissick, spitting, partly blood. She her self was under great Consternation.

The marriage had not got off to a promising start, but for as long as it lasted Sewall was satisfied. His new wife was "very helpfull," "very kind," but she was wracked by fits of the ague and suffered extreme shortness of breath. One night, seven months after the marriage, she was "oppress'd with a rising of Flegm that obstructed her Breathing." Sewall hurried out of bed, "lighted a Candle, made Scipio give me a Bason of Water (he was asleep by the fire) Call'd . . . Mr. Cooper, Mayhew [ministers]. About midnight my dear wife expired to our great astonishment, especially mine. May the Sovereign Lord pardon my Sin, and Sanctify to me this very Extraordinary, awfull Dispensation."

Next day (May 27, 1720) came sympathetic callers, one of whom, Mr. Williams, consoled Sewall with the thought that what had happened to him "was what befell the Prophet Ezekiel." The following Sunday Mr. Prince spoke from the twenty-fifth chapter of Matthew, sixth verse: "At midnight behold a Cry was made." Two days later Sewall's second wife was laid in the tomb and he was again alone.

After waiting three months he once again turned to Madam Winthrop, this time in full earnest. He was now sixty-nine and she fifty-six. Both had been twice married. The record of their courtship, though often given in summary highlights deserves to be presented entire. Its combination of innocent insight, humor, and pathos is unique.

On September 5 he sent Madam Winthrop a sermon, the opening gambit. On September 30:

Daughter Sewall [Joseph's wife] acquaints Madam Winthrop that if she pleas'd to be within at 3. p.m̄. I would wait on her. She answer'd she would be at home.

8: [October] 1. Satterday, I dine at Mr. Stoddard's: from thence I went to Madam Winthrop's just at 3. Spake to her, saying, my loving wife died so soon and suddenly, 'twas hardly convenient for me to think of Marrying again; however I came to this Resolution, that I would not make my Court to any person without first Consulting with her.*

October 3.2. Waited on Madam Winthrop again; 'twas a little while before she came in. Her daughter Noyes being there alone with me, I said, I hoped my Waiting on her Mother would not be disagreeable to her. She answer'd she should not be against that that might be for her Comfort. I Saluted her, and told her I perceiv'd I must shortly wish her a good Time; (her mother had told me, she was with Child and within a Moneth or two of her Time). By and by in came Mr. Airs, Chaplain of the Castle,† and hang'd up his Hat, which I was a little startled at, it seeming as if he was to lodge there. At last Madam Winthrop came too. After a considerable time, I went up to her and said, if it might not be inconvenient I desired to speak with her. She assented, and spake of going into another Room; but Mr. Airs and Mrs. Noyes presently rose up, and went out, leaving us there alone. Then I usher'd in Discourse from the names in the Fore-seat; at last I pray'd that Katharine [Mrs. Winthrop] might be the person assign'd for me. She instantly took it up in the way of Denyal, as if she had catch'd at an Opportunity to do it, saying she could not do it before she was asked. Said that was her mind unless she should Change it, which she believed she should not; could not leave her Children. I express'd my Sorrow that she should do it so Speedily, pray'd her Consideration, and ask'd her when I should wait on

---

* At this point occurs the "pleasant discourse," earlier noted, about ladies of the foreseat at South Church, Madam Winthrop "propound[ing] one and another" and Sewall saying that "none would do."

† The military installation at Castle Island in the bay.

her agen. She setting no time, I mention'd that day Sennight. Gave her Mr. Willard's Fountain open'd . . . saying, I hop'd if we did well read that book, we should meet together hereafter, if we did not now. She took the Book, and put it in her Pocket. Took Leave.

8ʳ 5. . . . Although I had appointed to wait upon her, Madam Winthrop, next Monday, yet I went from my Cousin Sewall's thither about 3. p.m̄. The Nurse told me Madam dined abroad at her daughter Noyes's, they were to go out together. I ask'd for the Maid, who was within. Gave Kattee [a grandchild] a penny and a Kiss, and came away. . . .

8ʳ 6.ᵗʰ . . . A little after 6. p.m. I went to Madam Winthrop's. She was not within. I gave Sarah Chickering the Maid 2ˢ, Juno, who brought in wood, 1ˢ. Afterward the Nurse came in, I gave her 18ᵈ, having no other small Bill. After awhile Dr. Noyes came in with his Mother; and quickly after his wife came in: They sat talking, I think, till eight a-clock. I said I fear'd I might be some Interruption to their Business: Dr. Noyes reply'd pleasantly: He fear'd they might be an Interruption to me, and went away. Madam seem'd to harp upon the same string. Must take care of her Children; could not leave that House and Neighbourhood where she had dwelt so long. I told her she might doe her children as much or more good by bestowing what she laid out in Hous-keeping, upon them. Said her Son would be of Age the 7ᵗʰ of August. I said it might be inconvenient for her to dwell with her Daughter-in-Law, who must be Mistress of the House. I gave her a piece of Mr. Belcher's Cake and Ginger-Bread wrapped up in a clean sheet of Paper; told her of her Father's kindness to me when Treasurer, and I Constable. My Daughter Judith was gon from me and I was more Lonesom—might help to forward one another in our Journey to Canaan. Mr. Eyre [Madam Winthrop's twenty year old son by her first husband] came within the door; I saluted him . . . and he went away. I took leave about 9 aclock. I told [her] I came now to refresh her Memory as to Monday-night; said she had not forgot it. In discourse with her, I ask'd leave to speak with her Sister [Madam Mico]; I meant to gain Madam Mico's favour to persuade her Sister [Madam Winthrop]. She seem'd surpris'd and displeas'd, and said she was in the same condition!

. . . .

8.ʳ 10.ᵗʰ . . . In the Evening I visited Madam Winthrop, who treated me with a great deal of Curtesy; Wine, Marmalade. I gave her a News-Letter . . . Proposals.*

8.ʳ 11.ᵗʰ I writ a few Lines to Madam Winthrop to this purpose: "Madam, These wait on you with Mr. Mayhew's Sermon, and Account of the state of the Indians on Martha's Vinyard. I thank you for your Unmerited Favours of yesterday; and hope to have the Happiness of Waiting on you to-morrow before Eight aclock after Noon. I pray GOD to keep you, and give you a joyfull entrance upon the Two Hundred and twenty ninth year of Christopher Columbus his Discovery; and take Leave, who am, Madam, your humble Servant.

S. S."

Sent this by Deacon Green, who deliver'd it to Sarah Chickering, her Mistress not being at home.

8.ʳ 12.ʳ . . . At Madam Winthrop's . . . Mrs. Anne Cotton came to door (twas before 8.) said Madam Winthrop was within, directed me into the little Room, where she was full of work behind a Stand; Mrs. Cotton came in and stood. Madam Winthrop pointed to her to set me a Chair. Madam Winthrop's Countenance was much changed from what 'twas on Monday, look'd dark and lowering. At last, the work, (black stuff or Silk) was taken away, I got my Chair in place, had some Converse, but very Cold and indifferent to what 'twas before. Ask'd her to acquit me of Rudeness if I drew off her Glove. Enquiring the reason, I told her twas great odds between handling a dead Goat, and a living Lady. Got

* His *Proposals Touching the Accomplishment of Prophecies.*

176

it off. I told her I had one Petition to ask of her, that was, that she would take off the Negative she laid on me the third of October; She readily answer'd she could not, and enlarg'd upon it; She told me of it so soon as she could; could not leave her house, children, neighbours, business. I told her she might do som Good to help and support me. [She] . . . said I had visited Mrs. Denison. I told her Yes! Afterward I said, If after a first and second Vagary she would Accept of me returning, Her Victorious Kindness and Good Will would be very Obliging. She thank'd me for my Book, (Mr. Mayhew's Sermon), But said not a word of the Letter. When she insisted on the Negative, I pray'd there might be no more Thunder and Lightening, I should not sleep all night. I gave her Dr. Preston, The Church's Marriage and the Church's Carriage, which cost me 6ˢ at the Sale. The door standing open, Mr. Airs came in, hung up his Hat, and sat down. After awhile, Madam Winthrop moving, he went out. John Eyre [Madam Winthrop's son] look'd in, I said How do ye, or, your servant Mr. Eyre: but heard no word from him. Sarah fill'd a Glass of Wine, she drank to me, I to her, She sent Juno home with me with a good Lantern, I gave her 6.ᵈ and bid her thank her Mistress. In some of our Discourse, I told her I had rather go to the Stone-House adjoining to her, than to come to her against her mind. Told her the reason why I came every other night was lest I should drink too deep draughts of Pleasure. She had talk'd of Canary, her Kisses were to me better than the best Canary. Explain'd the expression Concerning Columbus.

8ʳ 13. I tell my Son and daughter [Joseph] Sewall, that the Weather was not so fair as I apprehended.

. . . .

8ʳ 15. I dine on Fish and Oyle at Mr. Stoddard's. Capt. Hill wish'd me Joy of my proceedings i.e. with M——Winthrop; Sister Cooper applauded it, spake of Visiting her: I said her complaisance of her Visit would be obliging to me.

8ʳ 16. L. Day, I upbraided my self that could be so
solicitous about Earthly things; and so cold and indifferent as to the Love of Christ. . . .

8ʳ 17. Monday. . . . In the Evening I visited Madam
Winthrop, who Treated me Courteously, but not in
Clean Linen as sometimes. She said, she did not know
whether I would come again, or no. I ask'd her how
she could so impute inconstancy to me. (I had not
visited her since Wednesday night being unable to get
over the Indisposition received by the Treatment received that night. . . .) Gave her this day's Gazett. Heard
David Jeffries [a grandson] say the Lord's Prayer, and
some other portions of the Scriptures. He came to the
door, and ask'd me to go into the Chamber, where his
Grandmother was tending Little Katee, to whom she
had given Physick; but I chose to sit below. Dr. Noyes
and his wife came in, and sat a Considerable time. . . .
Juno came home with me.

8ʳ 18. Visited Madam Mico, who came to me in a
splendid Dress. I said, It may be you have heard of my
Visiting Madam Winthrop, [your] Sister. She answered,
if her Sister were for it, she should not hinder it. I gave
her Mr. Homes's Sermon. She gave me a Glass of Canary, entertain'd me with good Discourse, and a Respect-
full Remembrance of my first Wife. I took Leave.

8ʳ 19. Midweek, Visited Madam Winthrop; Sarah told
me she was at Mr. Walley's [Madam Winthrop's son-
in-law], would not come home till late. . . . Was ready
to go home: but said if I knew she was there, I would
go thither. Sarah seem'd to speak with pretty good
Courage, She would be there. I went and found her
there, with Mr. Walley and his wife in the little Room
below. At 7 a-clock I mentioned going home; at 8.
I put on my Coat, and quickly waited on her home.
She found occasion to speak loud to the servant, as if
she had a mind to be known. Was Curteous to me; but
took occasion to speak pretty earnestly about my keeping
a Coach: I said 'twould cost 100. per annum: she said

twould cost but 40. . . . Mr. Eyre came in and sat awhile; I offer'd him Dr. Incr. Mather's Sermons, whereof Mr. Appleton's Ordination Sermon was one; said he had them already. I said I would give him another. Exit. Came away somewhat late.

8.ʳ 20. . . . Madam Winthrop not being at Lecture, I went thither first; found her very Serene with her dater Noyes, Mrs. Dering, and the widow Shipreev sitting at a little Table, she in her arm'd Chair. She drank to me, and I to Mrs. Noyes. After awhile pray'd the favour to speak with her. She took one of the Candles, and went into the best Room, clos'd the shutters, sat down upon the Couch. She . . . said the Coach must be set on Wheels, and not by Rusting. She spake somthing of my needing a Wigg. Ask'd me what her Sister said to me. I told her, She said, If her Sister were for it, She would not hinder it. But I told her, she did not say she would be glad to have me for her Brother. Said, I shall keep you in the Cold, and asked her if she would be within to morrow night, for we had had but a running Feat. She said she could not tell whether she should, or no. I took Leave. As were drinking at the Governour's, he said: In England the Ladies minded little more than that they might have Money, and Coaches to ride in. I said, And New-England brooks its name. At which Mr. Dudley smiled. Governour [Shute] said they were not quite so bad here.

8.ʳ 21. Friday, My Son, the Minister, came to me p.m̄. by appointment and we pray one for another in the Old Chamber; more especially respecting my Courtship. About 6. a-clock I got to Madam Winthrop's; Sarah told me her Mistress was gon out, but did not tell me whither she went. She presently order'd me a Fire; so I went in, having Dr. Sibb's Bowels* with me to read. I read the two first Sermons, still no body came in: at

---

* *Bowels opened; or a Discovery of the Union betwixt Christ and the Church.*

last about 9. a-clock Mr. John Eyre came in; I took the opportunity to say to him as I had done to Mrs. Noyes before, that I hoped my Visiting his Mother would not be disagreeable to him; He answered me with much Respect. When twas after 9. a-clock He of himself said he would go and call her, she was but at one of his Brothers: A while after I heard Madam Winthrop's voice, enquiring something about John. After a good while and Clapping the Garden door twice or thrice, she came in. I mention'd something of the lateness; she banter'd me, and said I was later. She receiv'd me Courteously. I ask'd when our proceedings should be made publick: She said They were like to be no more publick than they were already. Offer'd me no Wine that I remember. I rose up at 11 a-clock to come away, saying I would put on my Coat, She offer'd not to help me. I pray'd her that Juno might light me home, she open'd the Shutter, and said twas pretty light abroad; Juno was weary and gon to bed. So I came hom by Starlight as well as I could. At my first coming in, I gave Sarah five Shillings. I writ Mr. Eyre his Name in his book with the date October 21, 1720. It cost me 8ˢ. Jehovah jireh!

October 22. . . . Little David Jeffries saw me, and looking upon me very lovingly, ask'd me if I was going to see his Grandmother? I said, Not to-night. Gave him a peny, and bid him present my Service to his Grandmother.

October 24. I went in the Hackny Coach through the Common. stop'd at Madam Winthrop's (had told her I would take my departure [for Salem] from thence). Sarah came to the door with Katee in her Arms: but I did not think to take notice of the Child. Call'd her Mistress. I told her, being encourag'd by David Jeffries loving eyes, and sweet Words, I was come to enquire whether she could find in her heart to leave that House and Neighbourhood, and go and dwell with me at the South-end; I think she said softly, Not yet. I told her it did not ly in my Lands to keep a Coach. If I should,

I should be in danger to be brought to keep company
with her Neighbour Brooker, (he was a little before
sent to prison for Debt). Told her I had an Antipathy
against those who would pretend to give themselves;
but nothing of their Estate. I would a proportion of my
Estate with my self. And I suppos'd she would do so.
As to a Perriwig, My best and greatest Friend, I could
not possibly have a greater, began to find me with
Hair before I was born, and had continued to do so
ever since; and I could not find in my heart to go to
another. She commended the book I gave her, Dr.
Preston, the Church Marriage; quoted him saying 'twas
inconvenient keeping out of a Fashion commonly used.
I said the Time and Tide did circumscribe my Visit.
She gave me a Dram of Black-Cherry Brandy, and gave
me a lump of the Sugar that was in it. She wish'd me
a good Journy. I pray'd God to keep her and came
away. . . .

8.ʳ 25. Sent a Letter . . . to my Son by Wakefield, who
delivered it not till Wednesday; so he visited her not
till Friday p.m̅. and then presented my Service to her.

. . . .

31. 2. [Monday. He had arrived back from Salem the
Saturday before] . . . At night I visited Madam Win-
throp about 6. p.m̅. They told me she was gon to
Madam Mico's. I went thither and found she was gon;
so return'd to her house, read the Epistles to the Gala-
tions, Ephesions in Mr. Eyre's Latin Bible. After the
Clock struck 8. I began to read the 103. Psalm. Mr.
Wendell [a relative by marriage to Madam Winthrop]
came in from his Warehouse. Ask'd me if I were alone?
Spake very kindly to me, offer'd me to call Madam
Winthrop. I told him, She would be angry, had been
at Mrs. Mico's; he help'd me on with my Coat and I
came home: left the Gazett in the Bible, which told
Sarah of, bid her present my Service to Mrs. Winthrop,
and tell her I had been to wait on her if she had been
at home.

November 1. I was so taken up that I could not go if I would.

November 2. Midweek, went again, and found Mrs. Alden there, who quickly went out. Gave her about ½ pound of Sugar Almonds, cost 3ˢ per. . . . She seem'd pleas'd with them, ask'd what they cost. Spake of giving her a Hundred pounds per annum if I dy'd before her. Ask'd her what sum she would give me, if she should dy first? Said I would give her time to Consider of it. She said she heard as if I had given all to my Children by Deeds of Gift. I told her 'twas a mistake, Point Judith was mine &c. That in England, I own'd, my Father's desire was that it should go to my eldest Son; 'twas 20 per annum; she thought 'twas forty. I think when I seem'd to excuse pressing this, she seem'd to think twas best to speak of it; a long winter was coming on. Gave me a Glass or two of Canary.

November 4.ᵗʰ Friday, Went again about 7. a-clock; found there Mr. John Walley and his wife: sat discoursing pleasantly. I shew'd them Isaac Moses's Writing.* Madam W. serv'd Comfeits to us. After a-while a Table was spread, and Supper was set. I urg'd Mr. Walley to Crave a Blessing; but he put it upon me. About 9. they went away. I ask'd Madam what fashioned Neck-lace I should present her with, She said, None at all. I ask'd her Whereabout we left off last time; mention'd what I had offer'd to give her; Ask'd her what she would give me; She said she could not Change her Condition: She had said so from the beginning; could not be so far from her Children, the Lecture. Quoted the Apostle Paul affirming that a single Life was better than a Married. I answer'd That was for the present Distress. Said she had not pleasure in things of that nature as formerly: I said, you are the fitter to make me a Wife. If she held in that mind, I must go home and bewail my Rashness in making more haste than good Speed. However, considering the Supper, I desired her

---

* Isaac Moses was an Indian.

to be within next Monday night, if we liv'd so long. Assented. She charg'd me with saying, that she must put away Juno, if she came to me: I utterly deny'd it, it never came in my heart; yet she insisted upon it; saying it came in upon discourse about the Indian woman that obtained her Freedom this Court. About 10. I said I would not disturb the good orders of her House, and came away. She not seeming pleas'd with my Coming away. . . .

Monday, November 7. My Son pray'd in the Old Chamber. . . . Twas on the Account of my Courtship. I went to Mad. Winthrop; found her rocking her little Katee in the Cradle. I excus'd my Coming so late (near Eight). She set me an arm'd Chair and mine. Gave her the remnant of my Almonds; She did not eat of them as before; but laid them away; I said I came to enquire whether she had alter'd her mind since Friday, or remained of the same mind still. She said, Thereabouts. I told her, I had made her an offer, without asking any advice; she had so many to advise with, that twas a hindrance. The Fire was come to one short Brand besides the Block, which Brand was set up in end; at last it fell to pieces, and no Recruit was made: She gave me a Glass of Wine. I think I repeated again that I would go home and bewail my Rashness in making more haste than good Speed. I would endeavour to contain myself, and not go on to sollicit her to do that which she could not Consent to. Took leave of her. As came down the steps she bid me have a Care. Treated me Courteously. Told her she had enter'd the 4th year of her Widowhood. I had given her the News-Letter before: I did not bid her draw off her Glove as sometime I had done. Her Dress was not so clean as somtime it had been. Jehovah jireh!

Midweek, 9.ʳ 9.ᵗʰ Dine at Brother Stoddard's: were so kind as to enquire of me if they should invite Madam Winthrop; I answer'd No. Thank'd my Sister Stoddard for her Courtesie. . . . Had a noble Treat. At night our Meeting was at Widow Belknap's. . . . She sent her servant home with me with a Lantern. Madam Winthrop's Shutters were open as I pass'd by.

. . . .

November 11. Went not to Madam Winthrop's. This is the 2ᵈ Withdraw.

. . . .

[no date] About the middle of December [1720] Madam Winthrop made a Treat for her Children; Mr. [Joseph] Sewall, prince, Willoughby: I knew nothing of it; but the same day abode in the Council Chamber for fear of the Rain, and din'd alone upon Kilby's Pyes and good Beer.

The story is not quite told. Sewall still noted Madam Winthrop's absence at lecture and was sensitive to imagined slights where she was concerned. In the summer of 1725 she fell ill and he came to the sick chamber: "I told her I found my Son coming to her [Joseph, that is, on a ministerial visit] and took the Opportunity to come with him. She thank'd me kindly. . . . At coming I said, I kiss your hand Madame (her hand felt very dry)." Two months later she died, with Sewall one of the bearers at her funeral.

After the breakdown in negotiations with Madam Winthrop, it wasn't long before Sewall wrote his friend Jeremiah Dummer to ask his "Prayers that GOD would . . . yet again provide such a good Wife for me that I may be able to say, I have obtained Favour of the LORD." To the Rev. Mr. Woodbridge at Hartford he wrote:

My dater Hannah is grievously fetter'd by Lameness; has not gon out of doors since last December was two years: So that I am left with my House-keeper, Mrs. Lydia Kay; which is disagreeable to me. I remember when I was going from school at Newbury, I have sometime met your Sisters Martha, and Mary, at the end of Mrs. Noyes's Lane, coming from their Schoole at Chandler's lane, in their Hanging Sleeves; and have had the pleasure of Speaking with them: And I could find in my heart to speak with Mrs. Martha again, now I my self am reduc'd to my Hanging Sleeves.* The truth is, I have little Occasion for a Wife, but for the sake of Modesty, and to cherish me in my advanced years (I was born March 28, 1652) Methinks I could venture to lay my Weary head in her Lap, if it might be brought to pass upon Honest Conditions. You know your Sister's Age, and Disposition, and Circumstances, better than I doe. I should be glad of your Advice in my Fluctuations.[3]

Nothing arriving from this quarter, he set upon the Widow Ruggles at Brookline, one who had figured in his speculations three years before. She expressed her "inability to be Servicable," however, and when Sewall pressed his case, finally said she would entertain him only if he would "solicit her no more; or to that effect."[4]

This was in the summer. The following January (1721/22) he made an "Epistolary Visit" to Widow Gibbs at Newton, asking her at once if she would marry him. Receiving what seemed a favorable reply, he arranged for a coach and set out. On his first visit he gave compliments ("told her . . . she writ incomparably well") and gifts ("a Quire of Paper to write upon . . . a good Leather Inkhorn, a stick of Sealing Wax . . . 200. Wafers in a little Box," shillings to the servants, cakes to the children). On the second visit—

Spake of the proposals I had intimated per Mr. H. Gibbs; for her Sons to be bound to save me harmless as to her Administration; and to pay me 100. provided their Mother died before me: I to pay her 50. per annum during her Life, if I left her a Widow. She said 'twas hard, she knew not how to have her children bound to pay that Sum; she might dye in a little time. Mr. [John] Cotton [her son-in-law, minister at New-

* That is, in his second childhood.

ton], whom she call'd, spake to the same purpose. . . .
I said I was peremptory as to the idemnifying Bond;
Offer'd to take up with that alone, and allow her 40.
per annum. . . . She said she would consider of it: I
said, I would also Consider. Afterward she excus'd her
speaking to me. I suppose she meant the word Hard.
Carried her a pound of Glaz'd Almonds, and a Duz.
Meers Cakes; Two bottles of Canary. . . . Had a very
good Legg of Pork, and a Turkey for Dinner. Mrs.
Gibbs help'd me on with my Coat at Coming away;
and stood in the Front door till the Coach mov'd, then
I pull'd off my Hat, and she Curtesied. I had moved to
be published next Thorsday; to carry in our names to
Col. Checkley [town clerk of Boston].

Publication of the banns was delayed a week while the
parties dickered over terms of the settlement. Agreement was
finally reached (her children to be responsible for the Widow
Gibbs' former debts, she to receive forty pounds a year in the
event of Sewall's death), and on March 1 "S.S. and M.G.
were Out-published" (that is, the necessary fourteen days had
expired), and on March 29, 1722, they were married by
Sewall's son-in-law, the Rev. William Cooper.

Sewall was happy in this third wife, finding her "a great
Blessing," especially in caring for his daughter Hannah,
"whoes Legg she dress'd once a day at least; To do which
required a great deal of diligence, Skill, and Courage."[5]

Making an End

When his daughter Hannah's painful, calamity-ridden life
came to an end in the summer of 1724, the next patient was
Sewall himself, who began now to find his "locomotive faculty
. . . very much enfeebled." He who had so rarely known in-
firmity was now burdened with "disorders of [the] Back . . .
weak Hands, and . . . feeble Knees." He had lost "many . . .
Organs of Music . . . Fore-Teeth, both upper and nether," a
fact which, he felt, "does . . . give me warning that I must

shortly resign my Head: the Lord help me to do it cheerfully."[1]

One by one, over the protests of colleagues and friends, he
resigned his offices, quickened in his resolve by an "Extraordinary Sickness of Flux and Vomiting the night after the
27. July [1728]." In one capacity or another he had spent
half a century in the public life of Massachusetts. Now, he
said, "it is high time for me to be favoured with some Leisure,
that I may prepare for the entertainments of another World."
During the next year (1729) he felt himself "mouldering down
apace" and in December took to his bed.

As the end drew near, his son Joseph stood watchfully by
to record its approach—

Dec 26. My father seems to grow weaker. At different
times He repeated to me the Creed and the Lord's
prayr. Mention'd that text, If any man Sin, we have an
advocate with the Father. When ask'd what wee should
Pray for—Answer, to this Effect, that he might follow
the Captain of his Salvation. In general, he speaks but
little.

Dec. 29. I read to him 11 John 23-27 &c. My Father
took notice and spake of what was read—that we were
beholden to Martha. Spake of the brazen Serpent—of
looking to Jesus—He the only remedy.

Jan 1. I was call'd up about 4 cl. (or something before)
found my Father dying. He seem'd to enjoy the use
of his reason, I pray'd with him, then Mr. Cooper.
C[ousin] Chauncy came in and Pray'd. My Honoured
and dear Father Expir'd about 35 minutes after 5 A.M.
Near the time in which 29 years agoe, He was so
affected upon the Beginning of the Century, when he
made those Verses to usher in the New Year, Once
more our God vouchsafe to shine.[2]

On January 7, "a fair cold Day," Sewall was "honourably
Inter'd" in the tomb to which he had accompanied so many
in life. Next day at South Church, Mr. Prince took the text

for his Thursday lecture from the seventh chapter of first Samuel, verses fifteen through seventeen: "And Samuel judged Israel all the Days of his Life; And he went from Year to Year in Circuit to Bethel and Gilgal and Mispeh, and judged Israel in all those Places: And his Return was to Ramah, for there was his House, and there He judged Israel, and there He built an Altar to the LORD."[3]

Notes

Bibliographical Note

Sources in a paragraph have generally been gathered into a single note. Since Sewall's diary and letter-book are chronological, references are mostly omitted when the date of a citation is apparent. These two chief sources of information are referred to simply as *Diary* and *Letter-Book*. Since notes have been kept to a practicable minimum, it may interest some readers to know that a more fully annotated form of the study is in the Michigan State University Library, East Lansing, Michigan. Full titles of works cited in the text or in the notes appear in the Bibliography with the customary facts of publication.

PREFACE
"The Prophecy of Samuel Sewall"

1. *Works*, I.
2. *History*, II, 99.
3. *A Sermon*, 35.
4. *An Address*, 5. The nineteenth century's one book on Sewall, Chamberlain's *Samuel Sewall and the World He Lived in* (Boston, 1897), despite its author's honest intent, is mostly genuflexion.

CHAPTER ONE: BACKGROUND AND EARLY YEARS

The Family Pattern

1. *Diary*, I, 484. The reference in Fuller (1811 edition), II, 404, is to a great flash flood of April 17, 1607, "in the Mayoralty of Henry Sewall."
2. Duff, *The Sewells* [sic] *in the New World*, 2-4; *Diary*, I, xi; Salisbury, *Family Memorials*, 154. The diary reference is to a letter dated September 21, 1720, which Sewall wrote to his eldest son, Sam junior, of Brookline. Of first importance in establishing family background, it is hereafter referred to as "Gen. Letter."
3. Salisbury, *Family Memorials*, 153-155.
4. Duff, *The Sewells*, 13.

5. Mather, *Magnalia,* I, 13; "Gen. Letter," xii.
6. Coffin, *History of Newbury,* 287.
7. *Records of the Governor and Company,* I, 149; Currier, *Ould Newbury,* 9.
8. *Records of the Governor and Company,* I, 163, 222, 233, 286.
9. Coffin, *History of Newbury,* 61.
10. Currier, *Ould Newbury,* 247.
11. "Gen. Letter," xii; Sewall, "Memoir," 239; Salisbury, *Family Memorials,* 257.
12. "Gen. Letter," xii; *Vital Records of Newbury,* I, 471; *Letter-Book,* I, 383.
13. "Gen. Letter," xii; Hutchinson, *History of the Colony of Massachusetts Bay,* Vol. I, app. 12. The evidence of Sewall's father being a minister is curious for several reasons. In the first place, we hear nothing about this occupation before he first left New England at the age of thirty-three, nor do we hear about it after he returned, in a country where ministers were in short supply. Also, nothing is said about formal training, and the Puritans were not given to a self-instructed clergy. Finally, strangest of all, his son makes no mention of the matter, when obviously it would have been of much importance to him.
14. Sewall, "Memoir," 239; *Letter-Book,* I, 294-295.
15. *Records of the Governor and Company,* Vol. IV, part 2, pp. 2, 41, 71, 274, 362, 448. The father's will is at the Essex County Courthouse, Salem, Mass., probate docket, file number 25077.
16. *Letter-Book,* I, 236; *Diary,* II, 15; Coffin, *History of Newbury,* 13.
17. *Diary,* II, 13, 14; *Letter-Book,* I, 265.
18. *Diary,* III, 365; Dunton, *Life and Errors,* 117; *Letter-Book,* I, 215.
19. *Diary,* I, xviii-xxi; *Letter-Book,* II, 181.

Newbury

1. "Gen. Letter," xiii.
2. Robinson and Dow, *Sailing Ships of New England,* I, 35; "Gen. Letter," xiii; *Diary,* III, 48, 222.
3. Coffin, *History of Newbury,* 15, 63-64; Currier, *Ould Newbury,* 16, 17.
4. Coffin, *History of Newbury,* 64-70; *Letter-Book,* II, 229-230.
5. Prince, *A Sermon,* 31.

Schoolboy

1. "Gen. Letter," xii; *Diary,* I, 344; Hoole, *New Discovery,* 20, 21-23, 33; Littlefield, *Early Schools,* 105, 121.

2. Hoole, *New Discovery*, 238-239.
3. *Ibid.*, 25-26, 240.
4. Littlefield, *Early Schools*, 241, 243, 245-246, 268, 273; *Diary*, II, 52; Hoole, *New Discovery*, 43; Murdock, "The Teaching of Latin and Greek," 28; *Letter-Book*, I, 238; Wendell, *Cotton Mather*, 35.
5. Coffin, *History of Newbury*, 398; Small, "The New England Grammar School," 518; Morison, *Harvard College*, I, 333-334; "Gen. Letter," xiii.
6. Mather, *Magnalia*, I, 480-487.
7. *Letter-Book*, II, 113; *Diary*, I, 41.
8. Locke, *Thoughts*, 225, 242, 264, 486; *Diary*, III, 163.
9. Mather, *Magnalia*, I, 480, 485, and II, 12; Morison, *Harvard College*, I, 81, 169, and II, 450.

CHAPTER TWO: HARVARD COLLEGE
AND INTELLECTUAL LIFE

Undergraduate Years

1. Johnson, *Wonder Working Providence*, 164; *Harvard College Records*, I, lxxiii, citing *New England's First Fruits* (1643), 12-13; Randolph, "Narrative" of 1676, in Hutchinson, *A Collection of Original Papers*, 501; Mass. Archives, LVIII, 32; Thomas, *History of Printing in America*, 84-85.
2. Mather, *Magnalia*, II, 13; Wertenbaker, *The Puritan Oligarchy*, 150; Morison, *Harvard College*, II, 391, 406-407; *Records of the Governor and Company*, V, 20.
3. *Diary*, I, 5-6; *Letter-Book*, I, 18.
4. Mather, *Magnalia*, II, 15.
5. *Ibid.*, I, 465, 468, 470; Boston *News-Letter*, January 8, 1730.
6. Morison, *Harvard College*, I, 81; Mather, *Magnalia*, I, 81, and II, 23-25; *Harvard College Records*, I, 37-38, 197-198.
7. Morison, *Harvard College*, I, 85, 189, 195; Neal, *History of New England*, I, 185; *Harvard College Records*, III, 332-333; Mather, *Magnalia*, I, 469.
8. Morison, *Harvard College*, I, 90-91; *Diary*, I, 3.
9. Morison, *Harvard College*, I, 94, 96, 109; Mather, *Magnalia*, I, 469, and II, 12.
10. *Diary*, I, 3, 4.
11. *Ibid.*, 4.
12. Morison, *Harvard College*, Vol. I, ch. 5, and pp. 144-145; *Harvard*

College Records, III, 333-334; Quincy, *History of Harvard*, I, 190-191.

13. Neal, *History*, I, 186; Mather, *Magnalia*, II, 25.

Master of Arts

1. *Harvard College Records*, I, 57, 227; *Diary*, I, 3; *Letter-Book*, II, 263; *Diary*, I, 2, 5-6, and III, 93.

2. Morison, *Harvard College*, I, 15, 19, 166; Mather, *Magnalia*, II, 12; *Diary*, I, 2.

3. *Harvard College Records*, I, 58, 223; Danckaerts, *Journal*, 266; Morison, *Harvard College*, I, 287-288, 296; Palfrey, *History of New England*, IV, 384, note 1; Potter and Bolton, *Librarians of Harvard College*, 3.

4. *Harvard College Records*, III, 335; Mather, *Magnalia*, II, 25; Morison, *Harvard College*, I, 148. In other words, the M.A. had no course requirements. The "staid three years" did not mean residence, except for a fellow of the college like Sewall, only "wait three years." The thesis requirement was perfunctory, and the "Synopsis, or Compendium" was little more than a useable outline and notes to provide freshmen with a "North-West Passage" to knowledge of the kind Puritans liked so well. (The phrase is Cotton Mather's. See Miller, *The New England Mind*, 102-103.) The "thrice problemed" refers to logical exposition of philosophical questions, and to "commonplace" was to deliver a brief sermon in Hall, the term being derived from the Puritan passion for organizing material under convenient headings or common places. Sewall, for instance, kept a commonplace book between 1677 and 1686 where he arranged excerpts from his reading under such heads as "De Infantibus," "De Oratione," "De Sabbato," "De Paulo Apostolo," "De Honore," "De Obedientia," "De Tempore," "De Resurrectione mortuorum," "De Conselatione," etc. (See Morison, *Harvard College*, I, 148-161, for discussion of the Master's requirements.)

5. *Diary*, I, 4; Sibley, *Biographical Sketches*, II, 345.

6. *Diary*, II, 190.

7. "Gen. Letter," xiii. Parrington, *The Colonial Mind*, 90, remarks of Sewall's marriage: "With excellent thrift he fixed his attentions upon the only child of a wealthy merchant, the richest heiress in the colony; no penniless 'waiting woman' for Samuel Sewall, such as had contented the unworldly Thomas Hooker. He understood how desirable it is to put money in one's purse; so he made a shrewd alliance." This is critical deduction with a vengeance, in

line with Parrington's treatment of Sewall as a kindly, small-minded representative of the school of rise and thrive.

Studies Sacred and Profane

1. Mather, *Magnalia*, II, 13; Neal, *History of New England*, I, 186.
2. Miller, *New England Mind*, 200.
3. Evans, "Literary References in New England Diaries, 1700-1730," unpublished thesis at Harvard; Wright, *Literary Culture in Early New England*, 148-150, 194; *Letter-Book*, I, 248, 261, 327-328, and II, 10-11, 53, 58, 253-254, 271; *Diary*, I, 284.
4. *Diary*, II, 1, 223, and III, 7, 289, 391; *Letter-Book*, I, 25, 38, 76, 204, 258, 324, 351, 396, and II, 3-4, 30, 31, 127.
5. Dykema, "Samuel Sewall Reads John Dryden"; *Diary*, I, 34, and II, 53; *Letter-Book*, I, 123, 199, 246, 297.
6. *Diary*, II, 167-168; *Letter-Book*, II, letter dated January 15, 1721/2.
7. Memorandum Book, part 2, pp. 1, 2, 14-15.

Alumnus

1. *Letter-Book*, I, 18, 20; *Diary*, III, 388-389.
2. *Letter-Book*, II, 105, 241, 270, 274.
3. Mather, *Ichabod*, 45-46; Wertenbaker, *Puritan Oligarchy*, 156.
4. *Letter-Book*, I, 260, 263-264; Quincy, *History of Harvard*, I, 198. In 1698 the Brattle Street Church separated from the principles of the Cambridge Platform, and the religious qualification for Harvard was negatived by Governor Bellomont the following year. The result was a general feeling that apostasy was abroad in the land. Brattle opposed public statement of religious experience as a requirement for church membership, preached at his own ordination, wouldn't allow an elder to lay a hand on his head during the ceremony, etc. Both Brattle and Leverett were outspoken critics of the witchcraft episode.

   Inasmuch as Sewall's and Addington's suggestions were incorporated into Yale's charter, it is odd that writers on the subject should differ as they do. Palfrey, *History of New England*, IV, 372, says: "Whether it was that arrangements had been already matured, or that a different judgment pervailed, their proposals do not appear to have influenced the projectors." But he cites Quincy, *loc. cit.*, whose conclusion is that "the founders of the College in Connecticut adopted, without any material alterations, the draft made by Sewall and Addington." Kingsley, *Yale College*, I, 22, says that though the suggestions arrived in time to be considered, "it appears that only the form and to some extent the phraseology was employed."

5. Winsor, *Memorial History of Boston,* II, 202; *Letter-Book,* I, 264; *Diary,* II, 43.

6. *Diary,* III, 298-299, 300, 311.

7. *Letter-Book,* I, 241-242, 354; *Harvard College Records,* I, 272.

CHAPTER THREE: MERCHANT AND MAN OF PROPERTY

Father Hull

1. Dow, *Every Day Life in the Massachusetts Bay Colony,* 150; Hutchinson, *Papers,* 485; Josselyn, *An Account,* 331. Among loose pages at the front of "Samuel Sewall His Ledger" is one headed: "An inventory of the Estate of [John] . . . Hull." The word "John" is torn away, but the contents clearly indicate the owner.

2. Mather, *Magnalia,* I, 314; Danforth, "Greatness & Goodness Elegized."

3. *Records of the Governor and Company,* II, 98, 260, and IV, part 2, pp. 363, 484, 507, 553, and V, 78, 131, 184, 210, 265, 308, 350, 407, 427-428, 434; Douglas, *Financial History,* 40-41; Hull, *Diary,* 122.

4. Dow, *Every Day Life,* 169; *Records of the Governor and Company,* Vol. IV, part 1, p. 84, and V, 43-44; Morison, *Builders of the Bay,* 153; Douglas, *Financial History,* 43-44; Hawthorne, *Works,* V, 45. The figure of thirty thousand pounds for the daughter's dowry is first given by Hutchinson, *History,* I, 178, who prefaces the statement with "as commonly reported."

The Meaning of Prosperity

1. Dow, *Every Day Life,* 149.

2. Johnson, *Wonder-Working Providence,* 43.

3. Hutchinson, *History,* I, 190.

4. Josselyn, *An Account,* 319-320; Greene and Harrington, *American Population,* 14; Maverick, *A Briefe Description,* 257-258; Winship, "Samuel Sewall and the New England Company," 65.

5. Miller, *New England Mind,* 42; Bebb, *Nonconformity,* 94; Parkes, "New England in the Seventeen Thirties."

6. Norton, *The Heart of New England Rent,* 79; Mather, *Ichabod,* 69, 71, 85; Ward, *A Trip to New England,* 5.

7. Mather, *A Serious Exhortation,* 9; Oakes, *New England Pleaded With,* 24, 30, 33; Mather, *A Discourse,* 55-56.

8. *Necessity of Reformation,* 2, 4, 5, 6, 7, 8.

9. *Records of the Governor and Company,* I, 136-139.

10. *Letter-Book,* I, 24; *Diary,* I, 123, 138-139.
11. Lodge, *Studies in History,* 30; *Diary,* I, 229-230.

The Marriage of Wealth

1. *Diary,* I, 5-12; Prince, *A Sermon,* 32.
2. "Diary and Commonplace Book, 1675—," foll. 13-14, 16-17.
3. Danckaerts, *Journal,* 274-275.
4. *Diary,* I, 5; "Gen. Letter," xiv.
5. Clarke, *John Hull,* 162-163; Dow, *Every Day Life,* 169; "Diary and Commonplace Book, 1675—," fol. 15.

Apprentice Years

1. Weeden, *Economic and Social History,* I, 249; Hull, *Diary,* 124.
2. "Diary and Commonplace Book, 1675—," foll. 10, 11; *Diary,* I, 35, 50; Hull, *Diary,* 253, note.
3. Littlefield, *Early Massachusetts Press,* II, 12-19; *Records of the Governor and Company,* V, 323-324; Winsor, *Memorial History,* I, 455-457; Thomas, *History of Printing in America,* I, 84-86; Evans, *American Bibliography,* I, 53-59. Sewall's letter to Nathaniel Dummer is printed in the *New England Hist. and Gen. Reg.,* IX, 287-288.
4. *Records of the Governor and Company,* V, 452.

The World of Business

1. *Diary,* I, 251; Suffolk Court Files, number 2190.
2. Record Commissioners of the City of Boston, *Reports,* I, 91-133; *Letter-Book,* II, 90; Ledger, foll. 25, 32, 39, 46, 54, 91, 99, 117, 126, 138, 145, 153, 157, 163, 168, 179. No attempt has been made to arrive at the meaning of figures given. They are a representative sample from entries covering several decades. Because of the frequent vagueness of property designations it would be extremely difficult to make even a rough estimate of Sewall's income in any one year or even at any one period. In his later years there was inflation, so that income from the Cotton Hill house, for example, went from ten pounds annually to forty. Even if a figure were arrived at for, say, 1685, there is no way of translating such a figure into meaningful terms. While it is true that the real value of money was, generally speaking, many times what it is today, it is also true that a man like Sewall was rich in terms of what he could afford of New England products and comparatively poor in terms of what he could afford of products from abroad.
3. Ledger, fol. 58.

4. Miller, *New England Mind,* 44; Knappen, *Tudor Puritanism,* 389, 397.

5. Weeden, "The Early African Slave Trade in New England," 16; *Letter-Book,* I, 64, 114, 133; Bill of Lading Book, *passim.*

6. *Letter-Book,* I, 33, 34, 44, 46, 67, 75, 96, 116, 118, 134, 154, 169, and *passim.*

7. "Diary and Commonplace Book, 1675—," fol. 26; Account Book entries for April 7, 1690, January 12, 1690/1, October 23, 1691, and November 30, 1691.

8. *Diary,* I, 312. Sewall's Bill of Lading Book shows that his work as an exporter lasted only about a decade and that much of this time he was not very active. This is also shown by the *Letter-Book,* I, 2-4, 84, 89, 90, 112, 114, 133, 141-142. The diary is almost silent on the subject. The best record of his importing is the *Letter-Book,* which shows that it virtually ceased around 1690.

9. *Diary,* II, 92, 93, 122, 218-219; Winship, "Samuel Sewall and the New England Company."

10. *Letter-Book,* I, 251-252, 274, 332, 341; Ledger, foll. 99, 159, 160, 183.

11. Pages 89-97, *passim.*

12. Ward, *A Trip to New England,* 45; *Diary,* II, 125-126.

13. *Letter-Book,* I, 26 (editors' note), 133, and II, 33, 134-135; *Harvard College Records,* I, 272; Hazard, *Judge Sewall's Gifts in the Narragansett Country,* 12-14, 17; Ledger, foll. 36, 135, 167, 174; *Diary,* II, 76 (editors' note), 165.

14. Fol. 171.

15. *Diary,* I, 69, 155, 173, 208, 210, 212, 367, 376, 389, 401, 478, 506, and II, 343, and III, 217, 225, 258.

16. "Diary and Commonplace Book, 1675—," foll. 1, 6; Ledger, fol. 35; *Diary,* I, 67, and II, 16.

CHAPTER FOUR: SERVANT OF COLONY AND PROVINCE

The Biblical Authority

1. Eliot, *Christian Commonwealth,* 143; Cotton, "Moses his Judicials," 29; Winthrop, *History,* I, 352, 388; *Records of the Governor and Company,* I, 174; Gray, "Remarks on Early Laws of Massachusetts Bay . . . ," 199; Lechford, *Plaine Dealing,* 86.

2. Morris, *Studies,* 26; Mather, *Magnalia,* II, 201-202; *Letter-Book,* II, 86-87. The last chapter of Calvin's *Institutes,* "On Civil Government," is a primer of Puritan political theory. "Magistracy," says Calvin, "is a calling not only holy and legitimate, but far the most sacred and honourable in human life." Again: "It is impossible to

resist the magistrate without, at the same time, resisting God himself." Under the laws of Massachusetts, anyone who "willingly
defame[d]" a magistrate for "Sentences and Proceedings" in the
line of duty was whipped, fined, imprisoned, disfranchised, or
banished, according to the offense.

3. Hilkey, *Legal Development in Colonial Massachusetts*, 62-63;
Records of the Governor and Company, II, 212; Mathews, "The
Results of the Prejudice Against Lawyers," 77; Grinnell, "The
Bench and Bar in Colony and Province," 171; Reinsch, "English
Common Law in the Early American Colonies," 385.

4. Knight, *Journal*, 51; *Diary*, I, 314, 410; Ledger, fol. 113. Sewall's
complaint that "persons often come upon me unawares" was addressed to Joseph Webb, "Clark of the Writts." He asked Webb
"to grant no Attachment for the Trial of any cause before me
except on the first Monday of the Moneth" and not to send any
"whoes Book-Debts are old enough to be senior Sophisters, being
of more than three years standing." Washburn, *Sketches*, 259-260,
treats these requests with great seriousness, taking them as an indication that Sewall had "a natural taste for legal science. . . . He
saw how chaotic was the system of legal practice at the bar, and
endeavored to introduce a corrective. . . . It shows a disposition
on the part of Mr. Sewall to introduce something like order into
the practice of the law." He may be right, but the evidence suggests otherwise.

5. *Records of the Governor and Company*, V, 453.

6. Dow, *Every Day Life*, 201; Lechford, *Plaine Dealing*, 86.

7. *Diary*, I, 140. Mathews, "The Results of the Prejudice Against
Lawyers," gives convincing demonstration of the charter's being
lost by default, there being no one qualified to challenge the
legality of steps taken by the crown. Every claim against land
titles, says Mathews, "could have been met by citing acts of the
Privy Council or the Crown . . . between 1660 and 1680."

Magistrate

1. *Letter-Book*, I, 357, and II, 173.

2. *Diary*, I, 39, 46.

3. Woodward, *The Way Our People Lived*, 24; *Col. Laws*, 163-164;
Records of the Governor and Company, II, 208.

4. *Diary*, I, 37, 125; *Col. Laws*, 154. The watch was patterned after
that in London. In the next century the town had five wards with
a watch house in each. The hours in summer were from ten in
the evening to daylight, in winter from nine in the evening to

eight in the morning. (See Cook, "Boston: the Eighteenth Century Town," 245.)

5. *Diary*, I, 57 (editors' note), 386; *Records of the Governor and Company*, V, 437. The number of assistants varied in number from fourteen to twenty, but in 1680 it was put at eighteen and remained there for the rest of the colonial period (*Records of the Governor and Company*, V, 437; Hilkey, *Legal Development*, 44). It has not seemed necessary to describe the colony's legislative and judicial setup. The charter statement was simple and explicit:

> Governor, Deputie Governor, and Assistants . . . shall . . . once every moneth, or oftener at their pleasures . . . [meet] for the better ordering and directing of their affaires. . . . Any seaven or more . . . of the Assistants, togither with the Governor or Deputie Governor . . . shalbe . . . a . . . sufficient Courte . . . for . . . all businesses, and . . . there shall or maie be held [on specified Wednesdays in each quarter] . . . one great . . . Generall Court . . . which shall have full power . . . to choose such . . . others as they shall think fit . . . to be free of the said Company . . . and to elect . . . such officers as they shall thinke fitt . . . and to make lawes and ordinances for the good . . . of the . . . Company . . . and the people inhabiting the same. . . . So . . . such lawes . . . be not contrarie or repugnant to the lawes and statutes of . . . England. [*Records of the Governor and Company*, I, 11-12.]

The key body was not the General Court, despite its being named "the chief Civil Power of this Commonwealth" (*Col. Laws*, 34), but the Court of Assistants. General Courts, except for the prescribed annual meeting, were held only "when the importancy of the business doth require it." Otherwise, business was "Ordered and dispatched by the Major part of the Council" (*ibid.*, 333)— that is, the Council of Magistrates, the records of which are lost. Dickinson, "The Massachusetts Charter and the Bay Colony," 115-116, says of this group:

> It is hardly too much to say that the entire administrative as well as the judicial machinery of the colony was gathered by the Assistants into their own hands. In a judicial capacity, they sat as judges in every one of the courts of the colony. Sitting as a body with the Governor and deputies they constituted the General Court. Sitting in a body they constituted the Quarter Courts. Sitting in small groups, or individually in company with commissioners, they constituted the county courts. Individually they had jurisdiction over small causes.

The best description of the colony's courts is in Washburn,

Sketches, ch. 2. Palfrey, *History,* Vol. II, ch. 2, has a useful summary, as does Hutchinson, *History,* Vol. I, ch. 5.

6. *Records of the Governor and Company,* VI, 421, 439-441, 450-451, 510, 516.

7. *Diary,* I, 77, 132; *Records of the Governor and Company,* V, 449, 465, 472, 494, 500, 506; *Col. Laws,* 36; *Records of the Court of Assistants,* I, 283-284, 294, 295.

8. Ward, *A Trip to New England,* 11.

9. *Diary,* I, 308, and II, 9*-10*; *Records of the Court of Assistants,* I, 302.

"Dolefull Witchcraft"

1. "Letters of Governor Phips," 196.

2. Hutchinson, *History,* I, 150-151, 187-188, and II, 12-15; Mather, *Memorable Providences,* 96; Drake, *Annals,* 187 ff.; *Diary,* I, 358; Council Records, II, 176; Nevins, *Witchcraft in Salem Village,* 71; *Acts and Resolves,* I, 10.

3. Calef, *More Wonders,* 373, 384; Upham, *Lectures,* 82-83.

4. *Salem Papers,* I, n.p.

5. *Ibid.,* and see the summary account in Drake, *Annals,* 187-208.

6. Drake, *loc. cit.;* Calef, *More Wonders,* 369.

7. *Salem Papers,* I, n.p. Nor does Sewall emerge from the general body of the witchcraft records, where all we learn is that he was present at some of the proceedings. His name is not even mentioned in Drake's comprehensive *Annals.*

8. Mather, *Magnalia,* II, 31; Nevins, *Witchcraft in Salem Village,* 131-134; *Diary,* I, 106, 340; Account Book, entry for March 14, 1692; *Salem Papers,* I, n.p.

9. Details of the examination are from volume one of *Salem Papers,* entry for May 9, 1692.

10. Mather, *Wonders,* 219.

11. *Ibid.,* 215.

12. Calef, *More Wonders,* 360.

13. *Ibid.,* 360-361.

14. Mather, *Magnalia,* I, 212; *Diary,* I, 367; Calef, *More Wonders,* 382.

15. Whittier, "The Prophecy of Samuel Sewall," *Works,* I, 210-211; *Diary,* I, 431, 433.

16. Mather, *Memorable Providences,* 95, and *Magnalia,* I, 207.

17. Drake, *Annals,* 207-208.

Provincial Councillor and Judge

1. *Acts and Resolves,* I, 10-12; *Diary,* III, 183, 357; *Letter-Book,* II, 247. Twenty-eight seems a large number of councillors, but the

Governor and seven constituted a quorum, and the Council Records, II-VIII (1692-1727), show about half the full number generally in attendance. The charter named the original members, but later election and re-election lay with the General Court, which is to say the Governor, Council, and Deputies. The tradition of continuity in office kept the same men serving year after year. Executive and judicial branches were now separate, but only in theory, for council members often served as judges.

2. Washburn, *Sketches,* 60; *Diary,* I, 419.

3. *Letter-Book,* II, 90.

4. *Ibid.,* 101; *Diary,* II, 143-149, and III, 65.

5. Prince, *A Sermon,* 34; Journal of Journey to Martha's Vineyard and Circuit Court Journal, entry for March 29, 1716; *Diary,* II, 39.

6. *Letter-Book,* II, 3; *Diary,* I, 126, 396, 486, and II, 340; Mather, *Magnalia,* II, 420-422.

7. Wertenbaker, *Puritan Oligarchy,* 170; Ward, *A Trip to New England,* 3. Morgan, "The Puritans and Sex," 595-596, says that fornication and adultery are "by far the most numerous class of criminal cases in the record," and concludes that the Puritans "became inured to sexual offenses, because there were so many. The impression one gets from reading the records of seventeenth century New England courts is that illicit sexual intercourse was fairly common."

8. There are at least ninety-five such entries, appearing in the Ledger, foll. 48, 86, 113, 146.

9. *Diary,* III, 81-83.

10. *Ibid.,* II, 291-293.

11. Council Records, V, 396; *Letter-Book,* II, 88-89; *Diary,* III, 183.

12. *Diary,* I, 405, 453, 482-483, and II, 75, and III, 102, 192, 261, 264, 348.

13. *Ibid.,* 56, 57, 76, 181. The passage quoted is from one of the small journals Sewall carried with him on circuit. Partly reprinted in the *Diary,* II, 425-440. The entry cited is for April 2, 1714.

14. One reason so many cases were trivial was that appeal was very freely used. The number of cases was enormous. Between April 1724 and February 1725, for example, the court sat about forty days and heard over three hundred (Superior Court Records, V, 170-252). Laws and penalties in early years of the Province remained about what they had been in the Colony.

15. *Letter-Book,* I, 364.

16. *Diary,* I, 396, 495, 496, and II, 254-255, 372, and III, 67, 110, 186, 287, 357; *Letter-Book,* I, 378. Sewall's faithful attendance appears

in the Council Records, II-VIII. He was, as he says, "the most constant attender." Over a period of thirty-three years (1692-1725) he attended around twenty-five hundred meetings.

17. *Diary,* I, 369, and II, 57-58, and III, 66, 84; *Letter-Book,* I, 212.
18. *Diary,* III, 85; *Letter-Book,* II, 55, 244-245.
19. *Diary,* II, 203-204. Pamphlets resulting from this and other charges against the Dudley administration are reprinted in the *Diary,* II, *31-*131.
20. *Diary,* I, 386, and II, 131, 143, and III, 87, 276-277.
21. Parrington, *Colonial Mind,* 92; *Diary,* II, 366, and III, 23-24, 35.
22. *Diary,* II, 365-366, and III, 87-88, 345. Parrington, *loc. cit.,* says that he even went "so far as to prefer barter to bills." It would be more accurate to say that he preferred barter to confiscatory inflation.

Militia Captain

1. Mather, *Memorable Providences,* 99; *Diary,* II, 143; Johnson, *Wonder Working Providence,* 10, 11.
2. Maverick, *A Briefe Description,* 237-238.
3. Roberts, *History of the Military Company,* I, 2; Whitman, *Historical Sketch,* 1. At first the company trained on the first Monday of each month. Later the number of training days was reduced to around half that number. The big training day was the first Monday in May, election day. The sermons given on this day (the so-called Artillery Sermons) and the "feasts" of the officers were in the English tradition. In dress as in method of selecting officers the military companies long remained very democratic. Up until the Revolution different colored ribbons were the only marks of office. (See Roberts, *op. cit.,* 3, and Whitman, *op. cit.,* 24, 38, 48.)
4. Whitman, *Historical Sketch,* 23. In early years the train bands had been called out as often as once a week. This was reduced to once a month, and the eight times a year here referred to later became four. Training in July and August was generally avoided for the "furtherance of husbandry." (See Hutchinson, *History,* I, 448, and Mook, "Training Day in New England," 680.) The military organization for the Colony may be seen in *Colonial Laws,* 108; that for the Province in *Acts and Resolves,* I, 128-133. They were about the same.
5. Randolph, "Narrative" of 1676, 485. See the discussion by Peterson, "The Military Equipment of the Plymouth and Bay Colonies."
6. *Diary,* I, 25, 310, and III, 157; *Letter-Book,* I, 113-114.
7. Knight, *Journal,* 52-55. See Mook, "Training Day in New England," for a description of the institution through its colorful

heyday and then its decline in the first half of the nineteenth century. By about 1820 it had become little more than a holiday and was abolished a few years before the Civil War.

8. *Records of the Governor and Company*, V, 426; Mass. Archives, LXX, 105-106.

9. *Diary*, I, 316, 335, 384; *Letter-Book*, I, 123. Roberts, *History of the Military Company*, I, 258, says Sewall was Major of the regiment in 1695-96, but I find no proof of this. Sibley, *Biographical Sketches*, II, 347, makes him Major of the regiment in 1675-76. I find no proof of this either, and the date makes it implausible.

10. *Diary*, I, 360, and II, 35-36, 54-55; *Acts and Resolves*, I, 129.

11. *Diary*, I, 369.

12. For this entire episode, see the *Diary*, II, 103-111.

13. *Letter-Book*, I, 5-8, 38, 45, 49, 77, 156, 177, 182, 191, 200; Mass. Archives, XXXVI, 8, 9; *Diary*, I, 317-319.

CHAPTER FIVE: WRITER

Humanitarian

1. Whittier, *Works*, I, 211-212; Locke, *Anti-Slavery in America*, 9-17; Moore, *Notes*, 109-110.

2. Weeden, "Early African Slave Trade," 106, 122; Adams, *Provincial Society*, 9, 164; Wertenbaker, *Puritan Oligarchy*, 198.

3. *Letter-Book*, I, 326, and II, 39. For a description of the Saffin case, see Goodell, "John Saffin and his Slave Adam."

4. *Letter-Book*, I, 326, and II, 182; *Diary*, II, 143; Johnson, *American Economic Thought*, 20-21, 109; Moore, *Notes*, 106. Greene, *The Negro in Colonial New England*, 41, makes the mistaken assertion that Sewall hypocritically engaged in the slave trade, citing the following advertisement in the Boston *News-Letter* for September 13, 1714: "To be disposed by Mr. Samuel Sewall Merchant, at his warehouse near the Swing Bridge in Merchants Row Boston, several Irish Maid Servants time, most of them for five years, one Irish Man Servants time, who is a good Barber and Wiggmaker, Also Four or Five likely Negro Boys." This was not the judge but "Samuel Sewall, *de Stephano*," as his uncle called him. In a letter to Samuel Storke dated October 29, 1717, Sewall says: "I suppose you are not unacquainted with Mr. Samuel Sewall Son of Major Sewall of Salem. He is an accomplish'd Merchant and dwells in Town."

5. *Col. Laws*, 164; J. Eliot, *The Day-Breaking*, 3 ff.; S. Eliot, "Early Relations with the Indians," 316-317.

6. Neal, *History*, I, 232-233, 257.
7. See the chapter on Eliot in Morison, *Builders of the Bay Colony*, for an agreeable sketch of early work among the Indians. Also: Barry, *History*, Vol. I, ch. 13; Love, *Samson Occam*, ch. 1; Hutchinson, *History*, I, 160-169.
8. Gottfried, "The First Depression in Massachusetts"; Winship, "Samuel Sewall and the New England Company," 56; Morison, *Builders of the Bay*, 298-300; Trumbull, "The Origin of Indian Missions," 27.
9. *Diary*, I, 502, and II, 29, 362-363, and III, 12, 115, 127, 188, 192, 216, 278, 281; *Letter-Book*, I, 231, 239, 250, 311, 338, and II, 162, 166, 177, 255, and III, 334, 395. The whole subject is thoroughly treated by Winship, "Samuel Sewall and the New England Company."
10. *Letter-Book*, I, 250; Morison, *Builders of the Bay*, 299; Palfrey, *History*, III, 501; Winship, "Samuel Sewall and the New England Company," 56-57.
11. Mather, *Magnalia*, bk. VI, ch. 6; *Letter-Book*, I, 22; Ford, *Some Correspondence*, 83-85.
12. *Phaenomena*, Dedication to Ashhurst, and pp. 55, 58.
13. *Ibid.*, the dedication and p. 53; *Letter-Book*, I, 22.
14. See the discussion of "gratuities" in "The World of Business," Chapter III.
15. *Memorial to the Kennebeck Indians*, 1-2, 4.

Poet

1. Morison, *Harvard College*, I, 132; Jantz, "The First Century of New England Verse," 395-408.
2. Matthiessen, "Michael Wigglesworth," 492.
3. *Diary*, III, 279.
4. Jantz, "The First Century of New England Verse," 312; *Diary*, II, 170; *Letter-Book*, II, 14; Journal of Journey to Martha's Vineyard and Circuit Court Journal, entry for March 31, 1715. See Murdock's *Handkerchiefs from Paul* for selections by some of the poets named.

Diarist

1. *Diary*, I, 42, 462, and III, 98.
2. *Ibid.*, I, 454, 458, and II, 219, and III, 280.
3. *Ibid.*, I, 417, and II, 170, 172, 193, 230, and III, 324-326.
4. *Ibid.*, I, 119-120, 476, and II, 46-47, 291, and III, 32.
5. *Nation*, XXX (February 26, 1880), 157-158.

Notes

CHAPTER SIX: PRIVATE LIFE AND LAST YEARS

The High Street House

1. Morison, *Builders of the Bay*, 137; Seybolt, "The Private Schools of Seventeenth Century Boston," 419; Dow, *Every Day Life*, 169; Howe, "The Abode of John Hull," 312-326; *Letter-Book*, I, 159-160, editors' note; Clarke, *John Hull*, 21-22; Winsor, *Memorial History*, II, xxv, no. 84 on the plan.
2. "Gen. Letter," xiv; Ward, *A Trip to New England*, 5.
3. *Letter-Book*, I, 137-138; *Diary*, I, 356, 376, 377.
4. *Diary*, I, 402, 412, 413, and II, 129, and III, 347, 348; Ledger, fol. 59.

The Marriage Relation

1. *Diary*, I, 418, and II, 50.
2. *Ibid.*, I, 67, 83, 84, 180, 187, 190-191, 454; *Letter-Book*, I, 35-36.
3. *Proposals*, 1. See George E. Ellis's digest of Sewall's *Talitha Cumi* in Mass. Hist. Soc., *Proc.*, XII (February, 1873), 380-384.
4. *Diary*, I, 237, 240, 259, 295, 269-270, and II, 403, and III, 113-114.
5. *Ibid.*, I, 295.
6. This poem, titled "Greatness & Goodness Elegized," is among the broadsides at the Boston Public Library.

Puritan Father

1. Commonplace Book, entry for May 21, 1680; *Diary*, II, 13*. For Hannah's calamity-ridden life see the *Diary*, I, 153, 166, 231, 320, 488, and III, 13, 48, 79, 209, 210, 339-342.
2. For the short and harrowing life of Hull Sewall see the *Diary*, I, 50, 68, 76, 78, 85, 101, 106, 110, 112, 114, 118, 122, 125, 127, 131, 135, 143. For Henry, *Diary*, I, 110, 113, 114, and *Letter-Book*, I, 22. For Stephen, *Diary*, I, 166, 181, 184.
3. For the birth of Joseph, see the *Diary*, I, 223. For Judith's short life, *Diary*, I, 328, 331, 332. For Mary's convulsions, *Diary*, II, 83. For the stillborn Jane, *Diary*, I, 381, 383. For Sarah, *Diary*, I, 394, 395, 410, 442. For the stillborn son, *Diary*, I, 426. For the birth of the second Judith, *Diary*, II, 50.
4. *Letter-Book*, I, 267-268, and II, 42, 94; *Diary*, I, 444-445.
5. *Ibid.*, 225, 369.
6. *Ibid.*, 344; *Letter-Book*, I, 44.
7. *Diary*, I, 308, 423; *Letter-Book*, I, 44.
8. Mather, *Magnalia*, II, appendix to ch. 7, bk. 6; *Diary*, I, 309, 328.
9. *Ibid.*, 492, 502; *Letter-Book*, I, 213.

10. *Diary,* I, 503, and II, 24, and III, 89-91.
11. *Ibid.,* II, 249; *Letter-Book,* I, 379.
12. *Diary,* III, 235-238, 243-244, 253.
13. *Letter-Book,* II, 105-107.
14. *Ibid.,* 261.
15. Joseph Sewall, "The Sins and Mercies of a Harvard Student"; Roberts, *History of the Military Company,* I, 259; *Diary,* III, 340-341; *Letter-Book,* II, 305.
16. *Diary,* I, 348, and II, 287.
17. *Diary,* I, 329, 400, and II, 348, 349, 360, 361, 388, and III, 17; *Letter-Book,* I, 255; Ledger, foll. 109, 197.
18. *Diary,* I, 420, and II, 371-372, and III, 78.
19. *Ibid.,* I, 397.
20. *Ibid.,* 452.
21. *Ibid.,* II, 60, 61, 63, 65; *Letter-Book,* I, 276-281.
22. *Diary,* II, 175, 371.
23. Knappen, *Tudor Puritanism,* 455.

The Observance of Religion

1. Pearson, *Thomas Cartwright,* 99.
2. *Col. Laws,* 239; *Records of the Governor and Company,* V, 59.
3. *Diary,* III, 270.
4. *Ibid.,* II, 171, 231, and III, 54.
5. *Ibid.,* II, 36-37.
6. *Ibid.,* 48-49.
7. Fowler, *Local Law,* 27; *Records of the Governor and Company,* II, 212, and V, 476.
8. *Diary,* I, 201, 178, 428, and II, 232; *Letter-Book,* I, 370-371.
9. *Diary,* I, 150-151, 152, 167, 173, 196.
10. *Letter-Book,* II, 29-30; *Diary,* III, 111, 158, 193.
11. *Ibid.,* 291-293, 294; *Letter-Book,* II, 182.
12. Knight, *Journal,* 52.
13. *Diary,* I, 143.
14. *Ibid.,* 84.
15. Danckaerts, *Journal,* 261; *Diary,* III, 140.
16. Entry for March 27, 1706. These lines were omitted from the published *Diary* as "unsuitable for publication," but since the editors explain the omission as involving "a mortifying accident which befel him in the night," the reader's fancy is bound at least to equal the amusing fact.
17. *Letter-Book,* II, 248, 257; *Diary,* I, 165, and II, 189, 314, 318, 319, 352-353, and II, 14, 50, 386.

18. *Letter-Book,* I, 52, and II, 78; *Diary,* I, 52, 127-128, 486, and III, 120, 215.
19. Tyler, *History,* II, 77; Miller, *New England Mind,* 213-214; Winthrop, *History,* II, 330.
20. This time of stress may be traced in the *Diary,* I, 32-37, entries from January 10, 1676/7, to the end of the first manuscript volume, the last pages of which are somewhat confused. The process of becoming a church member has been variously described. An early statement is in Lechford, *Plaine Dealing,* 65-67, and see Ellis, *Puritan Age,* 207; Dexter, *Congregationalism,* 449-450; Wertenbaker, *Puritan Oligarchy,* 66-67.
21. *Diary,* I, 319-320, 351, and II, 74, 189.
22. Neal, *History,* II, 590.
23. *Diary,* I, 34, and III, 11-12; *Letter-Book,* I, 44, 136-137, 152-153, 191-192, 199, 274, 299, 311, 331, 384, and II, 36-37, 53.
24. *Ibid.,* I, 153.
25. Miller, *New England Mind,* 41; *Diary,* I, 373.
26. *Ibid.,* II, 298, 355, and III, 86-87.
27. *Ibid.,* II, 71.
28. *Ibid.,* I, 143, 337, and II, 11-12, 43, 67, 151, 157, 176 (editors' note), 183, 192, 193, 223, 231, 246, 257, 319, 347, and III, 57, 196, 323.
29. *Ibid.,* II, 403-404.
30. *Letter-Book,* I, 149; *Diary,* I, 248, 260, 272, 305, 506, and III, 131.
31. Fisher, *Notes on Music in Old Boston,* 17.
32. *Letter-Book,* I, 314-316 (editors' note); Wertenbaker, *Puritan Oligarchy,* 129; *Diary,* I, 351.
33. *Ibid.,* II, 151.
34. *Ibid.,* III, 285, 323.
35. Weeden, *Economic and Social History,* I, 295; *Diary,* I, 98, 240, 255, 264, 288, and III, 257; Palfrey, *History,* III, 46.

A Widower's Life

1. Morgan, "The Puritans and Sex," 592, citing Cotton's *A Meet Help* (Boston, 1699).
2. *Diary,* III, 262.
3. *Letter-Book,* II, 122-123, 133-134.
4. *Diary,* III, 174-175, 290, 291.
5. *Letter-Book,* II, 146, 160, 162, 180.

Making an End

1. *Letter-Book,* II, 105, 211, 262.

Notes

2. I quote from Hill, *History of the Old South Church*, I, 443, the manuscript of this diary having been destroyed by fire. See the comment in Sibley, *Biographical Sketches*, V, 390.
3. Hill, *loc. cit.*; Boston *News-Letter*, January 8, 1730; Prince, *A Sermon*.

Bibliography

I. Primary sources other than those by Sewall, which are given in part III. Here, as in Section II below, the list includes only works cited.

Acts and Resolves of the Province of Massachusetts Bay, ed. Ellis Ames and A. C. Goodell, Boston, 1869-1922, 21 vols. (Vol. I cited.)

Boston *News-Letter* for January 8, 1730, No. 158. (Sewall obituary.)

Brattle, Thomas, Letter of October 8, 1692, in George L. Burr, ed., *Narratives of the Witchcraft Cases, 1648-1706*, Original Narratives Series, New York, 1914.

Calef, Robert, *More Wonders of the Invisible World*, London, 1700. *Repr. in George L. Burr, ed., *Narratives of the Witchcraft Cases, 1648-1706*, Original Narratives Series, New York, 1914.

Calvin, John, *Institutes of the Christian Religion*, Trans. John Allen, Philadelphia, n.d., 2 vols. (Vol. II cited.)

The Colonial Laws of Massachusetts, ed. William H. Whitmore, Boston, 1887. (A reprint of the 1672 edition with supplements through 1686.)

Cotton, John, "Moses his Judicials," publ. as *An Abstract of the Lawes of New England*, London, 1641.

Council Records, Archives Division, Statehouse, Boston. (Vols. II-VIII [1692-1727] cited.)

Danckaerts, Jasper, *Journal of Jasper Danckaerts*, ed. Bartlett B. James and J. Franklin Jameson, Original Narratives Series, New York, 1913.

Danforth, John, "Greatness & Goodness Elegized." (Broadside on the death of John Hull, at the Massachusetts Historical Society.)

———, "On the Death of Mrs. Mary Gerrish," Boston, 1719. *Repr. in *Broadsides, Ballads, &c. Printed in Massachusetts 1639-1800*, Mass. Hist. Soc., *Colls.*, ser. 7, V (1922).

———, "Greatness & Goodness Elegized," Boston, 1717. (Broadside on the death of Hannah Sewall.)

Dugdale, Sir William, *Antiquities of Warwickshire*, London, 1656.

*Edition used.

Dummer, Jeremiah, Letter to Samuel Sewall dated May 13, 1720, in *New England Historic and Genealogical Register*, II (1848), 146-147.

Dunton, John, *Life and Errors*, London, 1705. *Repr. in Mass. Hist. Soc., *Colls.*, ser. 2, II (1814).

Edwards, Jonathan, *Images or Shadows of Divine Things*, ed. Perry Miller, New Haven, 1948.

Eliot, John, *The Christian Commonwealth*, London, 1660. *Repr. in Mass. Hist. Soc., *Colls.*, ser. 3, IX (1840).

———, *The Day-Breaking if not the Sun-Rising of the Gospell with the Indians in New England*, London, 1647. *Repr. in Mass. Hist. Soc., *Colls.*, ser. 3, IV (1834).

Essex County Probate Docket, file no. 25077, County Courthouse, Salem, Mass.

Fuller, Thomas, *History of the Worthies of England*, London, 1662. *1811 edition.

General Court Records, Archives Division, Statehouse, Boston. (Vols. XI-XII [1689-1725] cited.)

Harvard College Records, in Col. Soc. of Mass., *Pubs.*, XV, XVI (1925), XXXXI (1935).

Hoole, Charles, *New Discovery of the old Art of Teaching School*, London, 1669. *Ed. E. T. Campagne, London, 1913.

Hubbard, William, *The Happiness of a People*, Boston, 1676.

Hull, John, *Diary*, Am. Antiq. Soc., *Trans.*, III (1857).

Hutchinson, Thomas, *A Collection of Original Papers*, Boston, 1767.

Johnson, Edward, *Wonder Working Providence of Sions Saviour in New England, 1628-1651*, London, 1654.

Josselyn, John, *An Account of Two Voyages to New England*, London, 1675. *Repr. in Mass. Hist. Soc., *Colls.*, ser. 3, III (1832).

Journals of the House of Representatives of Massachusetts, Boston, 1919-50, 25 vols. (Vols. I-VI cited.)

Knight, Sarah Kemble, *The Private Journal of a Journey from Boston to New York in the Year 1704*, Albany, 1865.

Lechford, Thomas, *Plaine Dealing, or Newes from New England*, London, 1642. *Repr. in Mass. Hist. Soc., *Colls.*, ser. 3, III (1832).

Ledger of Commissioners of the New England Company, Photostat copy at the Mass. Hist. Soc.

Locke, John, *Thoughts Concerning Education*, London, 1710.

Massachusetts Archives, Archives Division, Statehouse, Boston.

Mather, Cotton, *Diary*, Mass. Hist. Soc., *Colls.*, ser. 7, VII (1911), VIII (1912).

---

*Edition used.

————, *Magnalia Christi Americana,* Hartford, 1853, 2 vols.

————, *Memorable Providences, Relating to Witchcraft and Posses-sions,* Boston, 1687. *Repr. in G. L. Burr, ed., *Narratives of the Witch-craft Cases,* Original Narratives Series, New York, 1914.

————, *Nehemiah. A Brief Essay on Divine Consolations . . . ,* Boston, 1710.

————, *Wonders of the Invisible World,* Boston, 1693. *Repr. in G. L. Burr, ed., *Narratives of the Witchcraft Cases,* Original Narratives Series, New York, 1914.

Mather, Eleazer, *A Serious Exhortation,* Cambridge, 1671.

Mather, Increase, *A Discourse Concerning the Danger of Apostasy,* Boston, 1679.

————, *Ichabod: a Discourse Shewing what Cause there is to Fear that the Glory of the Lord is departing from New England,* Boston, 1702.

Maverick, Samuel, *A Briefe Description of New England . . . ,* Mass. Hist. Soc., *Proc.,* I (1884), 231-249. (Written around 1660.)

Minutes and Files of the Superior Court of Judicature, Suffolk County Courthouse, Boston.

The Necessity of Reformation, Boston, 1679.

Norton, John, *The Heart of New England Rent,* London, 1660.

Oakes, Urian, *New England Pleaded With,* Cambridge, Mass., 1673.

"Papers Respecting Pettiquamscut Purchase," R. I. Hist. Soc., *Colls.,* III (1835).

Phips, Sir William, "Letters of Governor Phips." In G. L. Burr, ed., *Narratives of the Witchcraft Cases,* Original Narratives Series, New York, 1914.

Prince, Thomas, *A Sermon at the Publick Lecture . . . Upon the Death of the Honourable Samuel Sewall, Esq; Late Chief Justice of the Circuits . . . ,* Boston, 1730.

Randolph, Edward, "Narrative" of 1676, in Thomas Hutchinson, *A Collection of Original Papers,* Boston, 1767.

Record Commissioners of the City of Boston, *Reports,* Boston 1876-1909. (Vol. I cited.)

Records of Salem Witchcraft, ed. William E. Woodward, Roxbury, Mass., 1864, 2 vols.

Records of the Court of Assistants of the Colony of the Massachu-setts Bay, 1630-1692, ed. John Noble, Boston, 1901-04, 3 vols. (Vol. I [1673-92] cited.)

Records of the Court of General Sessions of the Peace, Superiour

---

*Edition used.

Court Archives, Suffolk County Courthouse, Boston. (4 vols. covering the years 1702-32.)

Records of the Governor and Company of the Massachusetts Bay, ed. Nathaniel B. Shurtleff, Boston, 1853-54, 5 vols.

Sewall, Joseph (Samuel's son), *The Orphan's best Legacy . . .* , Boston, 1730.

———, "The Sins and Mercies of a Harvard Student," *More Books,* XI (September, 1936), 277-285. (Material from his diary.)

Some Correspondence between the Governors and Treasurers of the New England Company in London and the Commissioners of the United Colonies in America, the Missionaries of the Company and others Between the Years 1657 and 1712 . . . , ed., John W. Ford, London, 1896.

Suffolk Deeds. (Vols. XIII [Boston, 1903], XLV [unpubl.] cited.)

Superior Court Records, Suffolk County Courthouse, Boston.

Torrey, Samuel, *An Exhortation unto Reformation,* Cambridge, Mass., 1674.

Verbatim Transcriptions of Salem Witchcraft Papers, Essex County Courthouse, Salem, Mass., 1938, 3 vols. (Referred to as *Salem Papers.*)

Vital Records of Newbury, Salem, 1911. (Vol. I cited.)

Ward, Ned, *A Trip to New England,* London, 1699.

Weeks, L. H. and E. M. Bacon, eds., *An Historical Digest of the Provincial Press, Massachusetts Series,* Boston, 1911. (Reprint of material from the Boston *News-Letter* down to 1707.)

Winthrop, John, *History of New England,* ed. James Savage, Boston, 1853, 2 vols.

II. Secondary Sources Cited. Were this a list of
     sources consulted rather than cited, many
     names would obviously be added. Because of
     space and the fact that several full bibliogra-
     phies for the period are already available,
     I am not here adding to the number.

Barry, John Stetson, *History of Massachusetts,* Boston, 1855-57, 3 vols.

Bebb, E. D., *Nonconformity and Social and Economic Life: 1660-1800,* London, 1935.

Clarke, Hermann Frederick, *John Hull: A Builder of the Bay Colony,* Portland, Me., 1940.

Coffin, Joshua, *The History of Newbury,* Boston, 1845.

Cook, Sherwin L., "Boston: the Eighteenth Century Town," in *Commonwealth History of Massachusetts,* ed. Albert Bushnell Hart, II, Boston, 1927.

Dexter, H. M., *The Congregationalism of the Last Three Hundred Years, as Seen in Its Literature . . . ,* New York, 1880.

Dickinson, John, "The Massachusetts Charter and the Bay Colony (1628-1660)," in *Commonwealth History of Massachusetts,* ed. Albert Bushnell Hart, I, Boston, 1927.

Douglas, Charles H., *The Financial History of Massachusetts,* New York, 1892.

Dow, George F., *Every Day Life in the Massachusetts Bay Colony,* Boston, 1935.

Drake, Samuel G., *Annals of Witchcraft,* Boston, 1869.

Duff, Hector I., *The Sewells* [sic] *in the New World,* Exeter, England, 1924.

Dykema, K. W., "Samuel Sewall Reads John Dryden," *American Literature,* XIV (May, 1942), 157-161.

Eliot, Samuel, "Early Relations with the Indians," in *Early History of Massachusetts,* Lowell Lecture, Boston, 1869.

Ellis, George E., *An Address on the Life and Character of Chief-Justice Samuel Sewall,* Boston, 1885.

————, *The Puritan Age and Rule in the Colony of Massachusetts Bay,* Boston, 1888.

Evans, Charles, *American Bibliography,* New York, 1941.

Evans, Evan A., "Literary References in New England Diaries, 1700-1730," unpublished thesis at Harvard College Library. Dated 1940.

Fisher, William Arms, *Notes on Music in Old Boston,* Boston, 1918.

Fowler, William Chauncey, *Local Law in Massachusetts and Connecticut,* Albany, 1872.

Goodell, Abner C., "John Saffin and his Slave Adam," Col. Soc. of Mass., *Proc.,* I (1892-94), 85-112.

Gottfried, Marion H., "The First Depression in Massachusetts," *New England Quarterly,* IX (December, 1936), 655-678.

Gray, T. C., "Remarks on Early Laws of Massachusetts Bay . . . ," Mass. Hist. Soc., *Colls.,* ser. 3, VIII (1843).

Greene, Evarts B. and Virginia D. Harrington, *American Population Before the Federal Census of 1790,* New York, 1932.

Greene, Lorenzo Johnston, *The Negro in Colonial New England, 1620-1776,* New York, 1942.

Grinnell, Frank W., "The Bench and Bar in Colony and Province," in *Commonwealth History of Massachusetts,* ed. Albert Bushnell Hart, II, Boston, 1927.

Hawthorne, Nathaniel, *Works*, Nottingham Society edition, New York, n.d. (Vol. I cited.)

Hazard, Caroline, *Judge Sewall's Gifts in the Narragansett Country*, Providence, 1936.

Hilkey, Charles J., *Legal Development in Colonial Massachusetts, 1630-1686*, New York, 1910.

Hill, Hamilton Andrews, *History of the Old South Church*, Boston, 1890, 2 vols.

Howe, Estes, "The Abode of John Hull and Samuel Sewall," Mass. Hist. Soc., *Proc.*, ser. 2, I (1884), 312-326.

Hutchinson, Thomas, *History of the Colony of Massachusetts Bay*, London, 1760. (Vol. I cited.) Same, ed. Laurence S. May, Cambridge, Mass., 1936. (Vol. II cited.)

Jantz, Harold, "The First Century of New England Verse," Am. Antiq. Soc., *Proc.*, ser. 2, LIII (1943), 219-507.

Johnson, E. A. J., *American Economic Thought in the Seventeenth Century*, London, 1932.

Kingsley, William L., ed., *Yale College: A Sketch of its History*, New York, 1879, 2 vols. (Vol. I cited.)

Knappen, M. M., *Tudor Puritanism*, Chicago, 1939.

Littlefield, George Emery, *The Early Massachusetts Press, 1638-1700*, Boston, 1907, 2 vols.

————, *Early Schools and School-Books of New England*, Boston, 1904.

Locke, Mary Stoughton, *Anti-Slavery in America . . . , 1619-1808*, Radcliffe College Monographs, No. 11, Boston, 1901.

Lodge, Henry Cabot, "A Puritan Pepys," in *Studies in History*, Boston, 1884. Repr. from *Magazine of American History*, II (November, 1878), 631-642.

Love, William De Loss, *Samson Occam and the Christian Indians of New England*, Boston, 1900.

Mathews, Nathan, "The Results of the Prejudice Against Lawyers in Massachusetts in the Seventeenth Century," *Massachusetts Law Quarterly*, XIII (May, 1938), 73-94.

Matthiessen, F. O., "Michael Wigglesworth, a Puritan Artist," *New England Quarterly*, I (October, 1928), 491-504.

Miller, Perry, *The New England Mind: The Seventeenth Century*, New York, 1939.

Mook, H. Telfer, "Training Day in New England," *New England Quarterly*, XI (December, 1938), 675-697.

Moore, G. H., *Notes on the History of Slavery in Massachusetts*, New York, 1886.

Bibliography

Morgan, Edmund S., "The Puritans and Sex," *New England Quarterly*, XV (December, 1942), 591-603.

Morison, Samuel E., *Builders of the Bay Colony*, New York, 1930.

———, *Harvard College in the Seventeenth Century*, Cambridge, Mass., 1936, 2 vols.

Morris, Richard B., *Studies in the History of American Law*, New York, 1930.

Murdock, Kenneth B., *Handkerchiefs from Paul*, Cambridge, Mass., 1927.

———, "The Teaching of Latin and Greek at the Boston Latin School in 1712," Col. Soc. of Mass., *Proc.*, XXVII (1927-30), 21-29.

Neal, Daniel, *The History of New England*, London, 1720.

Nettels, Curtis, "The Menace of Colonial Manufacturing, 1690-1720," *New England Quarterly*, IV (April, 1931), 230-269.

Nevins, Winfield S., *Witchcraft in Salem Village*, Salem, Mass., 1916.

Palfrey, John Gorham, *History of New England*, Boston, 1876.

Parkes, Henry B., "New England in the Seventeen Thirties," *New England Quarterly*, III (July, 1930), 397-419.

Parrington, Vernon Louis, *The Colonial Mind, 1620-1800*, New York, 1927.

Pearson, A. F. Scott, *Thomas Cartwright and Elizabethan Puritanism: 1535-1603*, Cambridge, England, 1925.

Peterson, Harold L., "The Military Equipment of the Plymouth and Bay Colonies, 1620-1690," *New England Quarterly*, XX (June, 1947), 197-208.

Potter, A. C., and Charles K. Bolton, *The Librarians of Harvard College, 1667-1877*, Harvard University Library, Bibliographical Contributions, No. 52, Cambridge, Mass., 1897.

Quincy, Josiah, *History of Harvard University*, Boston, 1860. (Vol. I cited.)

Reinsch, P. S., "English Common Law in the Early American Colonies," in *Select Essays in Anglo-American Legal History*, I, Boston, 1907.

Roberts, Oliver A., *History of the Military Company of the Massachusetts*, Boston, 1895-1901. (Vol. I cited.)

Robinson, John, and George F. Dow, *The Sailing Ships of New England, 1607-1907*, Salem, Mass., 1922. (Vol. I cited.)

Salisbury, Edward E., *Family Memorials*, New Haven, 1885.

Sewall, Samuel (minister-descendant of Burlington, Mass., long the possessor of the MS diary), "Memoir of Hon. Samuel Sewall, Esq.," *American Quarterly Register*, XIII (February, 1841), 237-252.

Seybolt, Robert F., "The Private Schools of Seventeenth-Century Boston," *New England Quarterly*, VIII (September, 1935), 418-424.

Sibley, John Langdon, *Biographical Sketches of Graduates of Harvard University*, Cambridge, 1873. (Vol. II cited.)

Small, W. H., "The New England Grammar School," *School Review*, X (September, 1902), 513-531.

Thomas, Isaiah, *The History of Printing in America*, Worcester, Mass., 1810.

Tyler, Moses Coit, *A History of American Literature, 1607-1765*, New York, 1897. (Vol. II cited.)

Upham, C. W., *Lectures on Witchcraft*, Boston, 1832.

Washburn, Emory, *Sketches of the Judicial History of Massachusetts from 1630 to the Revolution in 1775*, Boston, 1840.

Weeden, William B., "The Early African Slave Trade in New England," Am. Antiq. Soc., *Proc.*, n.s., V (October, 1887), 107-128.

———, *Economic and Social History of New England: 1620-1789*, New York, 1890, 2 vols.

Wendell, Barrett, *Cotton Mather, Puritan Priest*, New York, 1891.

Wertenbaker, Thomas J., *The First Americans: 1607-1690*, History of American Life Series, New York, 1927.

———, *The Puritan Oligarchy*, New York, 1947.

Whitman, Zachariah G., *Historical Sketch of the Ancient and Honourable Artillery Company*, Boston, 1820.

Whittier, John Greenleaf, *Works*, New York, 1892. (Vol. I cited.)

Winship, George P., "Samuel Sewall and the New England Company," Mass. Hist. Soc., *Proc.*, LXVII (1941-44), 55-110.

Winslow, Ola, *Samuel Sewall of Boston*, New York, 1964.

Winsor, Justin, "The Literature of the Colonial Period," in *The Memorial History of Boston*, I, Boston, 1882.

Winthrop, Robert C., *A Difference of Opinion Concerning the Reasons why Katherine Winthrop Refused to Marry Chief Justice Sewall*, Boston, 1885.

Woodward, W. E., *The Way our People Lived*, New York, 1944.

Wright, Thomas Goddard, *Literary Culture in Early New England*, New Haven, 1920.

III. Works by Sewall, printed and in manuscript

A. Poetry. Though items have all been checked and minor additions and corrections made, this section is substantially the bibliography of Sewall's poetry in Harold Jantz's "The First Century of New England

Verse." Trivial though much of it is, the whole gives some idea of Sewall's activity as a maker of verse. So it may better do this, explanatory and descriptive matter has frequently been inserted.

"The Humble Springs of Stately Sandwich Beach." 6 lines. *Diary,* I, 27, entry of October 28, 1676. Revised version in the Boston *News-Letter* for March 28, 1723; repr. in the *Diary,* III, 322, editors' note.

"O great Menasseh, were it not for thee." 2 lines. *Diary,* I, 37, entry for March 6, 1677.

"Mrs. Mehitable Holt. A Person of Early Piety." (An aunt of Sewall's who died in England, September 30, 1677.) 6 lines. Broadside at the Mass. Hist. Soc. (probably printed at Boston, 1689-90) and in the Sewall Memorandum Book at the N. Y. Hist. Soc.

"Si Christum Discis, nihil est si caetera discis." 2 lines Latin. Printed book plate of around 1690. At the Mass. Hist. Soc., and it appears in Sewall's Memorandum Book at the N. Y. Hist. Soc.

"Mrs. Judith Hull." On Sewall's mother-in-law, who died at Boston, June 22, 1695. 1. 10 line broadside at the Boston Public Library. 2. 12 line broadside at the Am. Antiq. Soc. Repr. in Am. Antiq. Soc., *Trans.,* III (1857), 272.

"Causa parata mihi est, et vitae, et mortis, ibidem." 4 lines Latin. *Diary,* I, 426, entry for May 18, 1696. Lines written on being "grievously stung to find a sweet desirable Son dead [the thirteenth child, stillborn]. . . ."

"To be engraven on a Dial." 4 lines. Commonplace Book at Mass. Hist. Soc., fol. 112. 1690's. Printed in Jantz's "The First Century of New England Verse," 311.

"To horses, swine, neat cattle, sheep, and deer." 2 lines. *Diary,* I, 479, entry for May 10, 1698. Printed in Joshua Coffin, *The History of Newbury,* 166.

"Ecce antiphrasin vocitaris, Ductor Arundel." 4 lines Latin. *Letter-Book,* I, 245, letter to Josias Crow dated October 18, 1700. He sends his friend "a Taste of my Daughters Bride-Cake, wrapt up in two or three Latin Verses."

"Upon Mr. Samuel Willard, his first coming into the Assembly, and Praying, after a long and dangerous Fit of Sickness; November 21. 1700." 1. 8 lines. *Diary,* II, 26, entry for November 21, 1700. 2. 3 four-line stanzas. Broadside printed 1700 and 1720. Repr. in Mass. Hist. Soc., *Proc.,* ser. 2, II (1885), 42-43.

"Wednesday, January 1. 1701. A little before Break-a-day, at Boston of the Massachusetts." 1. 3 four-line stanzas. *Diary,* II, 28, entry for January 2, 1700/1, and broadside at Mass. Hist. Soc. 2. 6 four-line stanzas. Broadside at the Boston Public Library and Am. Antiq. Soc.;

appended to *Proposals Touching the Accomplishment of Prophecies* (Boston, 1713). Repr. in Mass. Hist. Soc., *Proc.*, ser. 2, I (1884-85), 14.

Epitaph on his granddaughter Sarah Sewall. Apparently lost. Mentioned in the *Diary*, II, 69, entry for December 8, 1702, as having been sent to Richard Henchman.

"Superannuated Squier, Wigg'd and powder'd with pretence." 4 lines. *Diary*, II, 79, entry for June 8, 1703. Satire against John Saffin, opponent of Sewall in the anti-slavery issue, not Governor Dudley as indicated in the index to the *Diary*, III, 562.

"Mitto tibi Psaltem CHRISTUM et sua Regna canentem." 1. 4 lines Latin. *Diary*, II, 136, entry for August 24, 1705. 2. 6 lines Latin. *Letter-Book*, I, 314, memorandum and editors' note. Verses sent to Richard Henchman with a copy of Calvin on the Psalms.

"Oceani Fluctus Anna Moderante superbos." 2 lines Latin. *Diary*, II, 137, entry for September 10, 1705, and *Letter-Book*, I, 314, letter to Cotton Mather dated September 10, 1705. An English version in the *Diary*, II, 140, entry for October 25, 1705, substitutes Christ for Anna.

"Roma simul coelebsque ruunt in tempore Petrus." 2 lines Latin. *Letter-Book*, I, 318, letter to Richard Henchman dated October 13, 1705. Sent to Henchman for "examination and censure."

"Roma inhonesta jacet, Sanctae gaudete puellae." 2 lines Latin. *Diary*, II, 140, entry for October 15, 1705. Revised and included in a letter to Governor Saltonstall, *Letter-Book*, II, 139, letter dated July 16, 1722.

"Desine Belshazzar Temple Omnipotentis abuti." 2 lines Latin. *Diary*, II, 141, first week of November, 1705.

"Sound! Sound! the Jubilean Trumpet sound." 2 lines English. *Diary*, II, 141, first week of November, 1705.

"On the burning of the Quebec Cross." 1. 2 lines Latin and 4 line English paraphrase, *Diary*, II, 143, entry for November 25, 1705. 2. 4 lines Latin. *Diary*, II, 150, entry for December 24, 1705. Printed in the Boston *News-Letter*, December 24, 1705, titled "In Obitum Crucis."

"Tom Child had often painted Death." 4 lines English. *Diary*, II, 170, entry for November 10, 1706, the day of Child's death.

"Feria Septima, Martij 8.° 1707. Anno Regni Annae Reginae Angliae &c. Sexto." 2 lines Latin, 4 lines English. *Diary*, II, 181, entry for March 8, 1707.

"Feria Sexta; Quintilis quarto, 1707." Broadside, apparently lost. See the *Diary*, II, 191, entry for July 4, 1707.

"Deo Servatori." 4 lines Latin. *Letter-Book*, I, 350, memorandum for July 14, 1707. Written in "Thankfull Remembrance" of Ipswich "and out of Respect to Mr. Jaffrey's Memory."

"Upon the Reverend Mr. Francis Goodhue, who . . . was surprised with a Fever at Rehoboth, and there died Sept. 15, 1707, Aetatis 29." 8 lines Latin. Boston *News-Letter*, February 28, 1723. Repr. *Diary*, III, 321, editors' notes.

"Verses on Mr. Clap." Mentioned, *Diary*, II, 243, entry for November 20, 1708. No copy known; possibly not by Sewall.

"Stylo Juliano, Bostoniae Novanglorum Feria Septima, Decembris 17, 1709." 1. 2 lines Latin. *Letter-Book*, I, 387, memorandum. Written inside the cover of a Commentary on the Book of Job presented to Charles Sucre, Governor of Carthagena, then resident in Boston. 2. 2 lines English "Upon the same Subject" (*ibid.*).

"In deditionem Castelli Portus Regalis Imperatori Excellentissimo Francisco Nicholsono Armigero, Octob. 2. 1710." 1. 16 lines Latin. *Letter-Book*, I, 399-400, inserted. 2. 20 lines Latin. See *Letter-Book*, I, 400, editors' note. 3. 22 lines English, titled "Verses on the Capture of Port Royal." See *Letter-Book*, I, 406, editors' note.

"Vive, doce, regna, semper, mihi CHRISTE Sacerdos." 2 lines Latin. *Diary*, II, 311, entry for May 16, 1711. "Left Jonathan [a nephew at Salem] my Distich transcribed by him at my bidding." Appended to verses addressed to Sewall by Rev. Nehemiah Hobart. Broadside repr. in the *Letter-Book*, I, 315, editors' note.

"Auris, mens, oculus, manus, os, pes, menere fungi." 2 lines Latin. *Diary*, II, 339, entry for March 8, 1711/12. ". . . gave Capt. Tuthill Mr. Tompson's, Heaven the best Country, with my Distich."

"Erroresque meos mihi condonate perosos." 2 lines Latin. *Diary*, II, entry for December 20, 1712. Lines added to the verses of Benjamin Larnell.

"To the Rev'd Mr. John Sparhawk on the Birth of his Son, August or September 1713." 12 lines English, 2 lines Latin. On an end page of the "Magunkaquog" Journal; printed by the editors of the *Diary*, III, 408.

"Imbres nocturni decorant Regalia Lucis." 2 lines Latin. *Diary*, III, 22, entry for October 5, 1714. Distich left for Mr. Stanton "Gone a Gunning."

"Isaac's withdrawn; my Laughter's done." 5 lines English. "Magunkaquog" Journal under date of March 31, 1715. On the death of his fellow judge and Councillor, Isaac Addington.

"Lines made to direct me in signing the Pound-plate." 3 lines Latin. *Diary*, III, 49, entry for July 5, 1715.

On the death of his sister, Mrs. Jane Gerrish, who died at Newbury, January 29, 1717. 4 lines Latin. In an interleaved almanac at the Mass. Hist. Soc. Printed in Mass. Hist. Soc., *Proc.*, ser. 2, VIII (1893), 214.

"A small Vial of Tears brought from the Funeral of JOHN WIN-

THROP, a very goodly Child." 10 line broadside at Mass. Hist. Soc. *Letter-Book,* II, 70, letter to the father dated April 8, 1717.

"Anglica Jana jacet germanis flenda duobus." 6 lines Latin. *Letter-Book,* II, 84, letter to Jeremiah Dummer dated January 25, 1717/18. He was moved by a consideration of the fact that "now my Brother, Mr. John Sewall, and Four Sisters and my Honoured Parents ly Buried at Newbury."

"What signify these Locks, and Bolts, and Bars?" 2 lines English. *Letter-Book,* II, 84, letter to Jeremiah Dummer dated January 25, 1717/18. On the death of his wife Hannah.

"Salem, Dec. 13, 1717. A specimen of New English Celibacy." 6 lines English. Boston *News-Letter* for February 13, 1721. Repr. in Mass. Hist. Soc., *Proc.,* ser. 2, III (1887), 380-381, and in *N. E. Hist. and Gen. Reg.,* XXIV (1870), 292.

"Nocte viatori comitem nix candida Lumen." 2 lines Latin. *Letter-Book,* II, 123, letter to Jeremiah Dummer dated December 13, 1720. Imitation of a distich of Ovid.

"Upon the drying up of that Ancient River, THE RIVER MERRY-MAK." 36 line broadside at Mass. Hist. Soc., dated January 15, 1719/20. Repr. in Mass. Hist. Soc., *Proc.,* ser. 2, IX (1894), 8-10. See the *Diary,* III, 240, entry for January 17, 1719-20.

"Upon the River Merrimak." 2 lines Latin. Boston *News-Letter,* February 21, 1723. Repr. in the *Diary,* III, 321, editors' note.

"Decembris 2. 1722." 2 lines Latin. Boston *News-Letter,* February 21, 1723. Repr. in the *Diary,* III, 321, editors' note. On Daniel Rogers, drowned in Black Rock Cove, December 1, 1722. See Sibley, *Biographical Sketches,* III, 358-359.

"Januarii 14, 15, 16. [1722/23.]" 4 lines Latin. Boston *News-Letter,* February 21, 1723. Repr. in the *Diary,* III, 321, editors' note. On the recovery of Roger's body. See Sibley, *loc. cit.*

"Upon the Reverend Mr. Samuel Pierpoint and Mr. Benjamin Gibson, learned and worthy Ministers, their dying in one and the same night." 8 lines Latin. Boston *News-Letter,* April 11, 1723. Repr. in the *Diary,* III, 322, editors' note.

"Boston, Feb. 1. 1723/4." 2 lines Latin. *Diary,* III, 330, entry for February 4, 1723/4, and Boston *News-Letter* for February 6, 1723/4.

"Dum Cererem et Bacchum meditaris, Ralle Sacerdos." 2 lines Latin. *Letter-Book,* II, 174, letter to Governor Saltonstall dated September 5, 1724. On Father Ralle and the defeat of the Kennebec Indians.

"Feria Quinta, Novembris duodecimo, 1724." 5 lines Latin. *Letter-Book,* II, 178, letter to Edmund Quincy dated November 12, 1724. A "short Epithalamium" on the marriage of Quincy's daughter.

"Nos simul occidimus, nostra recidente corona." 2 lines Latin.

Letter-Book, II, 193, letter to John Winthrop dated January 4, 1725/6. On the death of his brother, Stephen Sewall of Salem.

"Three Sams, two Johns, and one good Tom." 2 lines English. *Diary,* III, 375, second week of April, 1726. On the pallbearers of Mary Coney.

"In Remembrance of Mr. Samuel Hirst." Sewall's grandson, who died January 14, 1726/7. 24 lines English. Broadside at Mass. Hist. Soc.

B. Prose. Including ledger accounts, memorandum books, etc. Item 17, not examined, is listed as given by Ola Winslow, *Samuel Sewall of Boston,* 222.

Notes of sermons. 11 vols. (5 at Boston Public Library, 6 at Mass. Hist. Soc.). From May 1672. Small, 4 x 6 inch manuscript volumes, some in calf and some in vellum, with about 150 close-packed, double pages of notes in each.

Memoranda in interleaved almanacs. From 1673. The editors of the *Diary,* I, 292, note, state that "Sewall made notes in the Almanacs for each year, perhaps as aids to his more extended diary." The editors have included in notes to the regular diary "such extracts as served to increase [the] text." Some of these memoranda also appear in *N. E. Hist. and Gen. Reg.,* VII (1853), 205, VIII (1854), 314. Numerous of these slim 4 x 6 inch volumes at Mass. Hist. Soc.

Diary. From December 3, 1673 (first regular entry) to October 13, 1729 (last regular entry), lacking the years 1677-85 through loss of a manuscript volume. Printed in *Sewall Papers,* Mass. Hist. Soc., *Colls.,* ser. 5, V-VII (1878-82), of which it is the principal part. The manuscript diary is in four volumes, for 1672-77, 1685-1703, 1703-12, and 1712-20, respectively. The volumes are 6 x 8 inches and bound in calf, excepting the 1703-12 volume, which is approximately 9 x 14 inches and bound in vellum. Like all the Sewall manuscripts, in excellent condition. At Mass. Hist. Soc. An abridged edition is *Samuel Sewall's Diary,* ed. Mark Van Doran, American Bookshelf Series (New York, 1927).

"Diary and Commonplace book, 1675—" (so listed at Mass. Hist. Soc.). 8 x 12 inches, bound in vellum. What mainly distinguishes this miscellaneous volume is its record of Sewall's meetings with the South Military Company, kept from April 1681 to April 1686. The first 26 fol. pages are his accounts for February 11, 1675, to November 26, 1677 (the period of his apprenticeship with John Hull). Other items in the volume are a first draft of the *Phaenomena* and one of *Talitha Cumi,* a careful hand copy of Nicholas Noyes' "Reasons Against Wearing of Periwiggs," commonplace extracts from sources related to his prophetical inquiries, and copies of letters concerning the same.

"Commonplace Book, 1677 to—" (so listed at Mass. Hist. Soc.) 6 x 8 inches, bound in calf. Scattered diary entries for the years 1677-86 (arranged chronologically and printed, *Diary*, II, *12-*23), but mainly extracts from books arranged under appropriate heads—"De Resurrectione mortuorum," "De Ministerio," "De Oratione," "De Sacramentes," "De Infantibus," etc., the diary entries being mostly under "De Omene." At the beginning of the book is written: "Samuel Sewall, his Booke, Decemb. 29, 1677."

Notes of meetings of the Old South Society. From January, 1681. 3 x 5 inches, calf bound, bearing the initials, "S. S." A note by the Rev. Samuel Sewall of Burlington, Mass., in the end pages and dated 1830, describes it as "a Record of Texts of Scriptures, and of Questions deduced therefrom, discussed . . . at Private or Conference Meetings of Members of the Old South Society, Boston . . . held at each others houses in turn; and generally on Wednesday evening of each week." At Mass. Hist. Soc.

Letter, "For the Reverend Mr. Increase Mather, in Boston," dated March 23, 1682/3. *Mather Papers,* Mass. Hist. Soc., *Colls.,* ser. 4, VIII (1868), 516-517.

Bill of Lading Book. 5 x 8 inches, bound in calf. Bills from December 6, 1683 (John Hull died the preceding October 1) through March 5, 1698, at which time the book, with pages still unused, was taken over by James Torten. At Mass. Hist. Soc.

Ledger. Marked on the cover, "Samuel Sewall His Ledger." Bound in vellum; 200 fol. pages. Loose pages at the beginning are by John Hull. Sewall entries begin after Hull's death in 1683 and continue until shortly before his own death almost half a century later. At N. E. Hist. and Gen. Soc. library.

Letter, "For his much esteemed Friend, Mr. Cotton Mather, at Boston," dated December 25, 1684. *Mather Papers,* Mass. Hist. Soc., *Colls.,* ser. 4, VIII (1868), 516. Repr. in the *Diary,* I, 58, editors' note. Letter "under several heads" on "why the Heart of America may not be the seat of the New Jerusalem."

Letters to his uncle Stephen Dummer, dated simply 1684/5, and to his uncle Nathaniel Dummer, dated February 2, 1684/5, both in England. *N. E. Hist. and Gen. Reg.,* IX (1855), 287-288. About his being a compositor of books for press.

Letter-Book. One volume manuscript at Mass. Hist. Soc., 8 x 12 inches, vellum-bound, begun in February, 1685/6, and continued to September, 1729, a few months before his death. Miscellaneous matter at the beginning of the volume dates from as early as 1672. Printed in *Sewall Papers,* Mass. Hist. Soc., *Colls.,* ser. 5, I-II (1886-87).

Business Journal. Entries from September 18, 1685 to July 19, 1698.

Bibliography

Described by Winslow, *Samuel Sewall of Boston,* 222, simply as "MS
. . . owned by the Baker Library, The Harvard School of Business
Administration."

Account Book. Entries from March 30, 1688, to April 28, 1692. Like
the "Magunkaquog" Court Journal, a 4 x 6 inch, vellum-bound, pocket
book with a clasp binding. Not ledger accounts, but individual items
of "paid and rec'd." Extracts in Mass. Hist. Soc., *Proc.,* LII (1919),
334-340. At Mass. Hist. Soc.

Letter of Sewall and Isaac Addington to Col. John Pincheon of
Springfield about plans for raising troops against the "Maquas and
Sineques," dated May 2, 1690. In *Pincheon Papers,* Mass. Hist. Soc.,
Colls., ser. 3, VIII (1819), 238-243.

Letter to unnamed addressee dated May 21, 1690, concerning arrangements against the French and Indians. *Diary,* I, 320-321, editors' note.

Letter to Nehemiah Grew dated January, 1690/1, in "Letters of
Samuel Lee and Samuel Sewall Relating to New England and the
Indians," ed. G. L. Kittredge, Col. Soc. of Mass., *Pubs.,* XIV (1913),
152-153.

"Memorandum Book." (So listed at N. Y. Hist. Soc.) 74 pp., 8vo.
On the manuscript title page is written, "Samuel Sewall his book,
August the 15. 1695," and the material bears dates in 1695-96. Some
miscellaneous material but notable for its collection of New England
poetry of the period, the first part of which consists of eighteen
"tributes of tears" and "lamentations" of the kind Sewall himself spe-
cialized in, by Benjamin Tompson, Thomas Wally, William Adams,
and unidentified authors. One, "Mrs. Mehitable Holt. A person of
early Piety," is by Sewall. The second part of the collection is secular
and has particular interest for that reason.

Diary fragment of March 15, 1696/7, on the meaning and method
of name-changing among the Indians. In *Diary,* III, 399, editors' note.

*Phaenomena quaedam Apocalyptica Ad Aspectum Novi Orbis con-
figurata. Or some few Lines towards a description of the New Heaven
As it makes to those who Stand upon the New Earth . . . ,* Boston,
1697. 4to, 64 pp. Second edition, Boston, 1727.

The Selling of Joseph, Boston, 1700. 4to, 3 pp. Repr. in Benjamin
Lay's *All Slave Keepers that keep the Innocent in Bondage, Apostates,*
Philadelphia, 1737; G. H. Moore's *Notes on the History of Slavery in
Massachusetts,* New York, 1886; *Diary,* II, 16-20, editors' note, etc.

Diary fragment on a trip to Cape Cod and Martha's Vineyard as a
commissioner for the Society for the Propagation of the Gospel, in
April, 1702. In *N. E. Hist. and Gen. Reg.* XIV (1860), 13-15, and
Diary, III, 397-399, editors' note.

Bibliography

"Computation that the Importation of Negroes is not so possible as that of White Servants," Boston *News-Letter*, No. 112, June 12, 1706. Attributed to Sewall by E. A. J. Johnson, *American Economic Thought in the Seventeenth Century* (London, 1932), 20-21. Attribution acceptable only as reasonable speculation.

"Tuesday, Nov. 25. 1707. The Reasons of my withdrawing my Vote from what was Pass'd in Council, upon Saturday, November the First, relating to an Address offered to her Majesty . . . ," Boston, 1707. Broadside. Repr. in the *Diary*, II, *111-*112. At N. Y. Hist. Soc.

Account book kept as disbursing agent for the Company for the Propagation of the Gospel in New England and the Parts Adjacent in America. Covers the years 1708-19. 80 page manuscript ledger at Mass. Hist. Soc.

Talitha Cumi, or an Invitation to Women to look after their Inheritance in the Heavenly Mansions. Exists only in unfinished manuscript (see above, "Diary, and Commonplace book, 1675—"), but was apparently printed. An entry in the ledger (fol. 188, date of January 15, 1711 [?]) reads: "For printing . . . Talitha Cumi 2. 15. 0." A digest of the piece by George Ellis appears in Mass. Hist. Soc., *Proc.*, XII (1873), 380-384.

Letter to the Reverend Edward Taylor at Westfield, dated June 14, 1712. Copied, say the diary's editors, "from the fly-leaf of a manuscript volume of theology in the Library at Yale College," and printed, *Diary*, II, 351-353, editors' note.

Proposals Touching the Accomplishment of Prophesies . . . , Boston, 1713, 4to, 12 pp.

Journal of journey to Martha's Vineyard and Circuit Court Journal (listed at Mass. Hist. Soc. as "Diary, Notes of Sermons, etc. 1714-1716 and account book, 1723-29"). 4 x 6 inch, vellum bound and fastened with a clasp, with the words "MAGUNKAQUOG. October 11, 1715" on the cover. Apparently the journal Sewall refers to in connection with his trip to the Vineyard, when he says, "See my journal" (*Diary,* II, 425). Portion covering his circuit travels is for March 1714 to July 1716; partially printed in notes to the *Diary,* II, 426-440; III, 1-4, 24-25, 400-408. Sermon notes are for sermons heard on circuit. The "account book" section relates mainly to the estate of Madam Bridget Usher, for which Sewall was executor.

Probate Journal. Manuscript record of matters handled by Sewall as judge of probate from December 5, 1715, to December 19, 1728. 6 x 8 inch, bound in calf. At Mass. Hist. Soc.

Journal of voyage to Arrowsick and Circuit Court Record, August 1, 1717, to August 17, 1727. 4 x 6 inch, bound in calf. It is to this that

Sewall refers when he says, " For my Voyage to Arrowsick in Kenne-beck River, see my Octavo Paper Book" (*Diary*, III, 135) and "See my Court Journal" (*ibid.*, 185). The volume was acquired by the Mass. Hist. Soc. in 1869 but remained unidentified by the editors of the diary, who say: "Not among the books and papers now owned by the . . . Society." Contents much like the "MAGUNKAQUOG" volume.

Letter to his son Samuel dated August 26, 1720. In *N. E. Hist. and Gen. Reg.*, I (1847), 111-113, and repr. in the *Diary*, I, xi-xv. Impor-tant for genealogical information.

A Memorial Relating to the Kennebeck Indians, Boston, 1721. 4to, 3 pp.

Note: Two items have been wrongly attributed to Sewall. The first is *The Revolution in New England Justified, and the People there vindi-cated from the Aspersions cast upon them by Mr. John Palmer . . .* (Boston, 1691). Because a preliminary "To the Reader" is signed by "E. R." and "S. S." it has generally been ascribed to Edward Rawson and Samuel Sewall. While part of it could have been written by Sewall, there is no evidence to support the idea. On the contrary: 1. Sewall's role in the revolution against Andros, however sympathetic he may have been, was passive. 2. If he had a hand in so important a piece of work, it is remarkable that nowhere in all his detailed records does he mention it, a fact which would make this work unique in this respect among the more substantial products of his pen. Wash-burn, *Sketches*, 123, attributes it to Edward Rawson and Samuel Shrimpton.

The second is an item concerned with "Whether Trading for Negros i.e. carrying them out of their own Country into perpetual Slavery, be in it self Unlawful, and especiall contrary to the great Law of CHRISTIANITY?" appearing in *The Athenian Oracle, The Second Edition* (London, 1704), I, 545-548. This has doubtless been ascribed to Sewall because of a note in a contemporary hand on the first page of the copy at the Mass. Hist. Soc. which reads: "Capt. Sewall sent the following question over to the Athenian Society." But in the *Letter-Book*, I, 322-323, letter to Nathanael Byfield dated January 4, 1705/6, Sewall writes: "Sir, you may remember that Mr. Saffin Printed a Letter [of reply] to *The Selling of Joseph*. I did not trouble the Town with a Reply: but in stead . . . have now reprinted the Sentiments of the Athenian Society, which I had not seen nor heard of, till I saw it in a Book-Sellers Shop last Fall." See also the letter to John Higginson dated April 13, 1706.

Bibliography

Finally, a reference in Tyler, *History,* II, 103, to an item by Sewall with the title, "Answers to Queries Respecting America, 1690," presumably refers to the letter to Nehemiah Grew dated January, 1690/1, noted above.

Index

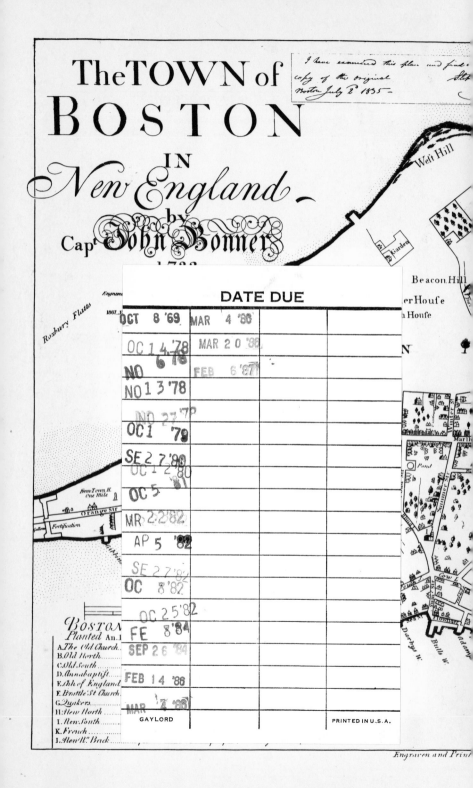